On The Structure Of The Strata: Between The London Clay And The Chalk, In The London And Hampshire Tertiary Systems

Joseph Prestwich

ON THE

STRUCTURE OF THE STRATA

BETWEEN THE

LONDON CLAY AND THE CHALK

IN THE

LONDON AND HAMPSHIRE TERTIARY SYSTEMS.

PART I.

FIRST DIVISION—" THE BASEMENT BED OF THE LONDON CLAY."

By JOSEPH PRESTWICH, Jun., F.G.S.

[*From the* QUARTERLY JOURNAL OF THE GEOLOGICAL SOCIETY OF LONDON *for* August 1850, VOL. VI.]

On the Structure of the STRATA BETWEEN THE LONDON CLAY AND THE CHALK *in the* LONDON *and* HAMPSHIRE TERTIARY SYSTEMS. By JOSEPH PRESTWICH, jun., F.G.S.

PART I.

WE are indebted, early in the history of geology, to Dr. Buckland, Phillips and Conybeare, Parkinson, Warburton, Webster, and others for many valuable illustrations and descriptions of separate and detached sections, as well as for some more general details of portions, of the London tertiary district*.   Further descriptions, in which I must necessarily go over again part of the same ground, may appear in some measure superfluous; but although the relative position which the whole of the series of beds known as the *plastic clay formation* bears to the *London clay* and the *chalk*, has long been well established, and is sufficiently apparent in several sections, the exact grouping and subdivisions of these lower Eocene deposits in their entire range, by which alone the precise co-relations of the strata can be determined, have not yet I think been clearly shown.

These beds have in fact been viewed as one deposit irregularly interstratified, and the sections at Herne Bay, Upnor, Lewisham, Woolwich, and Reading have been co-related "*en masse,*" but not in detail.   It has of late even been considered doubtful whether the larger original divisions into *London clay* and *Plastic clay* could be maintained; whether the latter were not merely the subordinate beds of the former formation.

The object therefore of this paper is both to describe several new sections, and also to show, that the variable series of deposits forming the lower tertiaries can be divided into distinct and separate, yet not altogether independent subdivisions, each marked by different conditions, indicating ancient hydrographical and palæontological changes of some importance.

The main body of the London clay presents throughout its whole range a uniformity of mineral structure so well marked and distinct, that either by this character alone, or else by its organic remains, when present, it can almost always be readily recognized.   But the case is far otherwise with the more varied deposits which intervene between the London clay and the chalk.   This series is not large, yet it exhibits in different places variations in its structure and in its fauna, which render the determination of the exact parallelism between distant sections difficult.   Thus below the London clay in the Isle of Wight† we find almost exclusively beds of compact mottled clays without organic remains.   In the neighbourhood of Newbury and Reading are mottled clays, interstratified with beds of sand, and generally underlaid by a bed abounding with the *Ostrea Bellovacina*. At Woolwich, Charlton, and Bromley the chalk is overlaid by unfossiliferous sands, succeeded by a mixed series of clays and sands with flint pebbles, and containing numerous organic remains of freshwater and estuary origin; whilst at Herne Bay and in the Isle of Thanet there exists a thicker and more important series of sands, sometimes in part very argillaceous, at other times much mixed with green sand, and many of the beds of which abound with marine fossils,—the fluviatile beds of Woolwich, and the mottled clays of the Western districts, having in these places completely disappeared.

Amongst the first questions therefore which arise, are,—with which portion of the Woolwich series are the mottled clays of the Reading

* See the early volumes of the Trans. Geol. Soc. from 1811 to 1825, and Phillips and Conybeare's Geology of England.   The separate references are made in the course of the paper, wherever the sections have been previously described.

† See Section of Alum Bay and White Cliff Bay, in the 2nd volume of the Quart. Jour. Geol. Soc. pl. 9, strata 1 and 2.

series the equivalent, and to which precise portion of the former is the *Ostrea Bellovacina* bed of the latter to be referred? what portion of the Isle of Wight strata represents the fossiliferous conglomerates of the neighbourhood of Bromley, and the extensive pebble-beds of Blackheath and Addington? and of what portions of the Herne Bay section are all the above-mentioned strata individually and jointly to be considered the representatives—if represented at all? The relative position of the Northaw "*Ostrea*" bed, and of the Kyson bed with its remains of the Monkey, in reference to those above-mentioned, is also to be determined.

I am aware that the series of mottled clays at Reading with their overlying seam of marine shells, has been referred as a whole to the series of sands, clays, and pebbles at Woolwich and Charlton, the marine upper bed at the former place being viewed as the representative of the fluviatile and estuary beds of the two latter; the thin but uniform stratum of impure green sand with large flints, which in both localities immediately overlies the chalk, at Reading with, and at Woolwich without, the *Ostrea Bellovacina*, being considered synchronous. It is true, that the series in each of these localities bear on a broad scale the same relative position to the chalk and the London clay; but, this admitted, it remains to be ascertained whether the whole of these series belong to one and the same group, occupying in an irregular manner this space in geological time, and varying in its thickness, in its mineral character, and in its organisms, without determinable order; or whether there are not subdivisions, each traceable over certain areas, and exhibiting essential modifications in structure, but yet invariably holding the same relative position one to another, and which may lead to the establishment of a more connected order and definite sequence in the phænomena. In this inquiry, we must take into consideration the physical condition of the surface at that early Eocene period, and ascertain how far it is probable that, as with the more recent London clay, which spreads uniformly over the whole area, the several and distant beds in this lower series originated in one sea, and were therefore likely to extend over co-extensive areas. The determination of this point is of material importance to the question of exact synchronism of the strata.

In the Isle of Wight and in the tertiary district westward of London, the London clay consists of tenacious brown and bluish-grey clays with layers of septaria, usually most abundant in the browner clays, and with small round black flint pebbles occasionally scattered through some of the darker and more sandy portions of the clay. Immediately at its base the London clay commonly contains a greater or lesser admixture of green and yellow sands, generally mixed with rounded flint pebbles, and not unfrequently cemented by carbonate of lime into semi-concretionary tabular masses. These mixed beds however never exceed a few feet in thickness, and pass upwards rapidly into the great mass of the London clay, to which they appear to be subordinate, being clearly and sharply separable from the sands and mottled clays both in mineral and zoological characters. (See Sections 1 to 6.) To the eastward of London, as at New Cross, Upnor, and Herne Bay, the mass of the London clay is apparently equally distinct, exhibiting a strong massive clay, reposing abruptly and without passage on a thick series of yellow and ash-coloured sands, with many subordinate beds of pebbles, and a few laminated clays, and containing a varied and irregular fauna. This series seems as independent of the London clay as do the sands and mottled clays to the westward of London; but it is a question whether the thin basement conglomerate bed, which in the latter district merges into the London clay, and has a character so entirely distinct from that of the underlying beds, does not, as it trends eastward, assume a lithological structure more entirely different from that of the London clay and not passing into it, but, on the contrary, assimilating so closely to the underlying sandy series, that in general appearance it seems an upper and subordinate member thereof. (See Sections 10 & 11.) I believe, however, this bed to be part rather of the *London clay* than of the so-called *plastic clays* with which it has been grouped. But although belonging to the former rather than to the latter, yet it forms in some of its characters a stratum separable from both. I purpose therefore to describe this bed ("*c*" of the Sections) before proceeding to an examination of the underlying deposits. This will follow in natural order the general description I have before given of the London clay; and as this will of itself constitute a subject of some extent, which it is important to our argument to examine in detail, I will subdivide the general question under different heads, and begin with this first division of it.

1st Division. *On the Basement bed of the London Clay ("c").*

In the fine section of Alum Bay there may be seen, at a distance of about ninety-four feet from the chalk, a thin and insignificant layer, not a foot thick, of rather large (egg-sized), rounded, black flint pebbles imbedded in a scanty yellow sand and brown clay, and separating the important mass of the London clay on the one side from that of the mottled clays on the other, and to the former of which it forms the base*. This pebble-band contains a few organic remains, of which the most common are the teeth of a species of *Lamna*; the *Ditrupa plana* also occurs, and traces of several species of shells. It reposes upon a somewhat uneven and worn surface of the underlying stratum. Small and unimportant, however, as this bed here is, it is nevertheless remarkable for the extent of its range, the uniformity of its lithological characters, and the permanence of its organic remains,—conditions of the more value from its position between the two main members of the Eocene series. It forms an excellent base-line, and its characters are so well marked, that it can be traced without much difficulty from the Isle of Wight to Woodbridge in Suffolk, a distance in a straight line of above 160 miles from S.W. to N.E.

In a former paper, when discussing the connection of the London

---

* See Section of Alum Bay, Quart. Journ. Geol. Soc. vol. ii. pl. 9. fig. 1. I have since applied the term "London Clay" to the division there called "Bognor beds," and have abandoned it for the strata higher in the series (see Quart. Journ. Geol. Soc. vol. iii. p. 355).

clay of Hampshire with that of the London district, I had occasion to allude frequently to this basement bed in the Isle of Wight and in the western part of the London district. In addition to the sections of the central and eastern area of the London tertiaries, which did not then come under notice, I purpose giving a few of the leading sections I then alluded to in more detail than I could in a paper which embraced a wider subject, and to which this point was only secondary.

I will take separately the sections and lists of the organic remains at each locality, and afterwards endeavour to show their co-relation*.

To resume in the Isle of Wight with the interesting section of this bed at White Cliff Bay. (See fig. 1.)

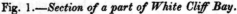

Fig. 1.—*Section of a part of White Cliff Bay.*

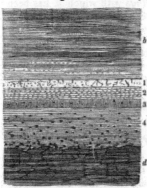

b. London clay; dark brown and grey clay; in descending becomes mixed with green sand. Fossils scarce.

1. Tabular septaria, with numerous fossils. 2. Mixed clay and green sand, like 4. 3. Dark green sand, full of the *Ditrupa plana.* 4. Brown sandy clay, much mixed with green sand, and passing downwards into a conglomerate with round flint pebbles, and partly rounded pebbles of chalk and red clay. Contains a few *Ditrupa plana.* 3 to 4 feet.

d. Mottled clays—dark red (upper part of).

The occurrence of pebbles of the underlying mottled red clay in the lower part of the basement of the London clay " *c* " is a fact here to be particularly noticed.

The organic remains found in this bed are as under :—

Cardium Plumsteadiense, *Sow.*
Corbula, a finely striated species.
Cytherea obliqua, *Desh.*
Ditrupa plana, *Sow.* sp.
Natica glaucinoides, *Sow.*
Traces of carbonized vegetables and wood.

Ostrea, a large undetermined species.
Pectunculus brevirostris, *Sow.*
Pyrula tricostata, *Desh.*
Rostellaria Sowerbyi, *Mant.*
Teeth of Lamnæ†.

Passing over to the northern part of the Hampshire tertiary district, the only good section of this bed that I am acquainted with was exposed in a cutting on the Railway at Clarendon Hill, three miles E.S.E. of Salisbury. (See fig. 2.)

* For an outline map of the tertiary strata, see Quart. Journ. Geol. Soc. vol. iii. pl. xiv.

† I have omitted the name of the species, as I feel in doubt as to which of Agassiz's species to refer it. It probably is the.*L. elegans*, or there may be more than one species. The same species accompany this bed throughout its entire range.

Fig. 2*.—*Section at Clarendon Hill.*

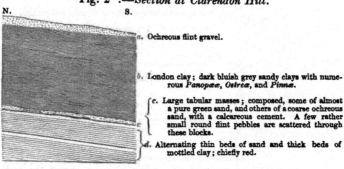

N.

S.

a. Ochreous flint gravel.

b. London clay; dark bluish grey sandy clays with numerous *Panopææ, Ostreæ,* and *Pinnæ.*

c. Large tabular masses ; composed, some of almost a pure green sand, and others of a coarse ochreous sand, with a calcareous cement. A few rather small round flint pebbles are scattered through these blocks.

d. Alternating thin beds of sand and thick beds of mottled clay; chiefly red.

The chalk outcrops lower down the hill at a depth apparently of about forty to fifty feet beneath "*c.*"

Organic remains of stratum "c," at Clarendon Hill.

Buccinum (? ambiguum, *Desh.*).
——, n. sp., large and globose.
Cancellaria læviuscula, *Desh.*
Cardium nitens, *Sow.*
——, n. sp., *a.*
Corbula longirostris, *Desh.*
Cytherea obliqua, *Desh.*
—— ovalis, var. ?, *Sow.*
—— lævigata, var. *a*?, *Lamk.*
Ditrupa plana, *Sow.* sp.
Fusus tuberosus, *Sow.*
——, n. sp., with plain costæ.
——, n. sp., large and smooth.

Natica glaucinoides, *Sow.*
—— Hantoniensis, *Pilk.*
Nucula, a small species.
Ostrea, large undetermined species.
Pectunculus brevirostris, *Sow.*
—— Plumsteadiensis, *Sow.*
Pyrula tricostata, *Desh.*
Pleurotoma comma, *Sow.*
Rostellaria Sowerbyi, *Mant.*
Tellina.
Turritella?
Teeth of Lamnæ.
Carbonized pieces of wood.

The fossils are extremely abundant, and occur in large blocks of clay and green sand with a calcareous cement. The most common species are the *Ditrupa plana, Natica glaucinoides* and *N. Hantoniensis, Cytherea obliqua, Pectunculus brevirostris, Rostellaria Sowerbyi,* and *Pyrula tricostata.*

It is not my intention to trace this bed any further in Hampshire : I may however observe, that I there know of no other good section of it. I have seen it, but not well exhibited, at Padnell, in Bere Forest, and also on the railway near Fareham.

Crossing the intervening chalk district to the most westerly extension of the London tertiaries, the first point, where we meet with some uncertain indications, without sections, of the basement bed of the London clay, is, capping the summit of Bagshot Hill between Great Bedwin and Hungerford. It is better exposed between Hungerford and Newbury, near the summit of Pebble Hill, one mile south of Kintbury. (See fig. 3.)

* This and the following sections (figs. 2 to 20) are all drawn upon the same scale; viz. 1 inch represents a thickness of 20 feet. Section fig. 1 is an exception to the rule. It is the fig. given in the Journal of the Society, vol. iii. p. 362, and is upon a much larger scale.

Fig. 3.—*Section at Pebble Hill.*

a. Ochreous gravel, composed chiefly of round flint pebbles.

b. { London clay; blackish sandy clay, passing downwards into brown clay; round flint pebbles and very friable shells dispersed irregularly throughout.

c. . . .Coarse ferruginous sand, full of round flint pebbles 1 to 12 inches in diameter; some chalk pebbles; many of the flint pebbles decomposed throughout into a white friable structure. This bed frequently passes into an iron sandstone conglomerate.

d. Mottled clays, chiefly of a light greenish colour, overlying an irregular bed of sand, below which succeed other irregular beds of mottled clays.

The chalk crops out about 50 feet below "*c.*"

Stratum "*c*" here contains no organic remains, except the teeth of the same species of *Lamnæ* which occur at Clarendon Hill, and which we shall find to accompany this bed very constantly in the London district.   This point forms the apex of a long and roughly triangular area, occupied by the tertiary eocene strata, and stretching eastward to the German Ocean.   The southern side of this triangle extends from Pebble Hill to the cliff near the Reculvers in Kent, a distance of about 100 miles, and the northern side from Pebble Hill to Woodbridge in Suffolk, nearly 140 miles.   Owing to the thickness of the London clay in the tract between these two lines, it is only by well-sections that we can learn anything of its basement bed.   If however we follow the outcrop of the beds, we shall find this stratum coming to the surface with much regularity along the southern edge of the tertiary area, whilst along its northern edge it forms a more broken and irregular line.   This arises from the tertiary deposits being, on the south from Inkpen to Croydon, tilted up at a considerable angle against the ridge of chalk hills, which throws them out suddenly and sharply, whereas towards the north they rise gradually, and form with the chalk a tolerably regularly inclined plane from their outcrop from below the London clay to the edge of the chalk escarpment, disappearing only gradually according as the chalk attains a higher level, and adapting themselves to all the irregularities and variations of the surface.

On this latter side, therefore, the tertiary strata often form hills overlooking the chalk district, whilst on the south side the chalk hills almost constantly command fine and extensive views over the tertiary area.

In following the basement bed of the London clay eastward from Pebble Hill, it will be convenient to take these two sides of the triangle separately.   It happens that many of the beds between the chalk and the London clay are of considerable economical value for their sands, and tile and pottery clays, and they are consequently worked to a great extent.   A zone of brick and tile fields in fact marks their outcrop from Marlborough to Ewell on the one side, and to Woodbridge on the other.   We are thus furnished with a series of sections, such as we obtain in no other part of the English tertiaries. They enable us to trace the sands and mottled clays without much difficulty over a large district; but although these lower tertiary beds are so frequently worked, and their relation to the chalk underlying them is often shown, the sections nevertheless rarely exhibit the overlying lower beds of the London clay.

At the base of the chalk hills between Inkpen and Basingstoke there are a considerable number of sections, more or less perfect, of these lower tertiary beds. One of the best and most illustrative is in a brick-field at Itchingswell, two miles westward of Kingsclere. (See fig. 4.)

Fig. 4.—Section at Itchingswell.

b. London clay; upper part bluish grey passing down into brown; sandy at base; a few calcareous concretions, and a few fossils. (The lower part of this bed should perhaps be included in " *c.*")
c. Ferruginous sand and iron sandstone mixed with green sand, and full of round flint pebbles, varying in size from 1 to 14 inches in diameter; no fossils except a few teeth of *Lamnæ*.
d. Mottled clay and sands.
The chalk outcrops at a distance of about 50 feet from " *c.*"

Organic remains of stratum "c," at Itchingswell.

Cancellaria læviuscula, *Desh.*	Nucula.
Cytherea obliqua, *Desh.*	Panopæa intermedia, *Sow.*
Ditrupa plana, *Sow.* sp.	Pectunculus Plumsteadiensis, *Sow.*
Ostrea, large species.	

These fossils occur at the base of " *b*," just above " *c.*"

A section at Chinham, one mile and a half north-east of Basingstoke, on the line of railway from that town to Reading, showed the basement conglomerate bed passing gradually upwards into the mass of the London clay. The organic remains were numerous, but in a very friable state. (See fig. 5.)

Fig. 5.—Section at Chinham.

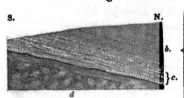

S.   N.

London clay; thin-bedded brown clay without fossils passing downwards into dirty yellow sands with seams of brown clay, and then into a sandy light-coloured clay " *c*," with seams of green sand and a few round flint pebbles occasionally concreted into small flat masses by carbonate of lime; traces of vegetable matter; shells abundant in the seams and patches of green sand, but very friable and generally in the state of casts. Average thickness of " *c* " 5 feet.

d. Mottled red and brown clays; upper surface slightly uneven and worn.

The junction with the chalk, which crops out immediately on the opposite side of the small valley formed in these lower sands, is not exposed.

Organic remains of stratum "c," at Chinham.

Cassidaria striata, *Sow.*	Fusus, small species.
Cardium Plumsteadiense, *Sow.*	Modiola elegans, *Sow.*
Cytherea ovalis, var.?, *Sow.*	Natica glaucinoides, *Sow.*
Ditrupa plana, *Sow.* sp.	—— Hantoniensis, *Pilk.*

Ostrea, small species.   Rostellaria ?
Pectunculus Plumsteadiensis, *Sow.*   Teeth of Lamnæ.
Pyrula tricostata, *Desh.*

Hence this bed may be traced by Old Basing, Odiham, Farnham*,
to Guildford, where an interesting section of it was exposed on the
line of railroad a few hundred feet north of the present station.
(See fig. 6.)

Fig. 6.—*Section at Guildford.*

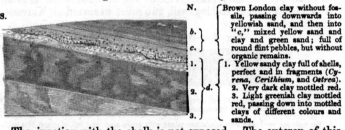

N.   ⎧ Brown London clay without fos-
S.   sils, passing downwards into
           yellowish sand, and then into
      b.   "*c*," mixed yellow sand and
           clay and green sand; full of
      c.   round flint pebbles, but without
           organic remains.
      1.   ⎧ 1. Yellow sandy clay full of shells,
              perfect and in fragments (*Cy-
              rena, Cerithium,* and *Ostrea*).
      2. d. 2. Very dark clay mottled red.
              3. Light greenish clay mottled
              red, passing down into mottled
      3.   clays of different colours and
              sands.

The junction with the chalk is not exposed. The outcrop of this
latter is however seen a few yards nearer Guildford. This section is
of much interest from the circumstance of a thin layer (1 of *d*) of
the fluviatile shells of the Woolwich beds occurring on the top of the
mottled clays and under stratum "*c.*" This is the most westerly
point at which these shells have, I believe, been yet observed. They
consist of several species of *Cyrena, Cerithium,* and *Ostrea.* The line
of separation between beds "*c*" and "*d*" is waved and irregular.

Passing by Leatherhead, Epsom, and Ewell to Croydon, no good
section of this bed is exhibited; indications of it occur only here and
there. It then trends suddenly to the north, but still it is not exposed
until we reach Lewisham, where, in one of the pits near the summit
of Loam-pit Hill, the London clay, with a thin basement conglomerate bed, may be seen overlying a bed of light-coloured sand. (See
fig. 7.)

Fig. 7.—*Section at Loam-pit Hill.*

a. Brown clay mixed with flint gravel.

b. London clay; laminated brown clay with septaria occasionally. No organic remains yet found.

c. Round flint pebbles in brown clay, and in places sand.
No organic remains.

d. .Light yellow and whitish sands.   8 to 10 feet exposed.

The pits lower down the hill show in disconnected sections the

* Two miles W.N.W. from this town I have recently found in a brook above
Lower Old Park Farm, detached blocks with numerous fossils of this " Basement
bed."

series of the Woolwich fluviatile beds, and the underlying sands reposing upon the chalk*.

At Counter Hill, stratum "*c*" is two feet thick, and shows very distinctly the irregular and worn surface of "*d*," on which it reposes; "*d*" is there thinner, of a nearly pure white colour, and contains numerous small patches of small round flint pebbles. On the line of the Croydon Railway immediately south of the New Cross Station, is a section of this bed, which has already been described by Mr. Warburton in 1844†. For the sake however of showing its connexion with the foregoing details, I here give a diagram of that part of the cutting, showing the conglomerate bed at the base of the London clay. (See fig. 8.)

Fig. 8.—*Section at New Cross.*

N.   8.

   b. London clay; tough brown clay with septaria, but without organic remains.

[remains.

c. Dark ochreous sand full of round flint pebbles. No organic

d. { Yellow sand and clays forming the upper part of the series of the Woolwich fluviatile beds hereafter to be described.

The chalk has been reached at a depth of about 100 feet beneath stratum "*c.*"

We must now make a slight deviation in order to examine a well-section at Hampstead, the particulars of which were communicated to the Geological Society in 1834 by Mr. Wetherell‡. It was shown, that the London clay was there underlaid by a compact rock, five feet thick, formed of green sand, with numerous round flint pebbles, and cemented by carbonate of lime, reposing upon a series of sands and mottled clays overlying the chalk.

The following are the organic remains he gives from this rock:—

Rostellaria lucida, *Sow.* (? Sowerbyi, *Mant.*)
Natica glaucinoides, *Sow.*
Nucula.
Panopæa intermedia, *Sow.*
Cardium nitens, *Sow.*

Pleurotoma.
Venus incrassata, *Desh.* sp. (? Cytherea obliqua, *Desh.*)
Scales and teeth of fishes.
Lignite.

We are now arrived at a point of considerable difficulty. So far the range of this stratum has been regular, and the line of demarcation between it and the upper part of the mottled clays and sands has been well-marked; but on reaching the neighbourhood of Croydon and London a different order of things commences. The mottled clays disappear except in small quantities, and in a few places; large and thick beds of round pebbles set in, interstratified with a peculiar series of fluviatile and freshwater beds. The London clay recedes further to the north, leaving a large and more

* For a better section than any now exposed of these beds, see Dr. Buckland's paper in the Trans. Geol. Soc. vol. iv. p. 285; also Phillips and Conybeare's Outlines of the Geology of England, p. 49.

† Quarterly Journal of the Geological Society, vol. i. p. 172. See also Phillips and Conybeare, Geology of England, p. 48.

‡ Trans. Geol. Soc. 2nd Series, vol. v. p. 131.

hilly district, stretching from Croydon to beyond Gravesend, occupied solely by this sandy and pebbly series reposing on a base of chalk, and only in a very few cases showing a capping of the London clay.   The difficulty is, whether we are to consider any of the peculiar fossiliferous, sandy or conglomerate beds of Woolwich, Bromley, and adjacent districts as a fuller development of the basement stratum of the London clay, or whether they all belong to a distinct and underlying series.   I am rather inclined, on structural evidence, to the latter opinion; nevertheless, on palæontological grounds it might be presumed that a passage here exists between the two series.   We however yet feel the want of a few good sections to settle clearly this point, to which I shall have occasion to revert more fully in another part of this paper.

At various points beneath the outlier of London clay at Shooter's Hill are indications of the basement pebbly bed of the London clay; and some years since there seems to have been at Plumstead a deeper and better section than any now existing; for in some of the early numbers of the 'Mineral Conchology,' Mr. Sowerby described a group of shells from this locality which bore a strong general resemblance to those of the bed we are describing.   The following is a list of the shells he enumerates :—

Cardium Plumsteadiense, *Sow.*	Fusus labiatus, *Sow.* sp.
Calyptræa trochiformis, *Lamk.*	Melania inquinata, *Defr.*
Cerithium variabile, *Desh.*	Neritina uniplicata, *Sow.*
Fusus latus, *Sow.* sp.	Panopæa intermedia, *Sow.*
—— costatus, *Sow.*	Pectunculus Plumsteadiensis, *Sow.*
—— gradatus, *Sow.* sp.	Planorbis (?) hemistoma, *Sow.*

Mr. Morris informs me that he has here found casts apparently of the *Cyprina Morrisii.*

From Mr. Sowerby's description, I cannot learn whether the fossils were all found in the same bed; I should be inclined to believe that they were not.   The *Planorbis hemistoma, Neritina uniplicata,* and some species of *Fusus,* I have never found associated with the *Panopæa intermedia* and *Cardium Plumsteadiense,* so characteristic of the basement bed of the London clay.   Still, if this bed was here accumulated under more fluviatile conditions, there would be no valid objection to such an association of organic remains in this part of the series.

About six miles to the north-west of this spot, a cutting on the Eastern Counties Railway, at Maryland Point, near Stratford-le-Bow, exposed a very illustrative section.   (See fig. 9.)

Fig. 9.—*Section near Stratford.*

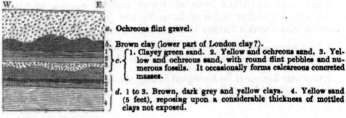

a. Ochreous flint gravel.

b. Brown clay (lower part of London clay?).

c. 1. Clayey green sand. 2. Yellow and ochreous sand. 3. Yellow and ochreous sand, with round flint pebbles and numerous fossils.   It occasionally forms calcareous concreted masses.

d. 1 to 3. Brown, dark grey and yellow clays. 4. Yellow sand (5 feet), reposing upon a considerable thickness of mottled clays not exposed.

Organic remains of stratum " c," at Maryland Point.

Cardium Plumsteadiense, *Sow.*
Cytherea obliqua, *Desh.*
Calyptræa trochiformis, *Lamk.*
Fusus.
Melania inquinata, *Defr.*
Natica glaucinoides, *Sow.*
Ostrea Bellovacina, *Lam.*
Pectunculus brevirostris, *Sow.*

Pectunculus Plumsteadiensis, *Sow.*
Pleurotoma, a small ribbed species.
Rostellaria Sowerbyi, *Mant.*
Tellina ?
Scalaria.
Teeth of Lamnæ.
A boring Mollusk, probably a Litho-
domus.

It will be observed that this bed is here as well characterized as at Clarendon Hill or Chinham, and that, with the exception of a single specimen of the *Melania inquinata*, its fauna does not at all resemble that of the Woolwich fluviatile beds. This solitary specimen had also the appearance of having been rolled and worn.

The low country along which this bed outcrops from Stratford to Horndon is covered with gravel and exhibits no sections. Some years since, however, a group of shells, similar to the above, was found at Stifford Bridge near Purfleet, and specimens of them are, I am informed by Mr. Morris, now in the Geological Museum at Cambridge.

On the south side of the Thames, another outlier of the London clay exists, I believe, on the Swanscombe Hills near Greenhithe, but although I have examined them closely, I have not been able to meet with a section of the basement beds.

We next arrive at the fine sections at Upnor on the banks of the Medway two miles north of Rochester. We there have nearly all the beds between the London clay and the chalk exposed in a few large sections. For the present it will be sufficient to exhibit the upper part of the section on the banks of the Medway, a short distance beyond the Castle*. (See fig. 10.)

Fig. 10.—*Section at Upnor.*

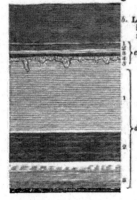

b. London clay ; upper part dark brown and very tenacious, passing down into sandy lighter coloured beds. No organic remains have been yet found in it.

c. 1. Brown clay and ochreous sand, with traces of lignite. 2. Light greenish sand, with a few patches of friable shells. 3. Fine yellow sand, with a few shells. 4. Indurated clay, with numerous shells and traces of plants. 5. Yellow sand, the upper part full of round flint pebbles, and the lower part abounding in shells. Concreted masses, full of shells, not uncommon.

d. 1. Light yellow and whitish sand ; upper surface indented by stratum " *c*;" contains a few shells (*Ostrea* and *Cyrena*) in irregular patches, and occasionally an underlayer of large Ostreæ. 2. A series of dark tough clays, with subordinate lignite and beds full of the fluviatile shells of Woolwich. 3. Variable yellow sands, reaching probably to the chalk, at a depth of 50 or 60 feet below " *c*."

* This section is described by Mr. Morris in the Proc. Geol. Soc. vol. ii. p. 451.

Organic remains of stratum " c," at Upnor.

Cardium nitens, *Sow.*
—— Plumsteadiense ? *Sow.*
—— n. sp. *a.*
Cytherea or Cyprina, large gibbous sp.
Calyptræa trochiformis ? *Lamk.*
Cerithium variabile, *Desh.*
Cyrena cuneiformis, *Sow.*
—— obovata, *Sow.* var.
—— tellinella ?, *Fer.*

Cytherea ovalis, var. ?, *Sow.*
Glycimeris or Panopæa.
Melania inquinata, *Defr.*
Natica Hantoniensis? *Pilk.*
Ostrea.
Pectunculus Plumsteadiensis, *Sow.*
Pleurotoma.
Rostellaria Sowerbyi, *Mant.*
Teeth of Lamnæ.

The undoubted admixture at this spot of several species of estuary shells of the Woolwich beds with the ordinary fauna of stratum "*c*" is to be noticed.

Thence through Sittingbourne to Faversham, I have met with no section of this bed. In the year 1841 Mr. Trimmer* called attention to a fossiliferous sandstone overlying the lower sands which repose on the chalk, on the hill above Boughton between Faversham and Canterbury, and mentions the occurrence there of four species of mollusks. I visited this locality with Mr. Rees in 1843, and we obtained from it a considerable number of other fossils, but owing to the state in which they are preserved, the following list must be received with some doubt. The bed consists of layers of very hard and compact siliceous sandstone with subordinate bands of iron sandstone. One of the upper seams of the latter contains rounded flint pebbles, and abounds with extremely well-marked impressions and casts of shells, but the substance of the shells is in all cases removed. The superposition of the bed is not shown. It is about five feet thick. At a short distance above it the London clay appears, and below it, in the valley, the chalk outcrops.

Organic remains of " c," near Boughton.

Astarte.
Calyptræa trochiformis, *Lamk.*
Cardium nitens, *Sow.*
—— Plumsteadiense, *Sow.*
——, n. sp. *a.*
Cerithium variabile, *Desh.*
Cyrena cuneiformis, *Sow.*
—— obovata ?, *Sow.*
Corbula longirostris, *Desh.*
Cytherea ovalis, var. ?, *Sow.*
Cytherea or Cyprina, a large gibbous sp.

Fusus latus ? *Sow.* sp.
——, long narrow species, same as at Upnor.
——, n. sp., same as the Hedgerley sp.
Melania inquinata, *Defr.*
Natica glaucinoides, *Sow.*
Panopæa intermedia, *Sow.*
Pectunculus brevirostris, *Sow.*
—— Plumsteadiensis, *Sow.*
Pyrula ?
Rostellaria Sowerbyi, *Mant.*

The estuary species of mollusks are here less numerous than at Upnor, and the marine species show an increase.

This bed thence passes by the north of Canterbury to the cliffs between Herne Bay and the Reculvers†, where a remarkably fine section of the lower part of the London clay and of a large portion of the underlying strata is exposed. These latter here put on a character very different to any we have hitherto observed. Both the fluviatile

---

* Proc. Geol. Soc. vol. iii. p. 457.

† See paper by Mr. W. Richardson, Proc. Geol. Soc. vol. ii. p. 78; also the paper before quoted of Mr. Morris.

beds of Woolwich as well as the mottled clays are entirely wanting. Still the physical or palæontological characters are such as to warrant our considering as the basement bed of the London clay the twenty feet of sands immediately underlying the London clay, although there is here no passage between them. This bed is well exhibited in the centre of the cliff east and west of the ravine at Bishopstoke, two miles east of Herne Bay. (See fig. 11.)

Fig. 11.—*Section near Herne Bay.*

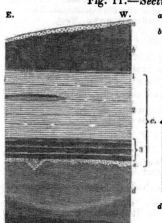

E.   W.

a. Brown and yellow clay, more or less mixed with ochreous flint gravel.

b. London clay; upper beds of a brown colour, and with a few small septaria covered with vermiform impressions, passing down into laminated dark grey clay, more or less sandy, with carbonized vegetable matter. Traces of *Ditrupa plana* and of two species of *Nummulites* occur in the lower part of this clay; other fossils are extremely scarce.

1. Thin irregular seam of green sand; ferruginous clay and a few round flint pebbles, 2 to 3 inches.
2. Very light yellow sands with tabular concreted masses of sandstone and iron sandstone; these are frequently overlaid by a mass corresponding in size of dark clay; very friable shells are irregularly dispersed throughout this bed in small layers and in patches; on the under side of the blocks they are particularly abundant, casts chiefly. 3 & 4. Small flint pebbles with a very irregular series of thin beds of clay and of ferruginous sandstone full of casts of shells. Teeth, vertebræ and bones of fishes of frequent occurrence.

d. Light greenish clayey sands; upper surface worn and indented by the pebble bed above. Beneath are some very fossiliferous clayey sands.

Organic remains of "c," in the Herne Bay cliffs.

Astarte.
Buccinum junceum, *Sow.*
Cardium nitens, *Sow.*
—— Plumsteadiense, *Sow.*
——, n. sp. *a.*
Cerithium variabile, *Desh.*
Cytherea obliqua.
——— ovalis, var. ?, *Sow.*
Cytherea or Cyprina, a large gibbous sp.
Cyprina Morrisii, *Sow.*
Corbula revoluta, *Sow.*
Fusus tuberosus ?, *Sow.*
——, n. sp.
Modiola.
Natica labellata, *Lamk.*

Natica glaucinoides, *Sow.*
—— Hantoniensis, *Pilk.*
Nucula margaritacea, var. β, *Desh.*
——, longer sp.
Ostrea, small sp.
Pectunculus brevirostris, *Sow.*
—— Plumsteadiensis, *Sow.*
Pleurotoma comma, *Sow.*
——, a second sp.
Pyrula.
Rostellaria Sowerbyi, *Mant.*
——, n. sp. large and striated.
Scalaria.
Vertebræ, bones and scales of fishes.
Teeth of Lamnæ.

The estuary species, it will here be observed, have almost entirely disappeared, and we have a fauna presenting a very close analogy with that of stratum "c" at Sonning Hill near Reading and Clarendon Hill near Salisbury. Still at Herne Bay, and more especially at Boughton and Upnor, the fauna differs in some measure from the one which I consider to be synchronous with it to the westward of London. The bed itself also appears more distinctly separable in mineral character from the London clay.

We will now return to our starting-point at Pebble Hill, and thence follow the northern outcrop of this deposit to Woodbridge. Taking a line by Newbury and then northward of Woolhampton to Reading, I know of but one tolerable section of this bed; it occurs in a brick-field on the summit of the hill at Englefield near Theale*. The London clay caps the hill to the depth of twenty to thirty feet. It is brown and sandy, and contains at its base a band of tabular septaria, very ferruginous and containing a few rounded flint pebbles. These septaria are occasionally full of the casts of the following shells :—

Cardium.	Panopæa intermedia, *Sow.*
Calyptræa trochiformis, **Lamk.**	Pectunculus Plumsteadiensis, *Sow.*
Ditrupa plana, *Sow.* sp.	Rostellaria Sowerbyi, **Mant.**
Nucula?	Soft, brown wood in fragments.
Natica.	Teeth of Lamnæ.

The sands and mottled clays outcrop immediately under these beds, and the chalk appears at the northern base of the hill.

At Reading Mr. Rolfe has pointed out a thin stratum overlying the *Plastic clay series,* and containing the following organic remains†:

Cytherea obliqua, **Desh.**	Ditrupa plana, *Sow.* sp.
Pectunculus brevirostris, *Sow.*	Modiola elegans, *Sow.*
Natica glaucinoides, *Sow.*	

In addition to these I have found

Cardium Plumsteadiense, *Sow.*	Scalaria.
—— nitens, *Sow.*	Ostrea.

But by far the best section, and one showing a considerable length of the basement bed of the London clay, was exhibited on the line of the Great Western Railway at Sonning Hill between Reading and Twyford. The cutting, which is sixty to seventy feet deep and about a mile long, traverses the mottled clays. These are covered in the highest parts of the cutting by three to four feet of brown clay with subordinate and irregular layers of yellow sand, the whole mixed with seams and patches of greensand and with some round flint pebbles. Irregular layers and masses of these materials, cemented by carbonate of lime and full of well-preserved shells, are of common occurrence. (See fig. 12.)   A thick bed of ochreous flint gravel caps the section.

Fig. 12.—*Section at Sonning Hill.*

a. Ochreous flint gravel.
b. Brown London clay, with septaria.
c. Yellow sand, with irregular seams of brown clay and green sand; a few round flint pebbles, and numerous tabular calcareous concretions. Fossils dispersed throughout, but peculiarly abundant in the calcareous blocks. Thickness varies from 4 to 5 feet.
d. Upper part of the sands and mottled clays. Surface worn and irregular.

The chalk lies at about 70 to 80 feet below "c," but is not exposed.

* I have found traces of this stratum at several places on the hills both to the N.E. and S.W. of Theale, but only in small road-side cuttings.

† Trans. Geol. Soc. 2nd Ser. vol. v. p. 127. The similarity of the organic remains of these beds at Reading, Watford, Hampstead, and some other places, has already been pointed out by Mr. John Morris so far back as January 1837 (Proc. Geol. Soc. vol. ii. p. 452). In the determination of the fossils of many of these lists I have to express my obligation to Mr. Morris.

Organic remains of stratum "c," at Sonning Hill.

Astarte.
Calyptræa trochiformis, *Lamk.*
Cardium Plumsteadiense, *Sow.*
—— nitens, *Sow.*
——, n. sp. *a.*
Cytherea obliqua, *Desh.*
—— ovalis, var.? *Sow.*
Ditrupa plana, *Sow.* sp.
Fusus.
Modiola elegans, *Sow.*
—— depressa, *Sow.*
Natica glaucinoides, *Sow.*
—— Hantoniensis, *Pilk.*

Nucula.
Ostrea pulchra, *Sow.*
Panopæa intermedia, *Sow.*
Pectunculus brevirostris, *Sow.*
—— Plumsteadiensis, *Sow.*
Pleurotoma.
Rostellaria Sowerbyi, *Mant.*
——, n. sp. *a.*
Scalaria.
Venericardia?
Voluta denudata? *Sow.*
Spatangus.
Teeth of Lamnæ.

The *Ditrupa plana, Cardium* n. sp., *Cytherea obliqua, Modiola elegans, Natica glaucinoides, Ostrea pulchra, Pectunculus brevirostris,* and the teeth of *Lamnæ,* were here particularly abundant.

The more hilly character of the country, and the slight dip of the strata, now cause the outcrop of this bed to expand over a wider area, and to take a very irregular line, which can only be followed at intervals.

At Holywell near Maidenhead a group of fossils from a bed of this age was described by Mr. Warburton[*] in 1821. These fossils are now in the museum of the Society, and consist of the following species :

Calyptræa trochiformis, *Lamk.*
Cardium nitens, *Sow.*
—— Plumsteadiense, *Sow.*
Cyprina or Cytherea.
Ditrupa plana, *Sow.* sp.
Fusus.
Modiola elegans, *Sow.*

Natica glaucinoides ?, *Sow.*
Panopæa intermedia, *Sow.*
Pecten.
Pectunculus Plumsteadiensis, *Sow.*
Pleurotoma.
Tellina.
Teeth of Lamnæ.

In the midst of the chalk district and nearly ten miles to the north of the main body of the tertiaries, I have met with a well-characterized outlier of the basement bed, underlying a capping of London clay, forming the high hill at Lane End four miles west of Wycombe. I found the fossils in blocks of very ferruginous septaria in some small shallow pits on Lane End Common. They were in the state of casts and impressions, and were extremely abundant in some places. They consist of the following species :—

Cardium nitens, *Sow.*
——, n. sp. *a.*
Cytherea obliqua, *Desh.*
Calyptræa trochiformis, *Lamk.*
Fusus.

Modiola elegans? *Sow.*
Natica glaucinoides, *Sow.*
Pectunculus Plumsteadiensis, *Sow.*
Teeth of Lamnæ.

No good section is exposed.

Another small but interesting outlier occurs on the chalk at Tilers' Hill, one and a half mile east of Chesham. Several brick-pits are worked on the summit of this hill, exhibiting in a series of clear sections the several beds from the chalk to the London clay, which here consists of a brown clay with large septaria. At the base of the London clay is a layer of one to two feet of rounded flint pebbles in sand and clay. To this succeeds a series of sands, with some pebble beds, reposing on the chalk. (The section of this hill will be

---

[*] Trans. Geol. Soc. 2nd Ser. vol. i. p. 52.

given in a future paper.)   The organic remains found here during a
very short visit were as under :—

Cytherea obliqua ? *Desh.*   Teeth of Lamnæ.
Natica glaucinoides ? *Sow.*

Returning to the main line of outcrop, we reach, about midway
between Maidenhead and Uxbridge, the small village of Hedgerley,
immediately to the south-west of which, in a brick-field on the slope
of the hill, is a very interesting section first visited by Mr. Morris
and myself in 1842, at which time the section was much clearer than
I found it last autumn.   The abundance and fine state of preservation of the organic remains at this place far surpass anything that
we had then, or that I have since, seen in any part of the tertiaries
westward of London, excepting perhaps Sonning Hill.   The fossils
are preserved in large tabular masses of calcareous clayey green sand
containing a few rounded flint pebbles, at the base of the London
clay, and immediately overlying the mottled clays. (See fig. 13.)

Fig. 13.—*Section at Hedgerley.*

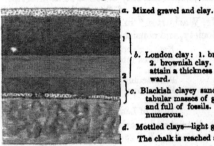

a. Mixed gravel and clay.

b. London clay: 1. brown and bluish clay with septaria;
   2. brownish clay. Fossils scarce in these beds, which
   attain a thickness of 35 feet at a short distance southward.

c. Blackish clayey sand and green sand, underlaid by flat
   tabular masses of green sand with a calcareous cement
   and full of fossils. The small round flint pebbles not
   numerous.

d. Mottled clays—light greenish grey and red.

The chalk is reached at a depth of 45 feet beneath " *c.* "

Organic remains of stratum " c," at Hedgerley.

Cardium nitens, *Sow.*
—— Plumsteadiense, *Sow.*
——, n. sp. *a.*
Cassidaria striata, *Sow.*
Corbula revoluta, *Sow.*
Cytherea obliqua, *Desh.*
—— ovalis, var. ? *Sow.*
Ditrupa plana, *Sow.* sp.
Fusus, large finely striated sp.
——, broad smooth sp.
Glycimeris ?
Modiola elegans, *Sow.*
Natica glaucinoides, *Sow.*
—— Hantoniensis, *Pilk.*
Nucula.

Ostrea.
Pectunculus Plumsteadiensis, *Sow.*
Panopæa intermedia, *Sow.*
Pleurotoma, large smooth sp.
Pyrula tricostata, *Desh.*
Rostellaria Sowerbyi, *Mant.*
——, n. sp. smaller.
Tellina.
Scalaria.
Vertebræ of fishes.
Teeth of Lamnæ.
Wood in fragments.
A boring Mollusk, probably a Lithodo-
mus.

The concretionary calcareous masses have a brown and weathered
appearance, and have been here and there bored into by some
mollusk. These blocks are literally full of shells, amongst which
the *Cardium* n. sp. *a, Cytherea obliqua, Natica glaucinoides, Nucula,
Rostellaria Sowerbyi,* and the *Ditrupa plana,* are most abundant.
The shells are well-preserved, some with their nacre, but, as at
Sunning Hill, their substance is rather soft and friable.

Proceeding by Uxbridge to Watford, occasional imperfect indications of this bed are met with.   On the Birmingham Railway, at Bushey near Watford, the mottled clays with the basement bed of the London clay were exposed, in a section which I was too late to see in a good condition.   The superposition, however, was sufficiently apparent.   The following organic remains were found there by the late Dr. James Mitchell :—

Cardium nitens, *Sow.*	Cytherea obliqua, *Desh.*
—— Plumsteadiense, *Sow.*	Nucula.
——, n. sp. *a.*	Panopæa intermedia, *Sow.*
Cytherea ovalis, var.? *Sow.*	Rostellaria Sowerbyi, *Mant.*

Diverging five miles to the south, the chalk comes so near to the surface in the valley at Pinner near Harrow, that it is worked by shafts sunk through the superincumbent tertiaries.   The following is a section of one of these shafts.   (See fig. 14.)

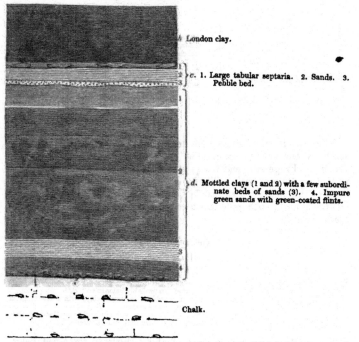

Fig. 14.—*Section at Pinner.*

b. London clay.

c. 1. Large tabular septaria. 2. Sands. 3. Pebble bed.

d. Mottled clays (1 and 2) with a few subordinate beds of sands (3).   4. Impure green sands with green-coated flints.

Chalk.

The works were not in operation at the time I visited this spot, and I was unable to procure any of the fossils said to occur abundantly in the stratum which I have marked " *c.* 1."

Passing eastward by Shenley Hill, no good section of this bed occurs until we reach a brick-field one mile east-south-east of Hatfield, and immediately adjoining the east side of Lord Salisbury's park.   This pit exposes a complete section from the lower part of

the London clay to the chalk.   It may, with fig. 14, serve to show
the general relative position of stratum "c" to the chalk, but exhibits neither the thickness nor the variety usual in this lower series.
(See fig. 15.)

Fig. 15.—*Section near Hatfield.*

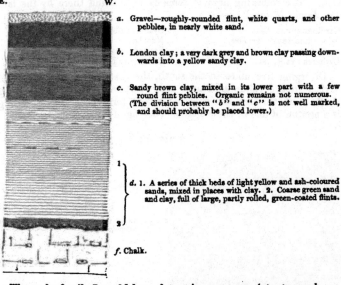

E.   W.

a. Gravel—roughly-rounded flint, white quartz, and other
   pebbles, in nearly white sand.

b. London clay; a very dark grey and brown clay passing downwards into a yellow sandy clay.

c. Sandy brown clay, mixed in its lower part with a few
   round flint pebbles.   Organic remains not numerous.
   (The division between "b" and "c" is not well marked,
   and should probably be placed lower.)

d. 1. A series of thick beds of light yellow and ash-coloured
   sands, mixed in places with clay. 2. Coarse green sand
   and clay, full of large, partly rolled, green-coated flints.

f. Chalk.

The only fossils I could here determine were an *Astarte* much resembling the species common at Herne Bay, *Ostrea*, and teeth of
Lamnæ.   Fragments and traces of other shells requiring further examination are met with.   Thence by Essenden* to Hertford no sections of this bed are exposed.   The next one is in a brick-field on
George's Farm, one mile south-east from Hertford on the London
road. (See fig. 16.)

Fig. 16.—*Section near Hertford.*

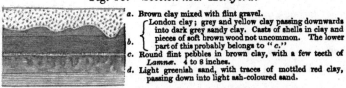

a. Brown clay mixed with flint gravel.
b. {London clay; grey and yellow clay passing downwards
   into dark grey sandy clay. Casts of shells in clay and
   pieces of soft brown wood not uncommon. The lower
   part of this probably belongs to "c."
c. Round flint pebbles in brown clay, with a few teeth of
   Lamnæ. 4 to 8 inches.
d. Light greenish sand, with traces of mottled red clay,
   passing down into light ash-coloured sand.

The chalk outcrops at a depth of about thirty to forty feet below
"c."   The organic remains here found in the lower part of "b" and
in "c" are not numerous, and are badly preserved in the form of soft
clay casts.   Sufficient, however, of them remains to determine with
but little doubt the undermentioned species :—

* In a well dug here, I am informed that a mass of shells ten feet thick occurred
immediately below the London clay, at a depth of 100 feet.

Panopæa intermedia, *Sow.*	Fusus.
Pectunculus Plumsteadiensis, *Sow.*	Ostrea.
Cardium, n. sp. *a* ?	Teeth of Lamnæ.
Astarte ?	

We now enter upon a tract of country, which is so thickly and uniformly covered by beds of gravel and boulder clay drift, that it is rarely that the smallest section of the tertiary beds is visible. Occasionally where the chalk is worked we find a small capping of the sands and mottled clays immediately overlying it; but taking the line of country by Stanstead, Bishop Stortford, Easton near Dunmow, to Great Yeldham, I have not been able to find a single section of the basement bed of the London clay.

Between Yeldham and Sudbury in Suffolk, however, in a brick-field on the brow of the hill near the village of Gestingthorpe, there is a small section in which the basement bed of the London clay may, I think, be identified, although the only fossils I could find in it were the teeth of the usual species of *Lamna*. (See fig. 17.)

Fig. 17.—*Section at Gestingthorpe**.

N.   S.

a. Boulder clay drift.

b. London clay; upper part of brown sandy clay, with the common bluish facets, and containing a few small sandy ochreous concretions; passes down into yellowish sand laminated with greyish clay. No organic remains yet found.

c. Round flint pebbles in sand and clay. Teeth of *Lamna* common. No other fossils.
d. Bright yellow sands.

The chalk outcrops near the base of the hill at a depth probably not exceeding sixty to eighty feet beneath " *c.*" Continuing over the same irregular hilly district, intersected by narrow and small river-valleys, we pass by Sudbury and Layland to Hadleigh. On a hill one mile E.N.E. of this town, the lower beds of the London clay are worked together with the underlying sands. (See fig. 18.)

Fig. 18.—*Section near Hadleigh*.

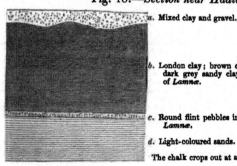

a. Mixed clay and gravel.

b. London clay; brown clay passing downwards into a dark grey sandy clay, with a few shells and teeth of *Lamnæ*.

c. Round flint pebbles in sand and clay, with teeth of *Lamnæ*.

d. Light-coloured sands.

The chalk crops out at a short distance below this pit.

* This section, with two near Hadleigh, and three or four near Ipswich, require further examination.

The next section is at Whitton Street, two and a half miles north-west of Ipswich. In some fields to the westward of the high road there are two pits, one of which exhibits the following section. (See fig. 19.) ·

Fig. 19.—*Section near Ipswich.*

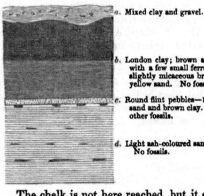

a. Mixed clay and gravel.

b. London clay; brown and occasionally light bluish-grey clay, with a few small ferruginous concretions, passing down into slightly micaceous brown clay laminated with ochreous and yellow sand. No fossils.

c. Round flint pebbles—1 to 10 inches in diameter—in ochreous sand and brown clay. Teeth of *Lamnæ* not uncommon. No other fossils.

d. Light ash-coloured sand, with a few small clayey concretions. No fossils.

The chalk is not here reached, but it crops out at a short distance lower down the hill, and at a level of not exceeding thirty to forty feet below stratum "*c.*" There are some pits adjoining Ipswich near the Woodbridge road which exhibit sections of the London clay over-lying sands which I believe to belong to the lower Eocene series. I have not examined these pits in detail.

Passing on to Woodbridge, we arrive, at a distance of one mile south from this town, and on the banks of the river, at the Kyson brick-field, a spot well known by the circumstance of the teeth of the Monkey having been found there[*]. The exact position of the bed in which these remains occur has been considered rather problematical, but I have little doubt that it belongs to the basement bed of the London clay[†]. (See fig. 20.)

Fig. 20.—*Section at Kyson*[‡]*.*

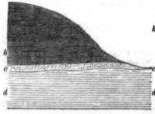

b. London clay. Above this clay, and a little higher on the slope of the hill, the red crag crops out.

c. Round flint pebbles in yellow sand. Teeth of *Lamnæ* common; those of a species of Monkey rare. This crops out on the level of the river.

d. Light-coloured sands; depth unknown. Large *Ostreæ* said to occur in some concretions in the upper part of this bed.

[*] Owen, Annals Nat. Hist. vol. iv. p. 191.
[†] It has been already assigned by several geologists to the beds beneath the London clay.
[‡] I cannot quite depend upon this section, as I have mislaid my original notes of it.

Organic remains of stratum " c," at Kyson*.

Macacus eocænus, *Owen.*	Cheiroptera.
Didelphys? Colchesteri, *Charlesworth.*	Teeth of Lamnæ.
Hyracotherium cuniculus, *Owen.*	

I have found slight traces of fossils in the clay bed " *b*," but they were too imperfect for determination.

A larger section of the London clay is worked near Melton Street, two miles north-east of Woodbridge.

Beyond Woodbridge to the coast the Eocene strata are continuously overlaid by the Crag, and sections of them become still less frequent. On the coast the cliffs at Bawdsley show a section of red crag reposing on the London clay, but these cliffs are not continued to that point (probably not far northward) where the beds below the London clay would crop out.

We have now traced this basement bed of the London clay at intervals in a belt wrapping round the tertiary series for the length of 250 miles.

In the central portions of the tertiary district, the base of the London clay, although not exposed, is reached in many well-sections. Everywhere the same leading features as we have shown to exist at the outcrop, present themselves at greater depths.

The organic remains found in this stratum, unlike those of the London clay, which so generally exhibit internally some form of pyritical or calcareous infiltration giving the fossil a solid form, are usually extremely friable, and have rarely undergone any mineral substitution. The ordinary material of the rock passes into the interior of the shell. The shell itself is almost always preserved, although in a very earthy and friable condition. Still, where care is taken, or when they are imbedded in calcareous masses, they can be obtained in a very perfect state.

Owing to the persistent range of this bed and its distinctive character, I have, to give it a definite designation for the convenience of reference, termed it " the basement bed of the London clay," although viewing it always merely as a subordinate member of the London clay.

Conclusion.

The preceding descriptions I believe embrace, with two or three exceptions, all the principal sections exhibiting the superposition of the basement bed of the London clay. Although, considering the extent of the line of outcrop, they are not very numerous, the intervals between them are sufficiently short to trace this deposit from place to place with considerable certainty. The details of each may vary

---

* These fossils are as rare as they are curious. They have been found chiefly by the careful and minute search instituted by Mr. Colchester, who, I believe, had the sands and pebbles (" *c* ") frequently sifted and examined on purpose. A like close examination might possibly bring to light similar fossils at other localities, especially at those where the structure so nearly resembles that at Kyson (as in figs. 17, 18, & 19). So scarce are these fossils, that in the short visits I have paid to all these pits (Kyson included), I have never found anything but the teeth of the *Lamna.*

in a few points, but they all present a general resemblance. This may not however be considered sufficient for our object—such thin and ordinary beds might be subordinate to some other portion of the Eocene series, and not peculiar to this part of them, and therefore some other proofs of their position may be thought necessary.

In the first place, all the sections in the tertiary district show, by evidence of the clearest kind, that the London clay forms a nearly homogeneous mass, several hundred feet thick, of tough clay of a predominating brown colour—that throughout its whole body it nowhere presents any subordinate beds of a mineral character essentially different from that of its ordinary argillaceous type—and that its organic remains are very irregularly dispersed, abounding in some parts and being entirely wanting in others. This clay occupies an area which is very well defined. Now wherever, without a single exception that I am aware of, the lower beds of this clay outcrop, there is found underlying them a basement bed of a conglomerate character and with or without organic remains—and these, if present, invariably belong to one and the same group of fossils. Further, if we go more into the chalk district, we shall find that whenever the outliers of the lower tertiary sands and mottled clays without organic remains, attain a thickness on an average of from 50 to 100 feet, the basement bed of the London clay invariably sets in. Again, this deposit always exhibits a peculiar mineral character, the chief feature of which is the presence of rounded flint pebbles, mixed with yellow, green, or ferruginous sands in variable proportions. Intermingled with the conglomerate bed, or in the thin sandy layer above it, are frequently found numerous organic remains belonging to a fauna of about forty species, many of which are persistent throughout the greater part of the range of this stratum. Now although the London clay does not always contain organic remains, nor is the basement bed always fossiliferous, neither is the mineral character of one or the other always exactly alike, nevertheless the concurrent testimony afforded in each case, either by position, or by organic remains, or by lithological structure, although the force and value of one or the other class of evidence may vary materially, is I consider, in all the instances I have adduced, sufficiently strong to prove the position assumed. I cannot admit, as has been urged, that the absence of organic remains in the lower beds of the London clay, at New Cross, Upnor, Gestingthorpe, Kyson, and elsewhere (see Sections 8, 10, 17, 20), is an argument against such beds forming part of the London clay. It is not possible to take up a position upon a mere negative fact—to use as substantive evidence that which of itself is but a difficulty arising from variable, and not from conflicting, conditions.

If the "*massif*" of the adjoining district consists of London clay, and the dip and position of the strata, as well as their mineral characters, lead us to suppose that these beds crop out in the position which should be occupied by the lower beds of the London clay, then I hold that as such they must be considered, unless they can be proved to be something else. Otherwise, in trying to avoid one difficulty a more formidable one will be raised, in having to reduce into harmony with the phænomena of the surrounding district that, which in this case would become an exceptional phænomenon.   We should rather seek, by an inquiry into the conditions regulating the distribution of organic remains in the London clay, whether a sufficient reason can be assigned for the absence of organic remains in these portions of the London clay, and to discover how far the phænomenon is a local or a general one.

In Hampshire and the western part of the London tertiary district, the organic remains of the London clay are dispersed with tolerable regularity throughout the whole of its mass, whereas eastward of London the lower beds of the London clay contain, as a general rule, few or no fossils.   The fact therefore of the scarcity of organic remains in the lowest clay beds of the London clay in a large portion of its range is a prevailing and not an exceptional feature.   It is not alone apparent in those sections where we find only a small extent of the London clay exposed, and on which consequently doubts have been thrown, but also in those sections where we have the successive beds of the London clay exposed from its base up to its well-characterized central beds.   Thus in the extensive section in the cliffs adjoining Herne Bay, the base of the London clay is almost, or entirely destitute of fossils, whereas as we reach the beds higher in the series, which are seen gradually setting in, the well-known fossils of this formation become far from scarce.   So also at Guildford the lower beds are unfossiliferous, but in proceeding along the dip of the beds towards Woking, organic remains become tolerably abundant.

I have in a previous paper* argued the probability of the London clay of Hampshire having been deposited during a period of a nearly constant, regular, and tranquil subsidence of the bed of the sea, whereby a nearly uniform condition of the sea-bottom, favourable to the prolonged existence of the same group of testacea, was maintained.   I also concluded that the subsidence had been greater to the north-east than to the south-west of the Tertiary district, and it therefore follows that it must have been more rapid in the former direction either throughout the whole, or else during particular intervals, of the London clay period ; and consequently if the rate of that subsidence was at any time more rapid than the silting up of the sea-bottom, it would result that at such times the sea would become deeper in the north-east than the south-west.   Under these conditions we might expect a distribution of the fauna in the north-east of the tertiary district different to that prevailing in the south-west.   Now, if the accumulation of the lower part of the great mass of clay forming the London clay commenced during a sudden or even a tolerably rapid subsidence of the sea-bottom in the north-eastern portions of the tertiary area, then the shallow sea fauna of the basement bed could not under these altered conditions of increased depth have been tranquilly transmitted upwards as in the Hampshire area, but must for a time have ceased to live in districts so affected, and, before a deeper sea fauna were introduced, strata might have been deposited with few or no organic remains.

* Quart. Journ. Geol. Soc. vol. iii. p. 354.

After a time, however, the inhabitants of deeper waters would gradually immigrate into these parts of greater depths, and there remain, until from some cause the sea became again sufficiently shallow to allow of the incoming of shallow sea testacea, and then that original fauna, which in the interval had been preserved in the same sea, in the distant Hampshire tertiary area, might have extended itself and reappeared in that part of it spreading over the more central and easterly parts of the London tertiary district.

This I consider to have been the succession of events at this period of the tertiary epoch. On this supposition I account for the absence or extreme scarcity of organic remains in the lower part of the London clay in the central and eastern divisions of the district, and for their abundance in the western divisions. In the neighbourhood of London, as we ascend in this formation, we meet with remains of Cephalopodous testacea in strata succeeding the lower unfossiliferous beds, and we find them further eastward with the remains of Cephalopoda, of Echinodermata, and of other denizens of deeper seas, in some abundance. The lower beds of the London clay overlying its basement bed, may therefore from this cause without difficulty be conceived to present, although synchronous, considerable modifications in their organic remains, whose presence or absence taken separately does not consequently afford a test in this case to the determination of the geological horizon.

We now have to consider the physical changes indicated by the structure of the basement bed itself, marking as it does the passage from the arenaceous beds below to the argillaceous ones above it. Of the conditions of the sea preceding this period we shall treat on a future occasion.

Indiscriminately over all the variable "Lower Eocene" deposits spreads the basement bed of the London clay. It is the first brush of uniformity, where previously all had been different. Extending from the Isle of Wight to Woodbridge in Suffolk, this bed presents some general characters of remarkable persistence. In the first place it is evident that it does not form a sequence in structure conformable to the beds which it immediately overlies. Yet no fresh element is introduced at first into its composition. Although the materials composing this bed are not in many cases found in any of the beds immediately below, yet they all exist in the underlying series in some part of their range, and are, I believe, derived from that source. The great depositary of the rounded flint pebbles in the underlying beds, are the estuary and fluviatile strata of Woolwich and Bromley, where they occur in remarkable abundance. Associated with these pebble beds are thick beds of yellow sand and also several subordinate beds of a strong coarse green sand (which become, however, much more important in East Kent), some beds of a deep ferruginous character, and a few clay beds—the mottled clays of the western districts also are interstratified with beds of yellow sands, but without pebbles. Now the pebbles of the basement bed of the London clay have been probably derived from those previously accumulated locally in these underlying beds, and, if the pebbles, then also

the various sorts of sand associated with those beds, were also likely
to have been thus derived.   I hold this opinion because this basement bed does not present these different substances in separate and
sedimentary order—the bed is composite, and its materials derived,
not by a river action bringing down sediment into the sea, but, if
I may so term it, by apparently a scouring and general sea action on
the pre-existing and underlying beds.   That the pebbles in this bed
are not in the position in which they received their present form, is, I
think, evident from the excessive and lengthened attrition which the
flints must have undergone to have formed pebbles of such uniform
roundness and finish—a state of things incompatible with the co-
existence and preservation of the remains of a delicate and abundant
fauna in the same stratum.   But we have other and independent
proofs of this bed having originated in the destruction of part of the
underlying beds.   Thus in Section, fig. 1, at White Cliff Bay, it has
been shown that rough pebbles of red clay, derived from the harder
parts of the underlying mottled clays, occur in this bed ; and in Section, fig. 11, at Herne Bay cliff, I have found in this bed specimens
of the peculiar uncouth green-coated flints, which form the characteristic bed, reposing almost everywhere in this country and in the
North of France immediately on the chalk.   These half-rolled green-
coated flints have an appearance so perfectly distinct and constant,
that their origin cannot for a moment be doubted.   Therefore it is
probable that the denuding action acted not only on the mottled
clays and the pebble beds forming the upper part of the underlying
series, but that it in places extended to the chalk itself.   It is doubtful however whether the latter suffered much denudation at this time.
There are but few traces of its direct debris in this bed.   The pebbles
of flint I suppose to have been derived from a long-continued wearing away of the chalk at a previous period.   The disturbance at the
period of the basement bed of the London clay does not appear to
have acted with sufficient power on the chalk, nor during sufficient
time on the flints, to have produced a large destruction of the former,
or to have reduced the latter to the state of such well-rounded flint
pebbles.

The irregular and worn upper surface of the lower beds of sands
and mottled clays, upon which the basement bed of the London clay
reposes, is a corroborative proof of their partial denudation prior to
the deposition of the latter.   The erosion is certainly not very great,
yet it forms an extremely well-marked phænomenon, as at Sonning
Hill and Guildford (see Sections 6 and 12), at which latter place it
has removed all but a few patches of the Woolwich beds.   In the
western parts of the London tertiary district it has worn to some
extent into the mottled clays.

That the setting-in of this denuding action was sudden, is evident
from the abruptness of the change ; of its force, the size of the
transported pebbles, and the amount of erosion, lead us to judge
that it was moderate ; and that it was not of long duration is evidenced by the thinness of the deposit.

The erosion is more apparent, and the exhibition of transporting
force greater, on the southern flank of the tertiary beds than on the

northern. It was at this period that the great break appears to
have taken place between the English and French tertiaries ; for up to
this point, the sands, mottled clays, and fluviatile beds are common
to both countries, and present much similarity of structure. But at
this level the resemblance ceases ; the London clay sets in with its
great argillaceous character, whilst in France this period is succeeded
by a series of light-coloured, calcareous, and generally very fossiliferous sands and earthy limestones. I do not think this separation
of the two districts to have been caused by the elevation of the
Wealden : in the first place, because the London clay is found in
nearly equal force on both sides of the Wealden elevation ; and
in the second place, because there is evidence (see Sections 4, 5,
and 6) that that elevation affected these Eocene strata equally with
the secondary ones. It would appear therefore, on physical grounds,
that the denudation acted from the southward, while it has been before shown, on palæontological evidence, that in this same direction
there was probably a considerable rise of the sea-bottom, accompanied
by a slight subsidence to the northward. To the disturbing action
of the waters flowing off from the sea-bottom thus raised to the
southward, I attribute the first spread of the basement bed of the
London clay and the partial denudation of the underlying strata.
The elevation of the bed of the sea was not sufficient to convert it
into dry land, nor was the change of that violence to destroy, over
the whole area acted upon, the animal life of the period. In distant
or in more sheltered parts of the sea, as before mentioned, some of
the testacea which inhabited it were preserved and transmitted into
the deposits formed subsequently to these changes.

The basement bed of the London clay contains altogether thirty-
one known species of testacea, and apparently eight to ten undescribed
species. In Hampshire and in the western division of the London
district there are in the underlying strata no remaining traces of any
older stock whence this new fauna could have been derived. From
London, however, through Woolwich to Upnor, this bed reposes upon
fossiliferous fluviatile beds, and here apparently there seems to be a
transmission upwards, from one period to another, of some of the
species, as the *Cyrena obovata, C. cuneiformis, C. tellinella, Cerithium variabile, Melania inquinata,* and *Pectunculus Plumsteadiensis,* which abound in the estuary and fluviatile beds of Woolwich*.
Some of the species also from the lower marine deposits of Herne
Bay and Sandwich range upwards into the "basement bed," as the
Corbula revoluta, C. longirostris, Natica glaucinoides, and *Pectunculus Plumsteadiensis,* and probably the *Cyprina Morrisii.* There
is this difference, however, between the species introduced from the
underlying beds, and those which constitute the typical and universal
group which will shortly be alluded to, viz. that the former are, with
the exception possibly of the *Cyprina Morrisii,* confined in their
range to a limited region, surmounting or not extending much beyond (*i. e.* at this period) that previously occupied by them, whilst
the latter have a general and unlimited range.

* Out of these six species four even lived on to the period of the freshwater
series of the Isle of Wight.

After deducting the Woolwich and Herne Bay species from the fauna of this period, there remains nineteen out of thirty-one described species which are not found in the underlying deposits. They form a distinct and well-marked group, and the individuals of the species are often extremely numerous. The principal species are the *Panopæa intermedia, Cytherea obliqua, C. ovalis,* var.?, *Cardium nitens, C. Plumsteadiense, Pectunculus brevirostris*, Natica glaucinoides, N. Hantoniensis,* and *Rostellaria Sowerbyi.* In the western districts the *Ditrupa plana* is also particularly abundant, and the *Pyrula tricostata* is common, but both these die out or become very scarce as they range eastward.

Between the eastern and western districts there is also a space (including Woolwich, Upnor, Boughton) where, owing probably to the more brackish state of the sea, as evidenced by the great and sudden abundance of *Melania* and the several species of *Cyrena,* many other marine-genera disappear. A few, as the *Panopæa, Rostellaria,* one species of *Cardium,* and *Calyptræa,* are however persistent throughout (see Table A.). Notwithstanding this interruption, the fauna at Herne Bay presents a remarkable similarity to that which flourished at the same period at Hedgerley, Reading, and Clarendon Hill, modified only by the introduction of the few shells before mentioned.

It is to be observed, however, that the fossils of this deposit, although they have so persistent a range from west to east, decrease rapidly to the north-east, and from their nearly total absence in Essex and Suffolk, an argument might be brought against the identity which I have there given to that deposit in Sections Nos. 17 to 20. On structural and lithological grounds I have before argued in favour of this identity, and I cannot view this absence of fossils as a militating argument of much weight against such a supposition. If it occurred on a line where the same bed in adjacent sections was very fossiliferous, then the question would be attended with some difficulty; but in this instance we are led almost naturally to anticipate their disappearance, from their rapid decrease as we proceed eastward on their northern line of outcrop from Hedgerley, where they abound, by Watford, where they are far less numerous, to Hatfield and Hertford, where they are comparatively scarce. Their decrease in this direction is in that ratio, that their rarity or absence in Essex and Suffolk presents no anomaly. The only fossil constantly present is the tooth of a species of *Lamna,* probably the *Lamna elegans* of Agassiz.

In order better to show the range of the organic remains of this bed, I have added the accompanying Table A. with a list of all the described species and of two or three of the more important undescribed ones. As a group, it will be observed that these species are essentially those which we find afterwards characterizing the London clay, and that the other species, which range from the beds below, are fewer in numbers, and possess usually a very wide vertical, although at this level they exhibit a very limited horizontal, range†.

* I do not give the *Pectunculus Plumsteadiensis,* as it seems to me to be doubtful whether this species is not a variety of the *P. brevirostris.*

† The breaks in the range of many of the species will probably decrease as the examination of this bed is made more complete at some of the localities.

With regard to the condition of the sea immediately anterior to the period of the deposition of the basement bed of the London clay, it is probable that the whole, or nearly so, of the south-east of England was occupied by the Eocene sea, studded with a few islands. An important one may have existed at some point between Woolwich and Newhaven (unconnected however with the elevation of the Wealden as it has since taken place). On the shores of these islands small rivers accumulated fluviatile and estuary deposits, such as those of Woolwich, New Cross, Upnor, and Newhaven, whilst further eastward marine deposits were accumulating in the open sea stretching to, and probably beyond, the now Isle of Thanet.

In this state of things a movement of depression probably took place over this district in a direction W.S.W. to E.N.E. from Hampshire to Suffolk, whilst a corresponding and coæval elevation took place perhaps on a parallel line further south, and passing, I am rather inclined to believe, south of the Isle of Wight towards the north of France, and not touching upon the area now occupied by England. From off this raised sea-bed to the south, a wave of translation (if the term may be applied to deposits of this period), of moderate power and having a N.N.W. flow, would be thrown, spreading over the bottom of the sea, debris derived chiefly from the older eocene sands and pebble beds forming the bed of the sea over which this wave moved. This wave would decrease in force as it receded from the axis of elevation, whence the diminished erosion of the surface, and the generally smaller size of the pebbles, in Essex and Suffolk. The spread of this debris would afterwards be further modified and extended by currents. At the same time, the sea, then of moderate and tolerably uniform depth, was extended over a larger area than it before occupied. The ancient river-courses were altered, their deposits ceased wholly or partially, and no new rivers yet came into full operation, for the fauna lived and flourished on a sea bed which evidently received but little addition of sediment during this period. Over the eastern part of Kent, however, the actions of currents and perhaps of small rivers still led to the accumulation of deposits of fine sands, increasing in thickness from two to three feet near London to twenty feet at Herne Bay.

Westward of London in no case does the basement bed of the London clay present a thickness of more than five feet, and in many places it does not exceed one foot. Where the passage from this stratum to the mass of the overlying London clay is gradual (see Sections 1, 5, & 12), fossils usually abound, especially near the line of junction; while if the argillaceous beds repose at once on a compact and separate layer of pebbles, few or no fossils are found (see Sections 3, 7, 8, 17).

This profusion in some localities of organic remains, and their dispersion over so wide an area, render it also probable that, after the first spread of the debris of pebbles and sand, a considerable interval of time elapsed before the argillaceous beds of the London clay began to accumulate, a process which however afterwards set in gradually and without any mark of further disturbance, the necessary physical changes having taken place at the period of its basement bed. At the same time the occasional presence in this bed of the remains of a boring mollusk would lead to the supposition that the first change after the interval of repose was one of a slight and tranquil elevation, by which the recently-formed deposit was raised either near to or above the surface of the sea, according to the irregularities of the sea-bottom.   On the emerged portions the *Lithodomus* might have lived, and there left traces of its existence, as exhibited in the borings in the calcareous masses of this age at Hedgerley, and in the large and thick oyster-shells of the same date at Maryland Point.   The places at which these remains occur, appear to me too detached and isolated to favour the supposition of a continued and extended line of coast.

The slight elevation here alluded to would also, by bringing fresh currents into action, account for the fact before-mentioned of the argillaceous beds of the London clay sometimes passing gradually downwards into this arenaceous and conglomerate bed, and at other times reposing abruptly on a mere layer of pebbles, the latter places having been more exposed to the denuding action of these currents whereby the lighter portions of the deposit might have been removed.   This movement I consider to have been but part of a very gradual and comparatively imperceptible oscillation, which, after producing a slight elevation, led to a long-continued subsidence productive of further and important changes in the distribution of land and water of that period. By these mutations new rivers would of necessity be formed, or the old ones would take a new course according as the watershed of the country was shifted, and thus probably originated that powerful fluviatile action, which swept down into this Eocene sea the vast argillaceous sediment, with its rich stores of land plants and marine animals, forming the London clay.

I conclude therefore that the basement bed of the London clay constitutes a well-marked horizon, dividing the London clay formation by a change, both in the palæontological conditions and in the ancient physical geography of the district, from the older Eocene deposits which intervene between the chalk and the London clay, its mineral mass being composed of the debris of the former, while its animal life belongs to the period of the latter.

I hope to treat of the remaining division of this series at a future period.

TABLE A.—London Clay through the Hampshire and

Note.—The line of ran[g]ent localities are placed approximately at their relative geographical [i]ndicates the greater or lesser abundance of the species at any given pla[ce].

		Upnor, near Rochester.	Boughton, near Faversham.	The Cliffs near Herne Bay.	Found in the London Clay, or in beds above it (marked o).	Found in the beds underlying the Basement bed of the London Clay.
Conchifera.	Ditrupa plana, *So[w.]*				*	
	Panopæa interme[d.]				*	
	Corbula revoluta,				*	*
	—— longirostris,					*
	Cyrena cuneiform[is]				o	*
	—— obovata, *Sou[w.]*				o	*
	—— tellinella, *F[e.]*					*
	Cyprina Morrisii,					*
	Cytherea obliqua,				*	
	—— ovalis, var.,					
	Cardium nitens, *S[.]*				*	
	—— Plumsteadie[nse]				*	
	——, n. sp........					
	Pectunculus brevi[s]				*	
	—— Plumsteadie[nse]					*
	Nucula margaritac[ea]				*	*
	Modiola depressa,				*	
	—— elegans, *Sow[.]*				*	
	Ostrea Bellovacina					*
Mollusca.	Calyptræa trochif[ormis]				*	
	Melania inquinata,					*
	Natica glaucinoide[s]				*	*
	—— Hantoniensis				*	
	—— labellata, *La[m.]*				*	
	Cerithium variabil[e]					*
	Cancellaria læviusc[ula]				*	
	Rostellaria Sowerb[yi]				*	
	——, n. sp.					
	Cassidaria striata,				*	
	Buccinum junceum				*	
	Fusus tuberosus, *S[.]*				*	
	——, n. sp.					
	Pyrula tricostata,				*	
	Pleurotoma comm[unis]				*	

ON THE

STRUCTURE OF THE STRATA

BETWEEN THE

LONDON CLAY AND THE CHALK

IN THE

LONDON AND HAMPSHIRE TERTIARY SYSTEMS.

PART II.
SECOND DIVISION—"THE WOOLWICH AND READING SERIES."

By JOSEPH PRESTWICH, Jun., Esq., F.R.S., F.G.S.

[*From the* QUARTERLY JOURNAL *of the* GEOLOGICAL SOCIETY *for* February 1854.]

LONDON:
PRINTED BY TAYLOR AND FRANCIS,
RED LION COURT, FLEET STREET.
1854.

On the Structure *of the* Strata *between the* London Clay *and the* Chalk *in the* London *and* Hampshire Tertiary Systems. By Joseph Prestwich, Jun., Esq., F.R.S., F.G.S.

Part II.—The Woolwich and Reading Series.

ᵛ[Plates I. II. III. IV.]

On two former occasions I have given some account of the deposit immediately underlying the London Clay, as well as of that which, to the eastward of London, lies upon the Chalk, and which I have respectively termed the "Basement Bed of the London Clay*" and the "Thanet Sands†." Between these divisions, which form the upper and lower portions of the *Lower London Tertiaries*, is a group of sands, pebble beds, and mottled clays, extending from Sandwich to Marlborough and from Newhaven to Dorchester. This group, with the two above-mentioned, completes the series of these Lower Tertiaries, and is the one which more particularly embraces the beds which have hitherto been described as the "*Plastic Clay Formation*," exhibiting in one part of its range the mottled clays of Reading and Newbury, and, in another, the clays and sands, with fluviatile and æstuarine shells, of New Cross,

* Quart. Journ. Geol. Soc. vol. vi. p. 252.   † *Ibid.* vol. viii. p. 235.

Woolwich, and Bromley. Some of the principal sections in these localities have been described by Parkinson[*], Webster[†], Dr. Buckland[‡], Phillips and Conybeare[§], Morris[||], Mitchell[**], Richardson[††], Warburton[‡‡], and more recently by the Rev. Mr. De la Condamine[§§]; whilst outlines of some underground sections have been planned by Mr. R. W. Mylne[||||], and a short notice relating to the superposition of these and the other Tertiary strata has lately been given by M. Hébert[***]. But nevertheless the correlation of the beds at the different sections has not, I conceive, been correctly shown, and the position which the strata of the Reculvers and Herne Bay hold with respect to those of Woolwich and Reading yet remains unsettled. At the same time, the lists of fossils even at the several best-known and often-explored localities admit of many additions and corrections. From the very circumstance of the band of green sand with the *Ostrea Bellovacina*, which underlies the mottled clays at Reading, having been referred to the band of green sand at the base of the Thanet Sands at Woolwich, and which likewise reposes upon the Chalk, it has had a tendency to place the Mottled Clays too low with respect to the fluviatile beds of Woolwich, and rather to correlate these latter with the Basement Bed of the London Clay at Reading. There was however another reason for this arrangement, inasmuch as in the sections at Blackheath, and elsewhere near London where the mottled clays show themselves, these latter underlie the Woolwich shelly clays ; but, as will be shown further on, this relative position is not permanent, for another and larger portion of the "mottled clays" set in upon these Woolwich beds as they trend westward from London.

It has been shown in my previous papers that both the "Basement Bed of the London Clay" and the "Thanet Sands" are respectively nearly uniform in their lithological and palæontological characters (when fossiliferous) throughout their entire range—the former being coextensive with the London Clay itself, whilst the latter extend only from the Isle of Thanet to a short distance westward of London—and that both are essentially of marine origin.

The middle division of the Lower Tertiaries, of which it now remains to treat, is, on the contrary, in different areas so very different in its lithological structure and in its organic remains, that it presents one of those cases where the evidence of superposition is indispensable. Were it not for the well-marked horizons afforded by the upper and lower divisions, which confine this group within distinct limits, it would in fact often be difficult or rather impossible to identify its synchronous beds, when viewed in detached sections, either by their

---

[*] Organic Remains, vol. iii. p. 171, and Trans. Geol. Soc. 2nd ser. vol. iii. p. 212.
[†] Trans. Geol. Soc. vol. ii. p. 196.   [‡] *Ibid.* vol. iv. p. 277.
[§] Geology of England, pp. 24–26 and 37–52.
[||] Mag. Nat. Hist. June 1835, p. 356, and Proc. Geol. Soc. vol. ii. p. 450, 1837.
[**] Proc. Geol. Soc. vol. i. p. 482 ; vol. ii. p. 551 ; vol. iii. p. 131.
[††] *Ibid.* vol. ii. pp. 78, 222, 449 ; Trans. Geol. Soc. vol. vi. p. 211.
[‡‡] Quart. Journ. Geol. Soc. vol. i. p. 172; Trans. Geol. Soc. 2nd ser. vol. i. p. 52.
[§§] Quart. Journ. Geol. Soc. vol. vi. p. 440.
[||||] Sections of the London Strata.
[***] Bulletin, Soc. Géol. de France, 2nd ser. vol. ix. p. 350.

mineral or palæontological characters alone. It is this feature which forms one of the chief points of interest of the group, for if it is important to identify strata by their organic remains or by their lithological structure, it is not less so to trace the changes of composition which can occur in strata on the same plane, to note the modifications in the fauna by which such changes are accompanied, and to determine the limits to which the variations may extend. The case now before us is, so far as it regards the dimensions of the deposit itself, one comparatively of small importance, but it is valuable from the clear and unmistakeable testimony which it affords on these points. It was the extremely variable character of this group, which putting on occasionally the appearance of the group beneath, and at other times assuming the character of the one above it, that led to the impression of a want of order and of irregularly recurring strata throughout the whole of the Lower Tertiaries. So deceptive, indeed, are these common points of structure, that it is only lately that I have been able to satisfy myself that these changes are confined essentially to one portion of the series, and that one restricted to the limits of the middle division, and that strata so very dissimilar are really equivalent. This once determined, and having eliminated the two more uniform groups, it becomes apparent that there is in the " Lower London Tertiaries " a defined order of superposition formed of three distinct and independent groups of strata.

At the same time there cannot well be strata varying more in appearance and character than we find forming this series in the separate sections at Reading, Deptford, Blackheath, and Herne Bay ; by tracing the group at short intervals it is seen that it is by actual alteration in some of its beds, effected as they range from west to east, as much as by the thinning out of others, that these changes are produced. The strata are, in fact, on the same horizon and clearly synchronous (see Pl. I. Diag. A & C.). Under these circumstances there are objections to giving this division a simple designation dependent either on mineral character or on place, for the former is constantly varying, and the type of the series in one district may be entirely different in another. Still a name taken from some well-known place is probably the least objectionable, or rather the more convenient, and I purpose therefore to term this division the " Woolwich and Reading series," as the two principal forms of structure are well exhibited in the sections at and around these localities*. I shall, however, in speaking of this group, sometimes use the name of that locality only, to the particular characters of which the observations may have reference.

The grouping of the " Lower London Tertiaries " will therefore stand thus :—

I. THE BASEMENT-BED OF THE LONDON CLAY.

II. THE WOOLWICH AND READING SERIES.

III. THE THANET SANDS.

----

* The Woolwich section has the inconvenience of exposing the three divisions of the " Lower London Tertiaries " together. The term applies only to the middle part of the section (see Pl. I. Diag. A. Loc. sect. 25).

The series of local sections forming the diagrams A, B, & C, Pl. I.
have been arranged with a view to show the original structure and
sequence of the beds of the Woolwich and Reading series, and of the
other two divisions of the Lower London Tertiaries at the commencement of the London Clay period, as also to prove the correlation of the
strata, and to render apparent the remarkable changes of lithological
character which the strata undergo in their range from Wiltshire to
the coast of Kent.   These sections are either described in the text,
or in the explanation of plates ; whilst a few others, which possess
features which those sections do not embrace, are given in separate
figures.

§ 1.   *Range and General Physical Features of the " Woolwich and
Reading series."*

Throughout the Isle of Wight and the western portion of the
London Tertiary district, this middle group consists of unfossiliferous
mottled clays passing into or alternating with non-persistent sands :
as it approaches near to London, strata of laminated and carbonaceous
clays, sands more calcareous, and thick shingle beds of flint pebbles,
with fluviatile and æstuarine shells, set in and replace the mottled
clays.   Following the group still further eastward we find it gradually becoming less pebbly and argillaceous, and at last passing entirely into light-coloured pure quartzose sands mixed with more or
less green sand, and containing in its extreme eastern range a distinctly
marine fauna.   Viewed horizontally this middle division may therefore be divided into three distinct areas of—

W.	C.	E.
Sands and Mottled Clays.	Pebble beds, Sands, and	Quartzose and Glauconi-
(*Reading and the Isle of*	laminated Clays.	ferous Sands.
Wight.)	(*Woolwich, Blackheath, and*	(*Herne Bay and Canterbury.*)
	Bromley.)	

These lithological changes are effected in an east and west direction
in both the London and the Hampshire districts.   In the latter,
the last (E.) form of structure is only partially developed.   It exists a
few miles east of Newhaven, and, with the second, is well exhibited
in an outlier on the coast three-quarters of a mile south of that town.
The latter shows again at the west of Brighton, but there merges
into the first (W.) form, which is continued by Lancing and Arundel to
Botley near Winchester, in a narrow belt marked by its generally
well-wooded surface, and by a succession of villages.   These beds then
pass two miles south of Salisbury, thence a few miles north of Wareham to near Dorchester, becoming more sandy as they proceed westward.   Returning along their southern outcrop they pass by Lulworth to Studland, and in the Isle of Wight range, as is well
known, through the centre of the island from Alum Bay to White
Cliff Bay.

Throughout its northern range this division only occasionally presents any marked surface-features, and the sections are small, indistinct, and far apart.   On its interrupted southern outcrop the vertical position of the strata restricts them to within so narrow a band,
that they can rarely be seen except in the coast sections.

Of the connection existing at this period between the Hampshire and London Tertiary districts there are few remaining traces : only here and there on the broad chalk tract a hill higher than usual may be found capped by some of the lower tertiary beds, which resume their range in the London Tertiary district at Marlborough Forest. The greater part of these fine woods are planted on a thin and irregular capping of the clays and pebble beds* on the Chalk. The tertiary strata here attain a height of 600 to 700 feet above the level of the sea and form a narrow zone, which gradually expands as it trends eastward and falls to a lower level. At a short distance E.S.E. of this Forest the chalk attains, on the downs above Inkpen to Highclerc, its greatest height, reaching at the former place an altitude of 1011 feet. The view from the fine open ridges of downs over the well-wooded, broken, tertiary lowlands, which, commencing abruptly at their base, stretches in an apparent plain far to the eastward, is one of considerable beauty. In this part of the district the sands and mottled clays form a large portion of the surface, and appear peculiarly favourable to the growth of timber trees. At a short distance further eastward the London Clay commences and the Bagshot Sands almost immediately follow, the latter forming more open tracts of heath and common.

Along their northern boundary the "sands and mottled clays" rise at a very gentle angle, and cover a considerable extent of ground on the chalk hills to the north of Newbury, and thence by Pangbourne, Reading and Sonning to Twyford, Maidenhead, and Taplow, where a further expansion of them forms the picturesque district known as the Burnham Beeches. The chalk hills which bound the tertiary area on the north, unlike the chalk of Salisbury Plains, present but a small extent of open downs, and are well-wooded on their summits ; this arises in part from a covering of clay drift and in part from thin cappings of the lower tertiary beds, the latter being especially frequent to the north and north-west of Reading, and again around Beaconsfield, Penn, and Amersham. They are also found to some extent near St. Albans, Welwyn, and to the north of Hertford, and between Ware and Bishop Stortford. Eastward of this latter place the mottled clays are less important, and at the same time the lower tertiaries become confined to a narrow belt, owing to which condition, and the spread of the Boulder-clay drift over so much of North Essex, these beds rarely present in this part of their course any marked features of surface.

The southern outcrop of these strata, in consequence of the steep angle at which they rise, is very narrow,—a feature persistently maintained from the neighbourhood of Inkpen, by Kingsclere, Old Basing, Farnham, and Guildford, to Croydon, along which line of country the "sands and mottled clays" form a belt generally from 50 to 200 yards broad, rarely exceeding a breadth of a quarter of a mile, and only occasionally showing any discernible independent character of surface. As this group, however, from its composite character of sands and clays, presents a more yielding surface than the homogeneous mass of

* Including also a clay and gravel drift.

London clay which succeeds and reposes upon it, or the chalk which rises from beneath it, its line of outcrop is not unfrequently marked by a narrow and shallow depression between the chalk and the London clay, as at Old Basing, Guildford, and Sutton; but in other places, the chalk, lower tertiaries, and London clay form one continuous slope or nearly continuous surface falling more or less rapidly from the former to the latter, as at Itchingwell, Ewell, and Carshalton.

Eastward of Croydon the middle division of the Lower Tertiaries changes its character, the mottled clays gradually thinning out, and great masses of pebbly sands setting in in their place, together with clays containing fluviatile and æstuarine shells. At the same time the Thanet Sands develope themselves, and the basement-bed of the London Clay becomes thicker. In consequence of this increased importance of the Lower Tertiaries, and of the decreasing dip of the strata, this series suddenly expands and forms that varied and most agreeable tract of country extending from the Addington Hills to Bromley, Chiselhurst, Blackheath, and Greenwich, and eastward to Bexley and Farningham: in the latter neighbourhood these beds merely cap the chalk hills between the valleys of the Cray and the Darent.

Eastward of this district the tertiary beds are more confined to the higher grounds, as to the Swanscombe Hills, Windmill Hill near Gravesend, and the hills of Cobham and Shorne, in all of which the beds of shelly clays form a constant feature. On the banks of the Medway, below Rochester, these beds dip northward beneath the London clay. Continuing however further eastward this series gradually passes, apparently entirely, into a light-coloured quartzose sand with more or less green sand, which crops out in the low ground at the foot of the chalk hills between Chatham and Faversham. It forms a broader belt by Boughton, Canterbury, and between that city and Sandwich, presenting sometimes a rather barren sandy surface; but it is in general too closely associated with the Thanet Sands, or covered by drift, to exhibit any independent surface-features.

§ 2. *Details of Structure and Local Sections.*

Hampshire District.—At the southern extremity of the vertical tertiary strata at White Cliff and Alum Bays in the Isle of Wight, and immediately adjacent to the chalk, is a fine massive deposit of bright-coloured tenacious mottled clays. Their prevailing colour is blood-red, especially at White Cliff Bay; but the rough indistinct beds into which this mass is divisible in Alum Bay, exhibit mixtures, some of light bluish grey and yellow, others of light and dark slate colour, of lavender, puce, and yellow, or brown and yellow. The tints are generally dark and the colours bright. These beds contain no animal remains, and mere traces of vegetable remains in the shape of small pieces and fragments of carbonized wood. They are almost free from any admixture of sand, and altogether their structure, for a deposit so variable as this shows itself elsewhere, is compact and homogeneous.

The entire space between the London clay and the Chalk in the Isle of Wight, varying from 90 to 140 feet, is occupied by this mass of clay, with the exception of an irregular bed of 2 to 4 feet of sand above and as much below it * ; the Basement-bed of the London clay existing here in a mere rudimentary state, while the Thanet Sands are wanting. This locality presents, in fact, the peculiar mottled argillaceous structure of the Reading series in its greatest and most exclusive development, being in fact almost as compact and impermeable as the London clay itself †.

Proceeding from this centre either westward or eastward, considerable changes take place in these strata. In the former direction we pass from the Isle of Wight over to Studland Bay ‡, where mottled clays of a rather light colour appear to succeed to the chalk, but the section is too obscure to determine the exact dimensions and superposition of the beds : they seem to be thinner and more sandy. Between this point and Lulworth Castle I am not aware that any sections of these beds are exposed §. At Lulworth there is a small section in the Park of light mottled red clays and some pebble beds overlying the chalk.

Proceeding toward Dorchester, the mottled red clays almost disappear, and are replaced by coarse sands, irregular pebble and shingle beds, and whitish clays. Two miles from this town towards Wareham, the road cuttings on the hill show the chalk capped by a few feet of tertiary beds, consisting first of brown ferruginous clay, with light brown-coated unrolled flints, covered by a bed of small pebbles, succeeded by brown clay, coarse sand, another fine conglomerate, and then mottled clay. The whole is not above 10 to 12 feet thick, and fills up a very irregular and deeply indented surface of the chalk ‖. About a mile further, near Little Maine, the chalk is overlaid by sands, which in one place are concreted into large blocks of sandstone,—the ordinary Druid sandstone. In a field adjoining the road there is a complete nest of them, fifteen to twenty in number, and varying in size from 2 to 6 feet in diameter. Westward of this locality there are several outliers of these lowest tertiary beds, which continue to show an increasing conglomerate character, the sands becoming coarser and the clays whiter and mixed with pebbles and

* Quart. Journ. Geol. Soc. vol. ii. pp. 255 & 259, and Pl. IX. strat. " b."

† In sinking one Artesian well at Portsmouth, a water-bearing sand bed was met with in this series ; whereas in another well sunk at a short distance from the first, the entire space between the London clay and the Chalk was occupied with a solid and compact mass of mottled clays without a seam of sand, and consequently without water.

‡ For particulars of this section, and various points connected with the tertiary geology of this district, see a paper by the Rev. W. B. Clarke in the Mag. Nat. Hist. new ser. vol. iii. p. 390.

§ The clays near Corfe are, I believe, higher in the series, and belong to the Bagshot Sands. They are brought by the disturbances affecting that district into close proximity to the Chalk.

‖ This section is, however, rather problematical. The conglomerate contains pebbles apparently of the palæozoic rocks. The whole district requires a closer examination. For a description of some Tertiary outliers to the west of Dorchester see Dr. Buckland and Sir H. De la Beche, in Trans. Geol. Soc. 2nd Ser. vol. iv, p. 4.

flints, the latter large and often but little rolled. The whole mass becomes also more irregular and variable, which, with its more shingly and coarser character, indicates a nearer approach to the source from whence these portions of the materials of this division of the Lower Tertiaries were derived. The exhibition, however, of these Lower Tertiaries throughout this district is very imperfect and unsatisfactory *.

If now we proceed northward from the Isle of Wight, we find that beneath Southampton the beds between the London clay and the Chalk consist essentially of mottled clays about 80 feet thick †. At Fareham the railway cutting exposed a good section of bright red mottled clays and the London clay with its fossiliferous Basement-bed above them. At the outcrop of this group at Kembridge, between Romney and Salisbury, we find the only instance I am acquainted with in the Hampshire Tertiary district of a character common to these beds in the western part of the London district, viz. the occurrence of a band of the " *Ostrea Bellovacina* " in a bed of greenish sand immediately over the chalk and beneath the mottled clays ‡. The following is the section taken from my former paper (Journ. Geol. Soc. vol. iii. p. 360) :—

Fig. 1.—*Railway-cutting, Kembridge.*

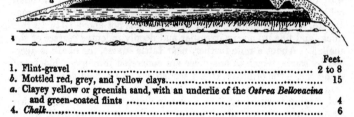

		Feet.
1.	Flint-gravel	2 to 8
b.	Mottled red, grey, and yellow clays	15
a.	Clayey yellow or greenish sand, with an underlie of the *Ostrea Bellovacina* and green-coated flints	4
4.	Chalk	6

At Clarendon Hill the strata are very similar to those at Alum Bay, but they are reduced in thickness to about 45 feet, and contain

---

* One of the best sections near Dorchester is at Yellowham hill, on the Blandford road.

† The section of these beds at the Artesian well of Southampton, as noted by Mr. R. Keele, is as follows :—" These mottled clays were remarkable from the almost entire absence of sand or water throughout the whole formation. No organic remains were found or indications of lignite. The clay was of extraordinary purity and hardness, and of almost every variety of colour. The last 6 or 8 feet of the lowest beds were of less degree of purity, the clay being mixed with a coarse flinty sand as they approached the main bed of chalk ; the last 5 feet of the bed was of a dark green colour, and mixed with water, with black flint, pebbles, and very coarse sand, all strongly tinted with the dark green colour above-mentioned."

‡ There is probably some other locality near Salisbury where this shell occurs, as the *O. undulata* figured by Sowerby from the neighbourhood of that city is apparently the *O. Bellovacina* of the Tertiary beds.

several subordinate beds of sand. At Bishopstoke, near Winchester, on the contrary, the mottled clays have nearly disappeared, and appear to be replaced, in part or wholly, as at Addington near Croydon, by sands and thick beds of rounded flint-pebbles in yellow sand. In one pit at Stoke Common they are 12 to 15 feet thick, and exactly resemble the shingle beds to the S.S.E. and E.S.E. of London.

Taking an easterly course from this line, the mottled clays and some associated pebble beds * range past Chichester, Arundel, to Highdown hill near Worthing, to the north of which, at the village of Clapham, a thick stratum of small rounded flint-pebbles overlies the clays as at Croydon; but whether these pebbles belong to the Basement-bed of the London clay or to the mottled clay group, there is at present no evidence to show. Wick House hill on the west of Brighton is capped by a few beds of mottled and carbonaceous clay reposing on sand over chalk—the section is incomplete, and no fossils have been found. Passing thence to the detached outlier at Newhaven, we find a totally different group of strata; a thick bed of sand overlying the chalk, succeeded by a series of laminated grey clays containing numerous fluviatile and estuarine shells.

Particulars of this section have been given both by Dr. Mantell† and Dr. Buckland‡. Owing to the frequent fall of the cliffs, the section, however, is constantly varying. I have never been able to see it in perfectly clear sequence; but still, as there are some points which I have noticed in addition to those described by former observers, I herewith give a rough account of the section, premising at the same time that, owing to the impossibility of approaching some parts of the cliff, it must be considered only as approximative.

Section, upper part of Cliff, Castle Hill, Newhaven.

	Feet.
Gravel of subangular flints and tertiary flint-pebbles in ochreous and ferruginous sandy clay, averages about	6
i. Grey clay passing into dark yellow sand and then again into grey clay : no fossils. [Were it not that part of the upper portion of this bed presents a mottled red appearance, I should have been disposed to consider it as the lower part of the London Clay; even now I am not satisfied but that the small quantity of mottled clay observed may not belong to the overlying drift, the line of separation being at that spot perfectly indistinct and very irregular.]	12
h. Round flint-pebbles in grey clay and yellow sand (Bt.-bed L. C.?) ...	1
g. Laminated grey clay with seams of yellow and ferruginous sand	8
f. Mass of concreted oyster rock (*Ostrea Bellovacina*).......................	2
e. Layers of comminuted shells, yellow sands, grey clays with well-preserved shells, and with an intermediate bed of grey clayey sand......	6
d. Yellow, light brown, and red sand in layers, with seams of laminated grey clay—traces of vegetable matter	5
Carry forward............	40

---

* It is uncertain whether these beds are continuous or not between Botley and Clapham.

† "On the Geological Structure of Sussex," and Trans. Geol. Soc. 2nd Ser. vol. iii. p. 204.

‡ Trans. Geol. Soc. vol. iv. p. 296.

		Feet.
	Brought forward...............	40

c. Dark grey laminated clays, sometimes fossiliferous, with thin layers of
  ironstone—vegetable impressions, and an underlie of ferruginous and
  carbonaceous clay—selenite common .... 20 ?

b. White sand 2 feet, to which succeeds ochreous sand 1 to 2 feet, passing down into light greenish sand* : no fossils......................... 25 ?

a. Green and ferruginous-coated flints in greenish sand† 2

Chalk to base of cliff.   87

The organic remains I have found in this section are as follows :—

Cyrena cuneiformis, *Fér.*	Melanopsis buccinoides, *Fér.*
—— intermedia, *Mell.?*	Ostrea Bellovacina, *Desh.*
Cerithium variabile, *Desh.*	Psammobia Condamini, *Mor.*
Dreissena serrata, *Mell.?*	Unio.
Hydrobia Parkinsoni, *Mor.?*	Cypris?
Melania inquinata, *Desh.*	

Leaves of plants figured by Dr. Mantell (in Stratum *c*).

Dr. Mantell also mentions the occurrence of the *Avicula media*, Sow., *Helix lævis*, Flem., and *Cytherea convexa*, Brong. (probably the *Dreissena*, *Hydrobia*, and *Cyrena cuneiformis* of the above list), and Fish-teeth resembling those of the Mustelus.
In addition to these there are in the collection of the Geological Society some curious specimens, apparently of cones and seed-vessels, found by Mr. Warburton. These beds require further investigation.

In consequence of this being a distant outlier, and of the absence therefore of connecting links, the relation of these fossiliferous grey clays and thick beds of sand to the mottled red clays of the Isle of Wight is not readily apparent. That they are in reality synchronous will be further on shown to be probable, by analogous changes in the same division in the London district.

The few foregoing observations merely give a sketch of this group in Hampshire. The rarity of sections and want of time have prevented me from working it out so fully as I could have wished. It will serve, however, to show the relation of this portion of the series to that of the same age in the London district, and which I purpose treating in greater detail. The number of sections exposed to the westward of London along both the north and south lines of outcrop of the Lower Tertiaries renders this a work of comparative facility, until we arrive in the neighbourhood of London. The chalk tract separating the Hampshire Tertiaries from those of the London district at their nearest point of approach is about twenty miles broad.

London District.—In entering upon this area we find the middle division of the Lower London Tertiaries resuming its position with characters almost identical with those under which it outcrops in the neighbourhood of Salisbury, as the two following sections will show :—

---

* At Seaford this sand contains masses of rough ferruginous sandstone concretions : and the flints of stratum *a* beneath it are often cemented into considerable-sized blocks.

† It is at the base of this bed that the *Websterite* and hydrate of alumina occur.

Clarendon Hill, Hampshire* (several small pits in a brick-field).

London Clay.   Feet.

    1. Basement-bed of the London clay (flint-pebbles in clay and sand) ...   1

    11.† { Mottled clays with a few subordinate beds of sand, about............   45

          { *a.* Flints and pebbles in green sand and clay   1

Chalk.

                                                                47

Pebble Hill, Berkshire (section from two pits in nearly adjoining brick-fields). Pl. I. Diag. A, Loc. sect. 2.

London Clay.   ft. in.

    1. Basement-bed of the London clay (flint-pebbles in clay and sand)   0 9

          { Light mottled greenish clay 10 0

          | Irregular bed of sand 5 0

          | Sandy grey and brown clay passing into slightly mottled clay ... 25 0

    11. { Red tile clay 5 0

          | Fine sand 3 0

          | Band of *Ostrea Bellovacina* 0 3

          { *a.* Flints and pebbles in green sand and clay.........................   1 0

Chalk.

                                          49 0

In Marlborough Forest the tertiary beds are so thin and so disturbed by, or mixed with, drift, that no good sections can be obtained; enough, however, is exposed to see that they consist of mottled clays with sands and pebble beds reposing upon chalk. At Bagshot Hill, two miles west of Hungerford, the series is more complete, but is badly shown, and consists of the following beds:—

Bagshot Hill (section from a few small pits and road-side cuttings). Pl. I. Diag. A, Loc. sect. 1.

                                                 Feet.

    1. Flint-pebbles in clay and sand, some blocks of puddingstone on surface...   3

    e. Laminated yellow clays and sands ....about   12

    d. Dark mottled clays, light green with bright red.......................about   35

    c. Imperfect iron-sandstone and sand   2

    b. Yellow sand and green clayey sand, with a thin seam of oysters at base...   8 ?

    a. Ferruginous clay with small flint-pebbles 0¼

                                               60¼

Chalk, with a very uneven surface.

The *Ostrea Bellovacina* is the only fossil found in this section, which is merely exposed in part and is given approximately. At Prosperous Wood these beds are more sandy, and contain subordinate layers of iron-sandstone 2 to 3 feet thick. At Inkpen mottled clays again preponderate and are worked to some extent: they are not fossiliferous. At Pebble Hill the irregular and undulating bedding of the Reading series is apparent, both in the section taken by itself, or viewed in relation to the Wickham and Newbury pits.

---

  * See Quart. Journ. Geol. Soc. vol. vi. pp. 257 & 258 for fig. of this and the following Section.

  † Group II. probably would admit of as many divisions as the mottled clays at Pebble Hill, but the section is too imperfect (the lower beds not being exposed when I was there) to give the exact sequence and thickness of each bed: on the whole also it is more argillaceous.

At a pit on Liquid Farm, three and a quarter miles E.S.E. of Aldbourne, and at Hopgrass Pit, one and a half mile W.N.W. of Hungerford, isolated masses of the mottled clays are worked, apparently in depressions or hollows on the summit of the chalk hills.   In both places the clays are interstratified with thick beds of sand, are extremely irregular in their stratification, and none of the beds contain any fossils.   At Wickham, five and a half miles north-west of Newbury, the section of these beds, showing a considerable change from the series at Pebble Hill, which is three and a half miles further south, is tolerably complete.

[*The vertical scale of this and all the following sections, except when mentioned to the contrary, is 50 feet to the inch.*]

Fig. 2.—*Wickham (section from three or four pits in the brick-field).*

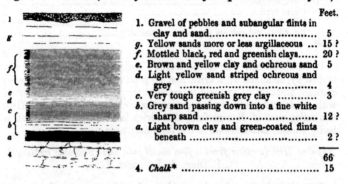

		Feet.
1.	Gravel of pebbles and subangular flints in clay and sand....................................	5
g.	Yellow sands more or less argillaceous ...	15 ?
f.	Mottled black, red and greenish clays......	20 ?
e.	Brown and yellow clay and ochreous sand	5
d.	Light yellow sand striped ochreous and grey	4
c.	Very tough greenish grey clay	3
b.	Grey sand passing down into a fine white sharp sand.......................................	12 ?
a.	Light brown clay and green-coated flints beneath	2 ?
		66
4.	*Chalk**	15

I have found no fossils in these pits.   The lower sand beds are more developed here than at the places before mentioned, being liable to rapid and considerable variations.   In some places they are 10 to 20 feet thick, and in others not more than 2 or 3.   Further, at Newbury, in the half mile of railway cutting, they pass (horizontally) from a nearly white colour to apple-green, and then to yellow. The same sands and clays are also worked in pits at Stock Cross and Donnington.

One (or rather two in adjacent works) of the best sections in this district occurs at Clay Hill, Shaw, one mile E.N.E. of Newbury. With the exception of a small break, the sequence from the London Clay down to the Chalk is complete.   No fossils are met with in the upper part of the Reading series, but in the lower part the bed of *Ostrea Bellovacina* is extremely well developed, and the shells in a fine state of preservation, although friable.   Many of them are very large, as much as 7 or 8 inches in diameter.   In the same bed are also found fish-bones, teeth of *Lamnæ* and other fish, a few bones of *Chelonia*, minute spine of *Echinoderm*, a few *Foraminifera* (*Globulina*), and *Cythere Mulleri*.

* The depth to which the Chalk is penetrated in this and the following sections varies of course from time to time, and is only given approximately.

Clay Hill, Newbury (connected section of two adjoining chalk and clay pits). Pl. I. Diag. A, Loc. sect. 3.

		Feet.
III.	Brown clay and traces of shells* (*London Clay and Basement-bed*).........	10
	j. Mottled red and bluish clay...	15
	i. White sand	1
	h. Mottled clay..	10
	g. Sands and loam, only partly exposed.......................................	10 ?
	f. Light-coloured and ochreous sand, laminated	3
II.	*e.* Laminated dark grey clay, grey and green sand, and a few pebbles†.	8
	d. Ditto, with *Ostrea Bellovacina*	1
	c. Dark grey clay mixed with green sand : no oysters	2
	b. Dark grey clay mixed with green sand, *oysters, teeth,* &c. : pebbly...	1
	a. Dark grey clay mixed with green sand, pebbles, and a few unrolled flints	1

                                                                          62
Chalk, with tubular surface-perforations filled with green sand 20

In this part of Berkshire the mottled clays preponderate on the south side of the Tertiary area, whilst on the northern outcrop the sands are more largely developed. This latter is especially the case at Courage and Oare, a few miles northward of Newbury.

At Red Hill, seven and a half miles west of Reading, the section is as follows :—

Red Hill (pit in brick-field). Pl. I. Diag. A, Loc. sect. 4.

		Feet.
e	Red and purple clay passing down into red and green mottled, and then red alone..	20
d.	Patch of angular chalk fragments, subangular flints, and flint-pebbles	1
c.	Mottled red and yellow sand..	0½
‡*b.*	Light-coloured sand	6 ?

                                                                          27½

The peculiarity of this section is the occurrence of a patch of angular chalk fragments and flints, resembling ordinary gravel, beneath the main mass of mottled clay §. I found no organic remains in this place. At Sulham near Pangbourne the sands overlying the chalk are more than 20 feet thick. At Rose Hill, and again at Woodcot Common, to the north of Reading, there is a considerable outlier of unfossiliferous mottled clays and sands. The section at Katesgrove pit, Reading, is well known from the description of Dr. Buckland ‖, who noticed also the rapid change by which, on the opposite side of the

* These were first noticed by Mr. Rupert Jones.   † I have recently found traces of fossils in this bed which require further examination.

‡ The letters affixed to the different beds of the Woolwich and Reading Series in the several sections do not mark equivalent strata, with the exception of " *a,*" which is always confined to the commencing or lowest bed of the series. Where the letters begin further on in the alphabet, it is merely to indicate that the series is not complete—that some of the lower beds are wanting.

§ In digging a well at Bradfield, between this spot and Reading, the mottled clays are said to have been above 130 feet thick; but this seems to me doubtful.

‖ Trans. Geol. Soc. 2 ser. vol. iv. p. 276. Since the period of Dr. Buckland's visit, the " Basement Bed of the London Clay " with its well-characterized fossils has been exposed by the extension of the pit further into the hill. (See Rolfe in Trans. Geol. Soc. 2nd ser. vol. v. p. 127.)

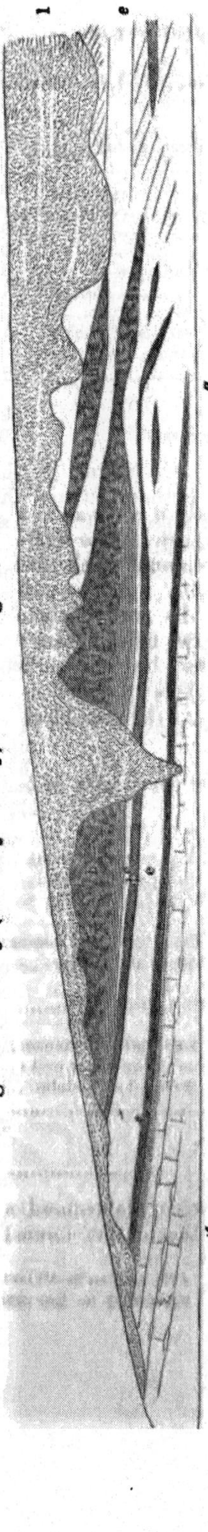

Fig. 3.—*Reading (Railway-cutting).* Pl. I. Diag. A, Loc. sect. 5.

valley at St. David's Hill, sands almost entirely replace the clays of the Katesgrove pit (Pl. I. Diag. A, Loc. sect. 6).

A feature of considerable interest connected with this series was exhibited in the railway cutting for the Newbury branch line through the hill west of and adjoining Reading. Under the mottled clays there were a few feet of sand, and then a local and lenticular mass of very finely laminated light greenish clay abounding, in places, with the most beautifully preserved impressions of plants. Beneath this bed were strata of yellow sand succeeded by the bed of green sand with the *Ostrea Bellovacina.* I give this section in full, both to show these points and also as a good instance of the irregular deposition of the mottled clay series. (For the plants see Pl. IV.)

	Feet.
1. Ochreous flint-gravel, varies greatly in thickness—averages	10
b. Mottled red and light bluish grey clay passing down into slightly laminated light grey clays	20
c. Laminated yellow sands	2
d. Thin layers of light grey and greenish clays more or less sandy; some of the seams consist of a very pure and fine clay slightly mottled with a tinge of red. Extremely perfect and very numerous impressions of leaves are found in this bed	4
e. Fine yellow sand with slight false stratification. Ferruginous clayey sand in patches —soft ferruginous casts of wood	8
a. Green sand with a band of *Ostrea Bellovacina* at *f*	2
	46
4. *Chalk*, with tubular surface-perforations filled with green sand at *f*	6

East of Reading the cutting of the Great Western Railway at Sonning Hill afforded an excellent section of the Reading series and of the Basement-bed of the London Clay. Here, the sands which, between Newbury and Reading, are often as fully developed as the mottled clays, disappear almost entirely, and pass into or are replaced by mottled clays. This section also shows the peculiar waved and irregular lines of bedding of these strata, which here as usual contain no organic remains*.

* The workmen however described to me a specimen which, from their account, would appear to have been the head or jaw of a fish that they had found in the middle of this series. The Basement-bed of the London Clay, which caps the hill, abounds in well-preserved fossils.

Sonning Hill (Railway-cutting).   Pl. I. Diag. A, Loc. sect. 7.

		Feet.
	Subangular flint-gravel, ochreous,—varies in thickness, averages.........	12
III.	*Basement-bed of the London Clay,*—fossiliferous brown clay with yellow and green sand, pebbles, and septaria	5
	l. Slightly mottled bluish and red, passing eastward into grey, clay ...	10
	k. An irregular seam of sand, in some places yellow, in others of a light bluish colour	2
	j″. Mottled brown and blue........................⎫	
	j′. Dark grey...⎬ clays................. 23	
	j. Mottled red and grey, the lower part lighter ⎭	
II.	*i.* Irregular seam of white sand..	2½
	h. Red clay	1½
	g. Light grey clay	0½
	f. Very dark grey clay	6
	e. Red clay	2
	d. Light grey clay	1
	c. Yellow sand with bands of brown clay*	2
		67½

At Twyford the section consists almost entirely of compact mottled green and red clay.   Northward of this district we find several outliers of the lower tertiaries reposing upon the elevated chalk district of Oxfordshire, Berkshire, and Buckinghamshire.   A very striking instance of this occurs at Nettlebed, nine miles due north of the main mass of the tertiaries at Reading, and only two miles distant from the edge of the chalk escarpment.   The tertiary beds here attain a height of 820 feet above the sea-level.   No fossils are found in this section, which is interesting, however, from its showing blocks of sandstone *in situ.*

Fig. 4.—*Nettlebed Hill (section from several small pits in brick-field).*

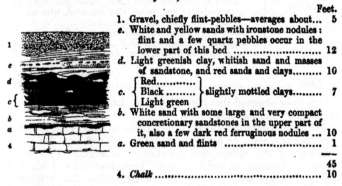

		Feet.
1.	Gravel, chiefly flint-pebbles—averages about...	5
e.	White and yellow sands with ironstone nodules : flint and a few quartz pebbles occur in the lower part of this bed	12
d.	Light greenish clay, whitish sand and masses of sandstone, and red sands and clays.........	10
c.	⎧ Red............⎫ ⎨ Black ....⎬ slightly mottled clays......... ⎩ Light green ⎭	7
b.	White sand with some large and very compact concretionary sandstones in the upper part of it, also a few dark red ferruginous nodules ...	10
a.	Green sand and flints	1
		45
4.	*Chalk*	10

The two high and conspicuous hills between Maidenhead and Henley are formed by tertiary outliers.   Another outlier forms the

* Beneath this bed, which was the lowest exposed, were said to be 10 feet of dark clay reposing upon 5 feet of ash-coloured sands, succeeded by the green-coated flints 1 foot, and then chalk.

high hills at Lane End, four miles west from High Wycombe. The summit of this hill consists of *London clay* with a thin layer of the "Basement Bed," with its characteristic fossils beneath it; this is succeeded by sands and mottled and laminated clays reposing upon the chalk. Sands predominate, and no fossils have been found.

On the chalk hills around Missenden, Amersham, and the Chalfonts, traces of the lower tertiaries frequently occur, but they are so covered and mixed with drift that it is rarely that clear sections can be obtained. One and a half mile east from Chesham is Tiler's Hill, where again we find, at a distance of nine miles north of the main mass of the tertiaries, an outlier of London clay reposing upon the lower tertiaries.

The falling in of the shaft of a chalk-pit has recently (1853) assisted in exposing a complete section of this hill from the London Clay down to the Chalk. Though not very accessible, it shows a clear unbroken sequence, and affords therefore a good key-section.

Tiler's Hill, Chesham (section from sand-pit and shaft of chalk-pit in the brick-field). Pl. I. Diag. B, Loc. sect. 1.

		Feet.
	Gravel, chiefly of flint-pebbles in clay, averages............	4
London Clay.	*b.* Brown clay with a few nodular septaria....................	10
	a. Layers of laminated grey and brown clay	3
I. *Basement-bed of the London Clay, 3½ feet.*	*c.* Layer of imperfect septaria full of fossils*	0¼
	b. Light brown sandy clay	2
	a. Flint-pebbles in clay..	1
II. *Woolwich and Reading Series, 31 feet.*	*h.* Umber-coloured clay, in places slightly mottled red and yellow..	2
	g. Fine siliceous sand, in places very white	3
	f. Light-coloured soft sandstone with an occasional pebble—variable	1
	e. Light-coloured siliceous sands with a few seams of grey clay, the lower part coarser, yellow, and brown	10
	d. Laminated grey and yellow clay and sand, with an under-seam of pebbles	1
	c. Yellow and ash-coloured sand with seams of grey clay	8
	b. Grey clay laminated with sand	4
	a. Large unrolled flints, apparently white-coated	2
		51¼
Chalk	....	25

It is to be observed that here a layer of the sand passes in places occasionally into soft sandstone.

Returning southward we fall in with the main body of the tertiaries near Beaconsfield. In a section at Pitlands Wood, one and a half mile east of this village, thin patches of subangular flints occur apparently beneath the mottled clays. From Starveall to Hedgerley is a succession of sections which are interesting from their exhibiting the very rapid structural changes which take place in these sands and mottled clays.

The two local sections, 12 and 13, in Plate I. Diag. A, are actual

* The *Ditrupa plana* abounds, together with *Ostrea Bellovacina*, a few *Natica glaucinoides*, a *Fusus*, and teeth of *Lamna*.

ones, less than half a mile apart. In this short distance the mottled clays almost entirely disappear and are replaced by sands *.

At Uxbridge and Pinner the mottled clays are largely developed. The shafts sunk to procure chalk at the latter place† give sections very similar to that at Hedgerley; but on Pinner Hill, in place of the mottled clays, sands and pebbles predominate, as shown on the side of the lane leading from the summit of the hill to Hamper Mill. At Watford a remarkable development of the rolled pebble bed immediately overlying the chalk occurs. It there forms a mass 15 feet thick, with a matrix of ochreous clayey sand, which gives it the appearance of the ordinary drift-gravel.

Fig. 5.—*Watford (general section on railway, Bushey cutting).*

3. *London Clay.*		Feet.
ɪ. Basement-bed of the London Clay with numerous fossils		5
II. { d. Sands		3 ?
c. Mottled clays with a few beds of sand		35 ?
b. Sand nearly white, with a few layers and patches of flint-pebbles		10
a. Shingle-bed of flint-pebbles in ochreous sand		15
		68
4. *Chalk*		5

At Welwyn this division consists essentially of sands with irregular subordinate beds of grey clays, occasionally mottled red and green, layers of flint-pebbles, and thin seams of iron-sandstone. At Hatfield‡ the mottled clays are entirely replaced by sands, which at Hertford again give way in part to clays. The oyster bed overlying the chalk is developed again in this neighbourhood. The sections are from pits in a brick-field at George's farm, one mile from Hertford, on the London road.

* For a section of the Hedgerley Pit (10) see Journ. Geol. Soc. vol. vi. p. 268.
† A section in full, taken by Mr. Morris, of the Pinner pits is given in Journ. Geol. Soc. vol. vi. p. 269.
‡ For the section at this place see Quart. Journ. Geol. Soc. vol. vi. p. 270.

Near Hertford (section from chalk-pit and pits in the brick-field).
Pl. I. Diag. C, Loc. sect. 2.

		Feet.
	Mixed clay and gravel	1
I. *Basement-bed of the London Clay, 6¼ feet.*	*b.* Brown sandy clay laminated with tougher clay, containing casts of *Panopæa*, &c.	6
	a. Flint-pebbles in clay	0¼
II. *Woolwich and Reading Series, 32 feet.*	*f.* Light greenish sand	4
	e. White or ash-coloured sand	6
	d. Light yellow sands	4
	c. Light-coloured mottled red and grey clays	10?
	b. Yellow sand with patches of the *Ostrea Bellovacina* in places at its base	6?
	a. Green-coated flints	1

39½

Chalk.. 12

At Seacombe and Collier's End, north of Hertford, mottled clays seem altogether to replace the sands (Pl. I. Diag. C, Loc. sect. 1). The section at the latter place is peculiar from the circumstance of the flint-pebbles, which usually form, with the quartzose sand, the shingle bed at the base of this series, being here enveloped in, and forming part of, the mottled clays, which therefore come down in actual contact with the chalk*. To the south of Hertford, on the contrary, sands predominate, as at Northaw, which is noted for its fine bed of the *Ostrea Bellovacina* (Pl. I. Diag. C, Loc. sect. 3).

The mass of lower tertiaries capping the chalk hills between Ware and Bishop Stortford affords no good sections. Several small pits, of which that at Patmore Heath is the best, show the prevalence of mottled red clays with sands and pebble beds.

Patmore Heath, three miles west of Manewden.

	Feet.
Brown clay and gravel	1
Mottled red, brown and grey sandy clay	2
Ash-coloured sand with laminæ of brown clay and a seam of flint-pebbles ...	2½
Flint-pebbles in light greenish grey clay	1½
The *Chalk* crops out at about 6 feet lower.	

I am doubtful whether the Thanet Sands range thus far north. If they do, they must be represented by the bed of sand which is to be seen reposing on the chalk in a few pits between Bishop Stortford and Newport. The sections, however, are so far between and so indistinct, that throughout Essex I do not know of one satisfactory exhibition of the Lower London Tertiaries; still enough is shown to lead to the belief that sands there prevail in this series almost exclusively. In Suffolk there are a few sections in the neighbourhood of Hadleigh and Ipswich†, where it appears that the space of 30 to 40 feet between the London clay and the chalk is occupied by sands only; but whether they belong to the Woolwich beds or to the Thanet

* This is the only spot in which I have seen the mottled clay come directly into contact with the chalk. Elsewhere it is always separated by a few feet of sand, green sand, or ferruginous clay.

† For sections of these pits at Gestingthorpe, Hadleigh, Ipswich, and Kyson, see my former paper in Quart. Journ. Geol. Soc. vol. vi. pp. 271, 272.

Sands, there is in these sections no evidence to show. I am inclined, however, to think that a portion, if not the whole of them, may possibly belong to the former group*. According to the Rev. W. B. Clarke, the evidence of its extension in Suffolk is more definite†. In well-sections at Harwich (p. 370) he mentions the occurrence of beds of *mottled clay*, sand, and shingle; also of vegetable impressions in a brown clay at Higham Bridge (p. 373)‡.

It would thus appear that mottled clays, irregularly interstratified with sands, prevail along the western portion of the northern outcrop of the Woolwich and Reading series, whilst north-eastward this series seems reduced generally to a simple thick bed (or beds) of sand. With the exception of the *Ostrea Bellovacina* found occasionally at the base of this group, no other shells are met with along that line. There is nowhere any appearance of the Woolwich group of fluviatile shells, but traces of vegetable matter and teeth of *Lamna* occasionally occur.

As the surface-sections do not afford us sufficient proof of the exact connection of the sands and mottled clays of Reading with the sands, clays, and pebble beds of Woolwich, we must retrace our steps to Uxbridge and Watford, and endeavour to follow the continuation of these beds underground to London and Woolwich. Although passing through a district in which several deep wells have been sunk, there are, owing to the want of correct details, but a few amongst the number which are available in evidence.

First is the well at the Hanwell Lunatic Asylum, of which general particulars were taken§ and rock-specimens‖ preserved.

---

* The foreman at the Kyson pit stated that large oysters (*Ostrea Bellovacina?*) were occasionally found in the sand beneath the pebble bed with the mammalian teeth.

† Trans. Geol. Soc. 2nd ser. vol. v. pp. 361–383.

‡ In many of this author's sections, some beds, which are described as " London Clay," " Plastic Clay," and " Plastic Sand," will, I believe, be found to belong to the Boulder Clay and the unproductive sands of the Crag (Nos. 33, 40 and 43, p. 376; Nos. 44 to 49, p. 377; Nos. 55, 56, 59, p. 378; No. 65, p. 379). At Balingdon Hill (p. 375) there should be 30 to 40 feet of the unproductive sands of the Crag and of the Lower Tertiary Sands between the diluvial clay and the chalk. These errors of description detract from the weight to be attached to this, in other respects, valuable document. Since writing the above, I have learnt that in an artesian well at Colchester the " Lower London Tertiaries " were only 30 feet thick (Brown, Ann. & Mag. Nat. Hist. for October 1853).

§ In the *well-sections* the names given by the well-digger are throughout retained. I have however, in most cases, added another column with the geological grouping, as I interpret the descriptions, in italics. The italics in parentheses are also introduced in explanation of some of the terms. It will be observed that the " Basement Bed of the London Clay " rarely appears in these sections. This I believe arises from the fact that, owing to its general thinness and not very striking mineral characters, it has been almost always overlooked in well-sections. Wherever specimens have been preserved, I have generally found evidence of its existence. I may remark that many of these deep wells have been sunk within the last ten, and all within the last thirty or forty years.

† Amongst the specimens which I have examined, there were the following London Clay shells, but they were loose and not placed :—*Cancellaria læviuscula, Cytherea obliqua, Fusus bifasciatus, Natica, Nucula Bowerbankii, Panopæa intermedia, Rostellaria Sowerbyi.*

Well-section, Hanwell. (*As the exact limits of the different beds are not given in a printed section, the measurements here assigned to them must be considered only as approximate.*) Pl. I. Diag. A, Loc. sect. 15.

Feet.

Surface soil and drift	{ Vegetable soil...... .... Gravel, sand, sand and gravel ...... }	21

London Clay	{ Brick clay ....
	 Blue or London clay ....
	 Piece of fossil wood ....
	 Vein of stone (*layer of septaria*) ...
	 Vein of stone (*septaria*) ....
	 Fossil shell ....
	 Several shells...........................
	 Vein of stone with shells imbedded
	    (*septaria with Cyprina planata, As-
	    tarte, and fruit-like impressions*).
	 Vein of stone (*septaria*) ....
	 Indurated mud and sand .... }
		190

I. *Basement-bed of the London Clay, 4 feet.*	{ Mud, sand, and pieces of wood (*also
	    tabular septaria with bivalve shells
	    not determinable*) ....
	 Pebbles (*flint*) and shells...............
		2
		 2

II. *Woolwich and Reading Series, 75 feet.*	{ Mottled clay (*red, grey, yellow, light
	    green and puce*) ....
	 Sand ....
	 Clay (*mottled light grey and red*)......
	 Indurated sand, clay, and mud (*light
	    brown sandy clays with a seam of
	    bituminous clay*) ....
	 Clay (*mottled brown and light green*).
	 Green sand and clay (*with some carbo-
	    naceous matter*).........................
	 Bed of oyster-shells as hard as rock...
	 Pebbles (*flint*) ....
	 Bed of flint-stones (*in green sand*) ...
		23
		 2
		 13
		
		 10
		 8
		
		 8
		 3
		 4
		 4

290

Chalk 30

In this section the mottled clays descend very near to the chalk, and are underlaid only by 3 feet of green sand, then by a concreted mass of the *Ostrea Bellovacina* reposing upon a bed of round black (flint) pebbles, under which comes the green-coated unrolled flints overlying the chalk. The next section is at Castlebear Hill near Ealing.

Well-section, Castlebear Hill. Pl. I. Diag. A, Loc. sect. 16.

(Communicated by Mr. R. W. Mylne*.) Feet.

London Clay.	Blue clay..	300
II. *Woolwich and Reading Series, 60 feet.*	{ e. Sand and silt... d. Coloured clays and black clays with pebbles ...... c. Black, yellow, and green sands .... b. Pebbles and black clay................................. a. Flints	30 15 5 9 1

To the Chalk 360

---

* For this and several succeeding well-sections I am indebted to Mr. R. W. Mylne, the author of " Sections of the London Strata," towards the further illus-

In the collection of the Geological Society is a series of specimens and a section of a well at Twyford near Acton, particulars of which are annexed. A bed of black bituminous clay with appearance of decomposed shelly matter occurs about 20 feet down in the mottled clays.

Well-section, Twyford.   Pl. I. Diag. A, Loc. sect. 17.

			Feet.
London Clay.	*b.*	Yellow clay	38
	a.	Blue clay	170
I. *Basement-bed*	*c.*	Rock	1
of the London	*b.*	Sand and clay with pebbles	1
Clay.	*a.*	Pebbles	1
II. *Woolwich and*	*f.*	Mottled clays	36
Reading Series.	*e.*	Sand	3
	d.	Clay, not traversed	2
			252

Stratum *b.* I. here contains, as at White Cliff Bay, small fragments or pebbles of the underlying mottled red clays, as well as flint-pebbles.

At Watford we have seen that the shingle beds of the Woolwich series repose immediately upon the chalk. The Thanet Sands are absent also at Pinner.

Section of a shaft at Pinner near Harrow.

(Mr. J. Morris.)

		Feet.
London Clay ...	Marly clay	12
I. *Basement-bed*	*b.* Sand with shells and septaria	1
of the London	*a.* Vein of pebbles...	1
Clay, 2 feet.		
II. *Woolwich and*	*d.* Soapy marl	5
Reading Series,	*c.* Mottled clay—red, blue, green, &c.	26
39 feet.	*b.* Pure white sand, sometimes ferruginous, and containing masses of sandstone, very irregular	4
	a. Green marly sand with flints	4
	To the Chalk...	53

At Willesden there are several deep wells, but I have not been able to obtain an exact section of any of them. From a good supply of water, however, being obtained before reaching the chalk, it is probable that the Thanet Sands have here commenced. At Notting Dale this deposit evidently exists; but in the following section it is probably confounded with the shingle beds of the Woolwich series; the "Pebbles and Sand" including, I believe, two distinct beds.

tration of which subject that gentleman has collected an amount of evidence of this description, as will, I expect, throw much light on the local changes which these beds undergo.

Well-section, Notting Dale, near Notting Hill.

(Mr. R. W. Mylne.)

	Feet.
Made ground	12
Gravel	5
London clay	154
Mottled clay	35
Pebbles and sand	38
	244
Chalk	12

This point is made clearer by the following more careful section near Westbourne Grove.

Well-section, Westbourne Estate Waterworks.
Pl. I. Diag. A, Loc. sect. 18.

(Mr. R. W. Mylne.)

			Feet.
London Clay.	{	*b.* Yellow clay	29
	{	*a.* Blue clay	188
II. *Woolwich and Reading Series,* 62 *feet.*	{	*f.* Mottled clay	40
		e. Pebbles...................................	2¼
		d. Green sand, pebbles, and clay	7½
		c. Sand and small pebbles	3½
		b. Green sand	2¼
		a. Sand, pebbles, and clay	6
III. *Thanet Sands,* 18 *feet.*	{	*b.* Grey sand	17
	{	*a.* Flints	1
			297
		Chalk...................................	15

Having thus traced the Woolwich and Reading beds into juxta-position with the Thanet Sands in this direction, we will now return to our starting-point at Hungerford and follow the former along their southern outcrop.

At Highclere, near Newbury, the section at the brick-pit is as under :—

Highclere.

		Feet.
	London clay	12
I. *Basement-bed.*	Large flint-pebbles in sand	1
II. *Woolwich and Reading Series.*	*e.* Fine ochreous sand	10
	d. Mottled light red, yellow and grey brick-clay, the upper part sometimes being a red tile clay..........................	25
	c. Whitish sand..	10
	b. Iron-sandstone	1

At Ewhurst the following section of a well near the church was given me from recollection by the man who had made it a few years previously*:—

---

* There is apparently some mistake in these measurements, although I believe the order of succession and the occurrence of *lignite* (*b*) to be correct.

Well-section, Ewhurst.

		Feet.
II. *Woolwich and Reading Series.*	*f.* Red and blue mottled clay	20
	e. Blue clay with pebbles	15
	d. Black clay with small oysters	15
	c. A bright ore (*iron pyrites*)	3
	b. Coal (*lignite*)	7
	a. Green sand and gravel (*flints*)	2
		62
Chalk		17

At Chinham, near Basingstoke, mottled clays prevail, as they do also at Old Basing, where they are 50 to 60 feet thick, with only one bed of yellow sand about 5 feet thick above and 2 feet of sand below them. It is uncertain whether about 20 feet of fossiliferous brown clay, overlying the sand and mottled clays, should not be included in this division, but the railway section, when I saw it, was too imperfect to admit of a satisfactory examination. A further investigation of the organic remains at this locality would be desirable.

At Odiham and Farnham these beds present but little variety, consisting almost entirely of mottled clays about 30 feet thick. The following is the section of a well at Dogmersfield Park near Odiham:—

Well-section, Dogmersfield Park.

(A. Bond.)

		Feet.
Bagshot Sand ...	*b.* Clay and sand	15
	a. Fine light bluish sand	25
London Clay	Blue clay with septaria	330
I. *Basement-bed of the London Clay?*	*b.* Sand, quite green	1½
	a. Stone (*septaria*)	2½
II. *Woolwich and Reading Series.*	*g.* Sand, quite green	1½
	f. Clay, yellow, mottled red with some grey ...	5
	e. Clayey sand, bluish grey striped red	10
	d. Chocolate-coloured clay mottled with grey...	11½
	c. Mottled light grey and red clay	15
		417

East of Farnham the band of *Ostrea Bellovacina* is found on the chalk. At Guildford we meet with the first traces of the Woolwich shell beds. They form on the top of the mottled clays a thin stratum with an eroded surface, on which reposes the "Basement-bed of the London Clay" (see Section in Journ. Geol. Soc. vol. vi. p. 260, and Pl. I. Diag. B, Loc. sect. 6 in this volume). At Fetcham the sand bed immediately overlying the chalk is said to be 35 feet thick*, and to be underlaid by a band of the *Ostrea Bellovacina*. On the chalk hills south of Leatherhead are several outliers of the "Lower London Tertiaries" consisting chiefly of sands and pebble beds. The most important one is at Headley-on-the-hill,

---

* In open sections I have never seen it above 10 to 12 feet thick.

where there is a considerable thickness of mottled clays, capped by
a thick pebble bed similar to that at Blackheath, and underlaid by
2 to 3 feet of sand with the *Ostrea Bellovacina*.

At Epsom the Thanet Sands commence : at least it is to that deposit I would refer the lower beds (III.) in the following section on
the railway, half a mile north-east from that town.

Fig. 6.—Railway Cutting, Epsom.

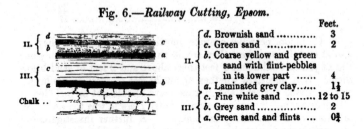

		Feet.
II.	d. Brownish sand	3
	c. Green sand	2
	b. Coarse yellow and green sand with flint-pebbles in its lower part	4
	a. Laminated grey clay......	1½
III.	c. Fine white sand	12 to 15
	b. Grey sand	2
	a. Green sand and flints ...	0¾

Near Ewell the mottled clays are worked at Nonesuch Park, but
the section is very imperfect.

Thus far the middle division of the "Lower London Tertiaries"
consists entirely of sands and mottled clays (with a comparatively small
quantity of flint-pebbles at their base), remarkable for the absence
of organic remains, excepting a bed of the *Ostrea Bellovacina* common, but not constant, in the thin stratum of sand and pebbles reposing immediately upon the chalk. We now, however, arrive at a
point where a very considerable, and rather sudden, change takes place.
Thick masses of rounded flint shingle, alternating with sands and less
frequently with grey and carbonaceous clays often laminated, and
characterized by a peculiar estuarine and freshwater fauna, now
intervene between the "Basement-bed of the London Clay" and the
"Thanet Sands." Into this mass the mottled clays, however, occasionally dovetail in a manner sufficiently clear to show the relation
and synchronism of these two very distinct-looking groups.

This change takes place nearly on a line passing N. and S.
through London. The Diagrams A. and C. Pl. I. exhibit the leading
phænomena. The following sections will serve further to show the
connection of these two groups of strata. It will be seen that the
mottled clays do not hold, as might be supposed from some of the
sections around Blackheath, any definite position either above or
below the Woolwich fluviatile beds, but that they alternate with the
whole series, sometimes appearing only above and sometimes only
below the latter, and at other times both underlying and overlying
them.

At Croydon there is no complete section of these beds, but the
following may be considered as the approximate sequence at Park
Hill, on the east of that town. It has been taken, with Mr. Flower's
assistance, on different occasions when the several beds have been
separately and partially exposed.

Fig. 7.—Park Hill, Croydon.

		Feet.
3.	*London Clay* (base not shown).	
I.?	Pebble beds ....about	10
II.	c. Clay with *Ostrea, Melania,* and *Cyrena*... „	6
	b. Mottled clay .... „	25
	a. Green sand and flint-pebbles .... „	5
III.	Thanet sands .... „	30
4.	*Chalk.*	

Owing to the number of *well-sections* which are necessary to trace the sequence of the beds across two other lines of section,—the one S. and N. from Croydon to London, and thence to Ware, and the other W. and E. from Esher to Chelmsford,—I have considered it better to remove them from this part of the paper, and to place them at the end, as an Appendix.

To resume now with the sections exposed by pits at the surface, eastward of the meridian of London.

Between a line drawn from Croydon to Orpington, and the Thames, is a district in which the pebble beds both of the Woolwich group and of the Basement-bed of the London clay* are largely developed. With the former group are constantly associated seams of fluviatile fossiliferous clays and occasionally even of considerable masses of the mottled clays. Very few sections are exposed in the central and south-western portions of this district: the whole series is extremely variable, and no very distinct order rules, except that on the whole mottled clays (thinning out eastward) prevail in the lower part, shelly beds in the central, and shingle in the upper part, but that not exclusively, of this group.

In proceeding eastward, the first sections of any consequence we arrive at are in the neighbourhood of Hayes Common. Two pits existed a few years since in a garden on the south side of the lane leading down from that Common to Nash Farm, whilst a more recent cutting made in deepening the same lane completed the section to the top of the hill. This general section, which showed tolerably well two zones of the Woolwich shells with the mottled clays between them, is rendered in Plate I. Diag. C, Loc. sect. 19. There is also a section showing the pebble beds, mottled clays, and shelly beds in the lane leading down from Hayes Common towards Wickham (Pl. I. Diag. C, Loc. sect. 18).

* The shingle beds of this division continue at intervals in considerable force, as at Abbey Wood near Erith, Rowhill Wood Hill south of Dartford, Windmill Hill, Gravesend, Shorne Hills, and Gad's Hill near Rochester.

At Orpington the Woolwich and Reading group decreases in importance. The following section was shown in a road-cutting at Crofton Pound near that village.

Orpington.

		Feet.
	l. Fine yellow sand	6
	k. Dark grey clay	0¾
	j. Mass of comminuted shells, chiefly *Cyrena cuneiformis*	1
	i. Yellow clay and concretionary slabs of earthy limestone, full of the *Ostrea Bellovacina*	1
Woolwich and Reading Series.	*h.* Light brown clay	0¾
	g. Rough thin concretionary limestone full of *Ostrea* and *Cyrena*	2
	f. Mixed brown and grey clay	1¼
	e. Mass of broken shells (*Cyrena, Melania, Cerithium*) in yellow clay	3¼
	d. Mottled bright red and light greenish clay	2¼
	c. Brown clay, full of small flint-pebbles	1
	b. Bright yellow clay	1½
	a. Dark clayey green sand, passing down into very light-coloured loose green sand, with a few thin layers of flint-pebbles	8

29¼

Traces of the mottled clays are visible yet here. The lower part of this group now often assumes the character of the Thanet Sands, from which it can only be distinguished by a few scanty seams of pebbles. On the hill west of St. Mary's Cray the separation of the two groups is however extremely well marked, as the pebbles form a dense mass in a bed of green sand.

Immediately north of the line just passed over is a district where, amidst a most variable series and a large development of unfossiliferous flint-shingle and sands, one section stands out in bold relief, and almost alone there preserves the fauna of the group : for a short distance near Bromley and Chiselhurst portions of the usually loose and sandy beds are rendered solid by a calcareous cement; and at Sundridge Park, where they are occasionally worked, they present a mass 25 to 30 feet thick of a hard light-coloured conglomerate, with a few subordinate sand beds, abounding in fossils. The upper beds in particular of this section show a strong false stratification shelving 12° to 22° northward. The exact position of these strata cannot be recognised in this section : I believe them, however, to be synchronous with the upper sands at Lewisham and the pebbly sands overlying the fossiliferous clays at Woolwich. The same beds are occasionally solidified nearer to London, but nowhere to the same extent as at Sundridge and beneath Chiselhurst Hill.

Organic remains, Sundridge Park Pit.

Cerithium variabile, *Desh.*
Corbula Regulbiensis, *Mor.*
Cyrena cuneiformis, *Fér.*
—— deperdita, *Sow.*
—— tellinella, *Desh.*
—— cordata, *Mor.*
—— intermedia, *Mell.*
Fusus latus, *Sow.*

Glycimeris ?
Melanopsis buccinoides, *Fér.*
Melania inquinata, *Desh.*
Modiola dorsata, *Mor.*
Natica glaucinoides, *Sow.*
Neritina globulus, *Def.*
Nucula fragilis, *Desh.*
Ostrea Bellovacina, *Desh.*

Ostrea tenera, *Sow.*	Crustacea (Cancer?).
Hydrobia Parkinsoni, *Mor.*	Teeth of Lamna.
Patella.	Scales of Fishes.
Pectunculus terebratularis, *Desh.*	Flustra.
Planorbis hemistoma, *Sow.*	Cythere?
Pholas.	Fragments of wood and imperfect
Serpula.	vegetable impressions.

Further northward in this district we meet with some better and well-known sections. The lower part of the Woolwich series is here generally formed of pebbly sands, remarkable on account of their variable and peculiar characters. At Loam Pit Hill, Lewisham, the section of which has been given both by Dr. Buckland* and by Conybeare and Phillips† (see Pl. I. Diag. C, Loc. sect. 10, and explanation of the same), these sands are in greater part ferruginous and 18 feet thick. On the hill between Lewisham and Lee the pebbles, instead of being imbedded in sand, are in a matrix of mottled clays, which elsewhere occasionally entirely replace both sands and pebbles. No fossils are found either at Deptford or Lewisham. At Woolwich this portion of the series consists of 1 foot of pebbles in an argillaceous green sand, with about 18 feet of a slightly pebbly greenish and ochreous sand above them. In the sand are a few calcareo-ferruginous concretions, and in these are found casts and impressions of the *Cyrena cuneiformis* and *Cerithium variabile*. In all these localities this bed, when exposed, is seen to repose upon an eroded surface of the Thanet Sands, but it is more especially to the east of Woolwich that this is apparent. The pebbly sands there come down on the Thanet Sands in great sweeps, as shown in the following section on the North Kent Railway, representing a length of 200 to 300 feet and a depth of about 12 to 20.

Fig. 8.—*Section on the Railway East of Woolwich.*

W. The vertical scale of this section is 100 feet to the inch. E.

II.
III.

II. Base of Woolwich and Reading series.   III. Thanet Sands.

But the clearest and most singular exhibition of this phænomenon is in a small pit on the left of the road ascending the hill from Plumstead to Abbey Wood Common, where this pebbly bed has been as it were splashed into the soft and yielding surface of the underlying Thanet Sands.

Fig. 9.—*Abbey Wood Common‡.*

} II. Dark pebbly argillaceous green sand.

} III. Light-coloured Thanet Sands.

* Geol. Trans. vol. iv. p. 287, and Pl. 13.   † Geology of England and Wales, p. 49.
‡ The last time (May 1853) I visited this spot this section was covered over.

This distinguishing feature is, however, so irregularly maintained, that at Erith, where in the Ballast pit this middle group overlies the Thanet Sands, the line of demarcation between them can hardly be traced : the two sands are almost exactly alike, and the pebble seams are wanting. But the organic remains here assist us, as a band, marked by the occurrence of the *Ostrea Bellovacina*, defines the line of separation of the two groups*.

Above this basement-bed are a series of fluviatile clays and pebbly sands generally abounding in fossils. It is in the lower part of this, or in the middle of the central division of the Lower Tertiaries, that the well-known fluviatile clays of Woolwich are placed. This stratum ranges from London† to Rochester, a distance of thirty miles, but with a breadth not exceeding five to six miles, except near London, where it extends from twelve to fifteen miles. The general character of this bed is well known from the descriptions of Dr. Buckland, Dr. Mitchell, Mr. Morris, and the Rev. H. De la Condamine, to whose papers I beg to refer‡ for some of the principal sections in this district.

As, however, the fossils of the Woolwich pits require both additions and corrections, I herewith annex a list of those found in the bed of dark grey clay (Nos. 7 & 8 of Dr. Buckland).

Organic Remains of the Woolwich Clay Bed, Ballast Pit §.

(Pl. I. Diag. A, Loc. sect. 25.)

Cyrena cuneiformis, *Fér.*	Nucula fragilis, *Desh.*
—— deperdita, *Sow.*	Ostrea Bellovacina, *Desh.*
—— cordata, *Mor.*	—— tenera, *Sow.*
Cerithium variabile, *Desh.*	Hydrobia Parkinsoni, *Mor.*
—— gracile, *Mor.*	Planorbis hemistoma, *Sow.*
Cypris?	Psammobia Condamini, *Mor.* ?
Fusus latus, *Sow.*	Small Corallines.
Melania inquinata, *Desh.*	Opercula (of Cerithium ?).
Melanopsis buccinoides, *Fér.*	Eggs of Molluscs ?
Neritina globulus, *Def.*	

The fossiliferous pebbly sands overlying this clay bed at the Woolwich pit must, I think, be referred to the upper part of this series. They contain the following fossils :—

Organic Remains of the Pebbly Sands, Woolwich Ballast Pit.

Arca depressa, *Sow.*	Buccinum (Pseudoliva) fissuratum,
Auricula pygmæa, *Mor.*	*Desh.*
Balanus ?	Calyptræa trochiformis, *Lam.*

---

* See also Journ. Geol. Soc. vol. vi. p. 443.

† Including the detached and isolated patch (which however belongs to a higher part of the series) at Guildford, the range of the fluviatile beds would be nearly sixty miles.

‡ *Ante*, p. 76.

§ The fossils of this pit have been most carefully worked out by Mr. De la Condamine, Mr. Lunn, and Mr. Rosser, in whose collections I found most of the rarer specimens of the accompanying lists.

Cardium Plumsteadiense, *Sow.*
Cerithium variabile, *Desh.*
—— Lunnii, *Mor.*
—— Bowerbankii, *Mor.*
Cyrena deperdita, *Sow.*
—— cordata, *Mor.*
—— cuneiformis, *Fér.*
—— intermedia, *Mell.*
—— tellinella, *Desh.*
Fusus latus, *Sow.*
—— gradatus, *Sow.*
—— planicostatus, *Mell.?*
Melanopsis ancillaroides, *Desh.*
—— buccinoides, *Fér.*
Melania inquinata, *Desh.*
Modiola Mitchelli, *Mor.?*
Murex foliaceus, *Mell.*
Natica glaucinoides, *Sow.*
Neritina consobrina, *Fér.*

Neritina globulus, *Desh.*
—— pisiformis, *Fér.*
—— viciua, *Mell.?*
Nucula fragilis, *Desh.*
Ostrea Beliovacina, *Desh.*
—— tenera, *Sow.*
Hydrobia Parkinsoni, *Mor.*
—— Websteri, *Mor.*
Pectunculus terebratularis, *Lam.*
Pholas?
Planorbis hemistoma, *Sow.*
Teredina personata, *Desh.*
Teredo antenautæ, *Sow.*
Teeth of Lamna.
Scales and teeth of Fishes.
Crustacea (Cancer).
Small seed-vessels (Carpolithes?).
Cythere &c. (Entomostraca, list, p. 120.)
Small Bryozoa.

There are also two undescribed sections to which I must allude, as they present several peculiar and interesting features. The first is one by the side of the new road leading down the hill from Charlton : it is taken from two or three small pits, but the sequence is perfectly clear. On the top of the hill is the Blackheath pebble bed ; then follows—

(Pl. I. Diag. A, Loc. sect. 24.)

			Feet.
	e.	Light yellow sands striped with clay	12
	d.	Light yellow sands with thin seams of iron sandstone ...	5
II.	*c.*	Dark grey clay with shells	6
	b.	Layer of hard concretionary limestone	2
	a.	Pebbly green sand...	10
III.	Thanet Sands.		

The beds " *a, b, d,* and *e* " are non-fossiliferous, but the clay bed " *c* " contains the same organic remains as at Woolwich.

The blocks of argillaceous limestone " *b* " are concretionary masses of frequent occurrence in this neighbourhood. They are exceedingly hard and tough, and contain here no organic remains. (This stratum is more fully developed beneath London, and is often a source of considerable difficulty to the well-digger.)

But the most important feature of this section is the occurrence on the upper surface of a thin seam of iron sandstone, interstratified in the upper part of " *d,* " of well-marked *ripple-marks,* the ridges of which run nearly E. and W. This is the only instance I have met with of a ripple-marked surface in the Tertiary series of the London district.

The second section is at the entrance to the Tunnel on the S. side of Blackheath, and differs in several points from the preceding Charlton section.

Fig. 10.—*Section on the Railway near the Blackheath Station.*

	Feet.
f. Blackheath pebble bed	10 to 12
e. Brownish sand	2
d. Comminuted shells in light-coloured clay with pebbles	4
c. Comminuted shells in greenish grey clay * ..	2
b. Light green sandy clays, mottled red and grey	7
a. Light greenish sands with a few pebbles...	6
III. Thanet Sands.	

Here the upper part of "*a*" of the preceding section passes into mottled clays. The fossils of "*c*" are similar to those of the same bed at Charlton and Woolwich: those of "*d* and *e*" are few and badly preserved, but at a distance of about half a mile further westward towards Lee these beds are richer in organic remains, which are for the greater part the same as those found in the "Pebbly Sands" at Woolwich, but not so well preserved. The main points of difference are, the far greater abundance of the *Modiola Mitchelli* at Lee,—a shell extremely rare at Woolwich,—and the absence or great rarity at the former place of the *Cardium* and *Pectunculus*.

In the neighbourhood of Blackheath this upper portion of the middle division of the Lower London Tertiaries often consists of alternating thin layers of light grey or brownish clays and yellow sand, which in the section of Loam Pit Hill, Dr. Buckland designated as "striped sands" and "striped loams"; and the former term has since been applied by Mr. De la Condamine to denote generally the upper part of this division,—a subdivision, however, which, although well-marked in that vicinity, can only be considered as a local feature.

The railway cutting at New Cross was interesting from its exposing a more freshwater condition† of the strata than usually prevails, and from its showing the relation of these upper beds of the Woolwich series to the London clay. Only the higher beds of the group were here exposed, consisting of—

(Pl. I. Diag. C, Loc. sect. 9.)

	Feet.
London clay	40
Basement-bed London clay (flint-pebbles in ochreous sand) ...	1 to 2
i. Yellow sand	2½
h. Clay and sand, with shells occasionally............................	3
g. Band of freshwater limestone (*Paludina*)	0½ to 1
f. Sand and shells	6
e. Clayey sand and shells	5

The order of succession of the lower beds was made known by a well sunk at the Naval School, New Cross.

* At a distance of a quarter of a mile E. this bed becomes 6 feet thick, of a dark grey colour, and full of shells.

† The same beds extend to Peckham on one side, and to Counter Hill and Lewisham on the other.

Well-section, New Cross.   (Pl. I. Diag. C, Loc. sect. 8.)
(Mr. R. W. Mylne.)

		Feet.
London	Yellow clay	10
Clay.	Blue clay	13
	i. Shells in sand	10
	h. Hard shells	3
II. *Woolwich*	*g.* Sand with water	1
and	*f.* Sand with shells	15
Reading	*e.* Shells and clay mixed	5
Series.	*d.* Sand	1
	c. Hard shells in sand	2
	b. Pebbles	15
	a. Green sand	2
III. *Thanet*	Hard sand	14
Sands.	Sand	34
		125
	Chalk	25

To the band of freshwater limestone, attention has been called by Mr. Warburton*.   It is full of the following fossils :—

Melanopsis buccinoides, *Fér.*
Paludina lenta, *Sow.* var. *a, Mor.*
Hydrobia Parkinsoni, *Mor.*

Teeth, bones, and scales of Fishes.
Unio (Deshayesii, *Wat.?*).
Traces of vegetable impressions.

The *Unio* has only been found at a very short distance to the E. and W. of this place.   The *Paludina,* which can scarcely be distinguished from the Isle of Wight species, hardly exceeds the limits of this area: it has been found however as far north as Limehouse. Beneath this bed are clays and sands also containing a somewhat different group of fossils.   The following is a list of those which I collected during the cutting of the railway :—

Arca depressa, *Sow.*
Calyptræa trochiformis, *Lam.*
Corbula Regulbiensis, var. β, *Mor.*
Cyrena cuneiformis, *Fér.*
—— cordata, *Mor.*
—— deperdita, *Sow.*
—— tellinella, *Desh.*
Cerithium variabile, *Desh.*
Melania inquinata, *Desh.*
Melanopsis buccinoides, *Fér.*

Modiola Mitchelli, *Mor.*
Ostrea Bellovacina, *Desh.*
—— tenera, *Sow.*
Hydrobia Parkinsoni, *Mor.*
Cypris ?
Bones and scales of Fishes.

Cythere, sp.
Foraminifera (last 3 sp. in list, p. 118).

To the above specimens may be added the following species from the Counter Hill pits :—

Pectunculus terebratularis, *Lam.*
Planorbis lævigatus, *Desh.*

Psammobia Condamini, *Mor.*
Impressions of plants.

When these upper beds contain subordinate seams of pebbles, it becomes difficult to separate them from the " Basement-bed of the London Clay," which reposes upon this division in a very irregular manner.

At Woolwich no line of separation can in the present section be drawn between the great mass of shingle, which I presume belongs to the Basement-bed of the London clay, and the fossiliferous pebbly sands ; but about twelve or fifteen years since, when the section

* Journ. Geol. Soc. vol. i. p. 172.

extended further southward, a waved irregular line generally separated these latter from some unfossiliferous pebbly beds above. The upper bed being derived in great part from the destruction of the lower, and the materials being so similar, renders it difficult to discriminate between them either here or anywhere in the immediate district. Viewed, however, on a large scale, this distinction is apparent. In conjunction with Mr. De la Condamine I had an excavation 10 feet deep made beneath the London clay at the north base of Shooter's Hill, and found that it reposed directly, and without admixture of pebbles, upon the great mass of sandy shingle spread over Plumstead Heath and Blackheath; just as at New Cross and Lewisham it reposes upon an equally compact bed of similar shingle, but which in these localities is only 1 to 2 feet thick. This latter bed I have before shown to extend uninterruptedly westward through the London district and as far as the Isle of Wight, maintaining throughout its range a general thickness not exceeding 2 to 5 feet. Although attaining such a remarkable thickness at Blackheath, still as no break or division can be detected in the mass, it may be considered as a development of the same bed,—a view confirmed by a constant character before shown to attach to the Basement-bed of the London clay, viz. that of reposing upon a worn and eroded surface of the underlying beds. This feature is very marked in the Blackheath district. Great hollows, swept out of the pebbly sands and fossiliferous clays, are filled up by these masses of shingle beds. In one locality on Blackheath the upper sands of the Woolwich group are 25 feet thick and come almost close to the surface, whilst in a pit a few hundred feet N.W. and on the same level the sands are entirely wanting, being replaced by the pebble beds. Very thick agglomeration of pebbles, and frequent false stratifications shelving down, generally northward, from 20° to 35°, mark these pebble beds, which in some places on Plumstead Heath attain the great thickness of 50 to 70 feet. Traces of shells are occasionally met with in them, but they are in so friable a state that it is difficult to determine their characters. The *Cardium*, *Nucula*, and *Cyrena*, all probably the same as the Woolwich species, have been recognised.

Proceeding eastward from Woolwich the Middle division of the Lower Tertiaries resolves itself more distinctly into—1st, upper beds of sand with subordinate layers of pebbles, clay, and containing many of the shells found in the pebbly sands of Lee and Woolwich; 2nd, beds of laminated brown or dark grey clay with *Ostrea*, *Cyrena*, *Melania*, and *Cerithium*, 6 to 10 feet thick; and 3rd, lower beds of pebbly light-coloured green sand varying in thickness from 10 to 30 feet.

The upper bed has, however, often been removed by the denudation preceding the deposition of the " Basement-bed of the London clay," —a denudation which has sometimes deeply eroded this middle division, as shown for instance in the section on the side of the lane leading from the Abbey Wood Station up the Abbey Wood hills, where the Basement-bed of the London clay reposes upon the lower beds of the Woolwich series. The middle bed (fossiliferous clays) exists further back (S.) in the hill and crops out by Wickham Church.

Fig. 11.—*Lane in Abbey Wood.*

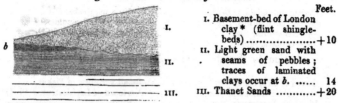

		Feet.
I.	Basement-bed of London clay * (flint shingle-beds)	+10
II.	Light green sand with seams of pebbles; traces of laminated clays occur at *b*.	14
III.	Thanet Sands	+20

Numerous small sections of the fossiliferous clays and associated beds may be seen on the higher hills between the valleys of the Cray and the Darent, as at St. Paul's Cray Hill, Well Hill, Croking Hill, Joyden Wood's Hill, and elsewhere; and again, east of the Darent, on the Swanscombe Hills near Greenhithe, on Windmill Hill, Gravesend, and on the Shorne and Cobham Hills near Strood. The section east of Bexley on the hill leading to Dartford Heath, the one between Green Street Green and Betsham, and that traceable on the path and road-sides in descending from the summit to the south side of Windmill Hill, Gravesend, are represented under the Loc. sect. 29, 30, 31, and 32, Diag. A, Pl. I. The section at Shorne, Loc. sect. 33, is taken in the lane leading from the high-road near Gad's Hill to Shorne Ridgeway.

At Upnor near Rochester the section, which is unusually clear and distinct, shows the London clay with its Basement-bed reposing upon the fluviatile sands and clays, which in their turn overlie the Thanet Sands. These latter, however, do not appear in the larger pit where there is the capping of London clay, but in the sand-pit by the brick-field to the S.W. of it. (See Journ. Geol. Soc. vol. viii. pl. 15.)

The general view of the pits is as follows:—

(Pl. I. Diag. A, Loc. sect. 34.)

		Feet.
	London clay	+25
I.	Basement-bed of the London clay	4½
II. *Woolwich and Reading Series.*	*c.* Light yellow and whitish sands, containing irregular patches of shells, chiefly *Ostrea* and *Cyrena*; occasionally the shells form a layer 1 ft. thick at the base of this bed. Upper surface worn and eroded by " I."	15
	b. Dark grey clay full of shells, both perfect and comminuted, and with a subordinate thin seam of sand, 3½ feet. Dark clay passing down into a brown sandy clay—a few casts of shells—selenite plentiful, 2 ft. Tough yellow clay, sand and ochre, and lignite, ½ ft.	6
	a. Fine white sand 2½ feet. Sand, grey and brownish-red at top, passing down into light yellow, 20 ft. Light ochreous sand, 3 feet. Small flint-pebbles in greenish sand, 2½ ft.	28
III.	Thanet Sands	+20

* In a cutting on the side of the new road just made a short distance east of this section, the "Basement-bed" reposes upon the pebbly sands of the Woolwich and Reading series. The division of these two groups is here perfectly well shown, the line of separation being distinct and irregular, and the pebbly sands, which are far more pebbly than at Woolwich, and contain numerous very friable and badly preserved shells, chiefly *Cyrena*, being in clear contrast with the overlying mass of non-fossiliferous and larger shingle.

The fossils* found in Stratum "*c*" are—

Cerithium variabile, *Desh.*	Melania inquinata, *Desh.*
Cyrena cuneiformis, *Fér.*	Melanopsis buccinoides, *Fér.*
—— deperdita, *Sow.*	Ostrea Bellovacina, *Desh.*
—— cordata, *Mor.*	

In addition to the above, the following fossils occur in Stratum "*b*" :—

Ostrea tenera, *Sow.*	Small vertebræ of Fishes.
Hydrobia Parkinsoni, *Mor.*	Vertebra of Lepidosteus. Pl. III.
Planorbis hemistoma, *Sow.*	fig. 1.
Psammobia Condamini, *Mor.*	Cypris or Cythere ?

In the light-coloured pebbly sands "*a*," no fossils have yet been found†.

The persistence of the fluviatile clays from Woolwich to Rochester is sufficiently apparent, but that of the associated pebbly sands beneath is not so. These latter, when the green grains and the pebbles are absent, assume so closely the appearance of the Thanet Sands, that in many places these two groups can scarcely be distinguished one from another ; and the clays "*b*" repose upon sands which may easily be mistaken for the Thanet Sands, and to which therefore they might be considered subordinate, instead of being, as I believe them to be, subordinate to the Woolwich group. The separation of the two sands is, however, shown in a sufficient number of instances to be marked and definite ; and even when this is not the case, a closer examination of them will generally show that some distinction in the mass does exist, however difficult it may often be in two such similar arenaceous beds to distinguish the line of separation.

Thus far either the mottled clays or the fluviatile clays of Woolwich have given a marked character to the middle division of the Lower Tertiaries, but these mineral and palæontological features cannot be traced eastward of Rochester, and we therefore become dependent upon other evidence for proof of the extension of the "Woolwich and Reading series" into East Kent. As before observed, the pebbly sands "*a*" at the base of this series often want distinctiveness even in West Kent, and this becomes still more apparent as the beds trend eastward ; there is a difficulty therefore in connecting the Woolwich and Upnor sections with those of Herne Bay and Canterbury, owing to our having to rely almost entirely upon these beds (*a*) in our traverse across the intervening district. The outcrop of the Lower Tertiaries between the Medway and Faversham rarely extends beyond the low ground at the base of the chalk hills, and consequently there are few of those long lane-sections so common on the hills in West Kent. I have not in fact been able to find one clear section of the whole of the middle division anywhere between the above-named places. Of the Thanet Sands there is no want of sections, and occasionally there are small sections of the lower part of the middle division ; scanty, however, as they are, they all exhibit the same features and prove the continued superposition

---

* For the fossils and details of "1." see Journ. Geol. Soc. vol. vi. p. 264.
† The fossils both of "*c*" and "*b*" require probably further working out. Both these beds vary slightly in structure in close adjoining pits.

of the two divisions, for wherever sections are open at 60 to 80 feet
above the chalk we invariably find the Thanet sands capped by the
pebbly sands "*a*" of the Woolwich series, the latter being distinguished from the former through this district by its coarser quartzose
character, by the admixture of green sand, of small concretionary or
tabular iron sandstone, of an occasional thin seam of a hard siliceous
sandstone, and sometimes by the presence of a few pebbles; but this
latter is a character which becomes less and less marked as we proceed eastward.   These beds may be seen on the hill in the marshes
W. of Ottersham Wharf, on those near Newington Street, and on the
hills W. of Faversham.   No organic remains have yet been found at
any of these places.

At Boughton, three miles east of Faversham, we arrive at a range
of hills extending from this village to Canterbury, and the summit
of which consists of London clay, while round its slopes the different
members of the Lower Tertiaries crop out and are tolerably well exposed.   From several sections we find that the middle division or
"Woolwich group" has here passed entirely into light ash-coloured
and greenish, and ochreous sands 30 to 40 feet thick.   At Boughton
the following section is exposed :—

(Pl. I. Diag. A, Loc. sect. 40.)

		Feet.
L.	London clay	+10
I.	*b.* Fine whitish sands with layers of pebbles and traces of shells, and a few teeth of *Lamna*	7
	a. Grey clay	1
II.	Light green, and ochreous, sharp sands	30

No fossils are found in Strata " II."   Just before the publication of
my paper on the Thanet Sands, I discovered some silicified fossils in
a hedge-bank at Oakwell.   The superposition of the bed is not shown,
and from the occurrence of the *Cucullæa crassatina** and *Cytherea
Bellovacina*, I considered that it was probably a part of the Thanet
Sands.   From subsequent examination of the ground I am, however,
led to believe that this bed belongs to the pebbly Woolwich sands
("*a*"), the more especially as I have since found similar fossils in a
bed whose superposition to the Thanet Sands is clear.   This is the
first indication we have of a distinctly marine fauna in this part of
the Woolwich group.   The following are the species found there :—

Cardium.
Corbula Regulbiensis, *Mor.?*
—— (Arnouldi, *Nyst?*)
Cucullæa crassatina, *Lam.*
Cyprina Morrisii, *Sow.*
Cytherea Bellovacina, *Desh.*
Dentalium.

Ostrea.
Flustra.
Sponge spicula.
Nodosaria bacillum, *Defr.*
A very small undeterminable univalve,
and some small bivalves, apparently
Cytherea.

* The occurrence of this silicified shell in this neighbourhood was noticed
some years since by Mr. Crowe of Faversham, and is mentioned in the ' Min.
Conch.'; but the exact locality was not given, and its position has remained uncertain up to the present time.   It appears to have been found nearer to Faversham, or there were formerly some excavations in Nash Park near Boughton
whence some fossils are said to have been obtained.

These fossils are, however, very rare: I have not found them elsewhere on this side of Canterbury.

On Shottenden Hill, three miles S. of Boughton, is an outlier of the
Lower Tertiaries capping the chalk, and singular in that it exhibits
the only instance in this district of the occurrence of the shingle-beds
of the Basement-bed of the London clay, forming a mass as distinct
as that on Blackheath, and from 30 to 40 feet thick.

Another interesting phænomenon is also met with at this place:
beneath the shingle are the light-coloured quartzose pebbly sands of
the Woolwich group, and in the upper part of this bed are occasional
small masses of a soft concreted sandstone, the upper surface of
which is often full of the holes of a boring mollusk, apparently a
Lithodomus. I have found no other traces of organic remains in
these beds.

The next clear section, or rather series of sections, is at the village
of St. Stephen's, one mile N.W. of Canterbury. In one pit, the
London clay reposing upon the Basement-bed, and in another the
latter on the faint-green sands of the Woolwich group, may be seen:
But the most complete section occurs at the entrance to the tunnel on
the Whitstable Railway, where the sequence of the Lower Tertiaries
from the London clay to the Thanet Sands is well exposed.

Fig. 12.—*Section on the Whitstable Railway, near Canterbury.*

(Pl. I. Diag. A, Loc. sect. 42.)

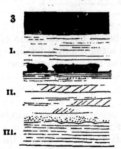

3. London clay.
ɪ. Basement-bed (light sands with large
    blocks of pebbly ironstone *).
ɪɪ. Woolwich series (light-coloured sands
    mixed with some green sand and a
    few pebbles).
ɪɪɪ. Thanet Sands.

The fossils in the "Basement-bed" "ɪ." are numerous; but none
occur in the pebbly sands "ɪɪ." : traces of sponge-like ferruginous
concretions are, however, common. Both are about 20 feet thick.

The most important section, however, in this district is on the coast
between Herne Bay and the Reculvers. Here, in addition to the large
surface exposed, the beds are more fossiliferous than usual. The
following is a description of the cliff immediately east of Bishopstone
ravine (see Journ. Geol. Soc. vol. viii. p. 239. pl. 15).

* These blocks of ironstone extend to Boughton, from which locality the organic remains enumerated in my paper in the Journ. Geol. Soc. vol. vi. p. 264,
were obtained. This bed has since been found to be sufficiently rich in iron to
be profitably worked, and it is now, I understand, quarried and sent to the Staf-
fordshire furnaces.

(Pl. I. Diag. A, Loc. sect. 43.)

		Feet.
Drift	Ochreous flint gravel	4 to 6
London clay	Tenacious brown and bluish clay, with few or no fossils	10 to 15

I. *Basement-bed of the London clay* (for the fossils of this division, see Journ. Geol. Soc. vol. vi. p. 265).

b. Fine light-coloured siliceous sands, with occasional large tabular masses of sandstone, white, grey, ferruginous, and brick-red. Lenticular twin-crystals of sulphate of lime, and small soft concretionary lumps of the black oxide of iron, common. Seams of flint-pebbles of occasional occurrence. False stratification of the sands not uncommon. Fossils common, occasionally dispersed in the sands, but more commonly in irregular patches, and in the sandstone blocks 22

a. A layer of flint-pebbles in sand, (yellow, green, and ferruginous,) often concreted ; abounds in organic remains .... 1 to 2

II. *Woolwich and Reading Series.*

c. Argillaceous green sand, passing down into yellowish sand with less clay 12

b. Dark grey argillaceous sand, full of small ferruginous sandy tubular concretions and lumps, passes down into a brownish sandy clay, and then into a light greenish-grey clayey sand, with a very few small flint pebbles. Nodules and lumps of iron pyrites, with coarse green sand and very small quartz pebbles, are common. Wood in fragments and pieces in the state of lignite are of frequent occurrence. A very few teeth and palates of Fishes are found. 7

a. Light ash-green and yellow sands with casts of shells, passing down into a coarser green sand, near the base of which a thin band of very coarse and bright green sand, sometimes concreted and abounding in silicified shells, occurs............................. 9

III. *Thanet Sands.* (Journ. vol. viii. p. 262.)

Yellow, greenish, and grey fossiliferous sands. These only just appear at this spot.

The strata *a, b,* and *c,* II. of this section I take to represent the Woolwich and Reading series. In its lower bed " *a* " there is a group of organic remains, consisting of the following marine species :—

Ampullaria subdepressa, *Mor.*
Cardium Laytoni, *Mor.*
—— Plumsteadiense, *Sow.*
Corbula Regulbiensis, *Mor.*
Cucullæa crassatina, *Lam.*
Cyprina Morrisii, *Sow.*
—— scutellaria, *Desh.*
Cytherea Bellovacina, *Desh.*

Dentalium.
Glycimeris Rutupiensis, *Mor.*
Pectunculus terebratularis, *Lam.*
Sanguinolaria Edwardsii, *Sow.*
Teredo antenautæ, *Sow.*
Thracia oblata, *Sow.?*
Teeth of Lamna.

Fragments and pieces of wood in the state of lignite, frequently bored by the Teredo, are not uncommon, and in an ironstone concretion I found a fine specimen of a Fir Cone (Pl. III. fig. 4). This bed also contains, nearer to the Reculvers, specimens of silicified wood likewise sometimes bored by the Teredo, and with the structure beautifully preserved.

The middle bed " *b* " passes towards Herne Bay into a dark clayey sand full of traces of vegetable matter and with a large number of concretions of iron pyrites. This may possibly represent the carbonaceous and fluviatile clays of Upnor and Woolwich. The only other fossils I have found in this bed were in the cliff at Bishopstone ravine. They consisted of a few rare fragments of *Myliobates, Edaphodon,* and *Chelonia,* but the specimens were too small and imperfect to distinguish the species. A few fish-vertebræ and teeth of *Lamna* also occur.

The upper bed " *c* " is an argillaceous green sand without fossils.

Although rather dissimilar in appearance, the base of these three beds is nevertheless alike, consisting in each case of quartzose sands and green sand. This common character becomes more apparent as the beds trend towards the Reculvers, where they pass into a light greenish quartzose sand easily separable from the Basement-bed above, but without any well-marked line of separation from the Thanet Sands beneath. This want of clear divisional surfaces, and the occurrence of several of the same species of shells in the two series, might be considered an objection to their being thus separated. The fossils, however, taken as a group, are different from those of the Thanet Sands, whilst the sands are more siliceous and contain a larger proportion of green sand and some disseminated flint-pebbles—two mineral characters deriving some importance from their breadth and constancy.

The indistinctness of the separating surfaces is, I believe, to be attributed merely to the lithological structure of the beds ; for, owing to the soft and yielding nature of the Thanet Sands on which the sands of the Woolwich series were deposited, the upper surface of the former would be liable to be moved and stirred up by the currents which brought down the latter, and as both must have been in the state of muddy sand, an intermixture of the surfaces in contact would be almost inevitable. An illustration in point is furnished in the same cliff-section between the Bishopstone ravine and the Reculvers. There, in one place, a *drift* of light brown brick-earth reposes upon the Woolwich sands. The difference of age of these two deposits will not be disputed, but nevertheless there is no defined line of demarcation between them, and the " Drift " appears to pass down into these old Tertiary beds.

At Richborough the division of the Thanet Sands from the Woolwich group is still less apparent. A close examination will, however, show the prevailing sharp quartzose and slightly green-sand character of the latter, whilst a thin seam of green sand full of the *Corbula Regulbiensis,* and with an occasional large *Cyprina,* occurs precisely in the position as the same fossiliferous band at Herne Bay. I have recently had this view confirmed by the small but beautiful series of fossils obtained from this bed by the Rev. James Layton of Sandwich at the railway ballast-pit, adjoining Richborough Castle. They consist of the following species :—

Ampullaria subdepressa, *Mor.*	Cyprina Morrisii, *Sow.*
Cardium Plumsteadiense, *Sow.*	Cytherea Bellovacina, *Desh.*
—— Laytoni, *Mor.*	Dentalium.
Corbula Regulbiensis, *Mor.*	Glycimeris Rutupiensis, *Mor.*
Cucullæa crassatina, *Lam.*	Pectunculus terebratularis, *Desh.*
Cyprina scutellaria, *Desh.*	Sanguinolaria Edwardsii, *Mor.*

All these species are silicified, and many of them in the most perfect and delicate state of preservation. (For the description of this section see Journ. Geol. Soc. vol. viii. p. 251 and pl. 15.)

On Woodnesborough Hill and at Ash the Woolwich sands are 26 to 30 feet thick, and consist entirely of one mass, nearly uniform throughout, of light-coloured quartzose sands with green sand in disseminated grains and patches, and with a few dispersed pebbles and slight ochreous patches and concretions. No shells have been found at these latter places, but Mr. Layton has procured from several pits in that district, especially the one at Marshborough, a number of specimens of silicified wood with the structure beautifully preserved. Some of them are pierced by the Teredo, which in one specimen is quite in its young state, just adhering to the wood. These specimens appear identical with those found in these beds at the Reculvers.

I have not met with any beds of the Woolwich group in the Isle of Thanet.

§ 3. *Organic Remains.*

As local lists of the organic remains have been given in the preceding pages, it now only remains to consider their general distribution, association, and condition, and to tabulate the whole.

It has been shown that the Woolwich and Reading series, far from being characterized throughout by similar fossils, exhibit peculiar assemblages in different districts. Where the mottled clays prevail, as over the greater part of the Hampshire and throughout all the London district west of London, organic remains seem altogether wanting, with the exception of the irregularly distributed layer of the "*Ostrea Bellovacina*" at the base of this group, and of the local plant remains at Reading, a few feet higher in the series, but still near its base.

The Woolwich beds continue comparatively barren until they reach the neighbourhood of London. Concomitant with the lithological change before-described, the peculiar group of fresh and brackish water shells of Woolwich appear, and attain their maximum development at London, New Cross, Deptford, Woolwich, Bromley, Chiselhurst, and then decrease in variety and abundance as the beds range to Rochester and Upnor. The species are not many, but the individuals of several are very numerous.

The more strongly marked freshwater conditions are confined to nearly the upper portion of this series at New Cross and a short distance around, where the *Unio*, the *Paludina*, the small *Hydrobia Parkinsoni*, and the *Melanopsis buccinoides* are abundant. The sands, pebbles, and clays just beneath the above contain a more mixed group, of which the prevailing species are the *Cerithium variabile*, *Melania inquinata, Neritina globulus,* the two species of *Melanopsis* and of *Fusus,* the several species of *Cyrena,* especially the *C. cordata, Modiola Mitchelli, Planorbis hemistoma,* and *Ostrea Bellovacina.* To these succeeds the well-marked and wide-spread Woolwich clay-bed characterized by the *Cyrena cuneiformis* and *deperdita, Hydrobia Parkinsoni, Melania inquinata, Cerithium variabile, Melanopsis buccinoides, Ostrea Bellovacina* and *tenera,* and *Planorbis hemistoma.* The other species given in the list p. 117, as occurring in this area (C.), are comparatively scarce.

Traces of plants and seed-vessels have been found in this series at Lewisham, apparently nearly in the same part of it as at Reading; but the earliest mention of plants from this group is by the late Dr. Mantell, who, in his description of Castle Hill, Newhaven, figures one or two specimens which agree apparently with some of the Reading species*. Coniferous wood, in the condition of patches of lignite, occurs in the pebbly sands just above the Thanet sands.

The remains of vertebrate animals are of rare occurrence. I have found fish-bones and a few scales in the Paludina-limestone of New Cross, and they occasionally occur together with teeth of *Lamna* and some smaller fish-teeth in some of the Woolwich beds. Small fish-vertebræ are not uncommon at Upnor, where also the vertebra of a large species of *Lepidosteus* has been found. Remains of the *Edaphodon* and *Myliobates* exist near the Reculvers. Mr. Alport has made known the occurrence in one of the conglomerate beds of this series of the remains of a *Coryphodon* or *Lophiodon,* a tooth of this animal having been found in sinking a well at Sydenham†; and Dr. Mitchell alludes in his manuscripts to the circumstance of the bones of some large animal having been discovered about 15 feet beneath the limestone band at the Counter Hill pits, Deptford. Fossils of this latter description have never come under my notice; but it is to be observed that this pit is only occasionally opened down to these beds. Of the remains of Crustacea I have only found part of the claw of a Crab at Sundridge Park‡.

The fauna of the Woolwich and Reading series in this area (C.), though rich, is very irregularly distributed, the strata being by no means continuously fossiliferous; in some places the organic remains are extremely numerous, whilst at others close adjacent they are wanting§. The fossils are more persistent in the clays than in the

---

* "Geology of Sussex," p. 257, and pl. 8.

† The Geologist, vol. i. p. 66.

‡ Mr. Rosser has since found a similar specimen at Woolwich.

§ Although the pits in the neighbourhood of London have been so long known, few additions were for a long time made to the list of shells collected by Parkinson and Sowerby. Within the last few years, however, the zeal and industry of the Rev. Mr. De la Condamine, of Blackheath, has brought to light several new species. In addition to the *Lepidosteus* mentioned above, he has discovered the *Psammobia Condamini, Planorbis lævigatus,* and a species of *Cythere,* with some peculiar vegetable remains, at Counter Hill, apparently in or near the same bed as that in which Dr. Mitchell noticed the remains of bones. This *Planorbis* has been found nowhere else in England, whilst the *Psammobia* has only been observed in one other specimen at Upnor by Mr. De la Condamine, and one at Newhaven by myself. The *Teredo personata* is a single specimen, also found by Mr. De la

sands. With regard to their state of preservation, the Paludina limestone exhibits well-preserved specimens. In the beds beneath this there are considerable bands formed almost entirely of comminuted fragments of shells, whilst in some associated beds the shells are preserved entire, but they are generally very friable. In the clays, although not unfrequently crushed, they are sometimes in an excellent state of preservation. In both these parts of the series the several species of *Cyrenæ* are often found with their two valves together. This fact was especially observable in the pebbly calcareous rocks of Deptford*, where scarcely a single valve either of the *Cyrena* or *Modiola* is found separate.

A very interesting example of this description, and of tranquil entombment, has been pointed out by Mr. De la Condamine at Woolwich, where, in one part of the pebbly sands overlying the bed of clay, the *Cyrena tellinella*, in an excellent state of preservation and the two valves united, occurs in its normal vertical position, as when living it bored into the sands.

The perfect condition of the *Ostrea Bellovacina* at Woolwich and Sundridge has often been noticed†.

In the neighbourhood of Bromley, Chiselhurst, and Lewisham there are beds or bands abounding almost exclusively with this oyster, frequently with the two valves united, and in the position in which it lived. The lowest bed of pebbly green sand immediately overlying the "Thanet Sands" is in this area also characterized by the *Ostrea Bellovacina*; not that it is so generally abundant as in some of the upper beds of this group, but it there constitutes, as in the western area, almost the sole fossil. It has been found in this position in sinking several wells in London (Barclay and Perkins's, Truman and Hanbury's, the Bank, the Mint, and others). It is nevertheless scarcely ever met with in this stratum at its outcrop in Kent ; at Erith it occurs occasionally in this bed and of a large size ; and I think it exists also at Oakwells near Boughton. North of London this old eocene Oyster-bed is largely developed at Northaw, where it lies, as it does also at Hertford, immediately upon the chalk without the intervention of the Thanet Sands. On the south of London it is again found overlying the chalk at Headley-on-the-hill and Fetcham. These fossil oysters frequently exhibit a much-worn and

Condamine at Woolwich. The upper part of the Woolwich series at Lee and Blackheath has likewise furnished him with several rare species of *Neritina* and a Bracheux *Buccinum*. These latter, together with some new species of *Cerithium* and a *Murex* of the neighbourhood of Laon, exist also in the fine collection from the Woolwich pits made by Mr. Lunn. It was not until the recent close and careful investigation of Mr. Rosser, that *Cytheræ* were known to occur in such abundance in the pebbly sands of Woolwich, together with well-preserved fish-scales, numerous small indeterminable bones, the eggs and opercula of Molluscs, a variety of small *Bryozoa*, and *Foraminifera*. These were chiefly found in the interior of the larger shells.

* In the railway cutting.

† Dr. Buckland, in particular, alludes to this circumstance, and to the frequent agglutination of several of these oysters together on some of the large flint pebbles.

eaten surface full of the small holes made by some minute boring sponge.

The surface of the chalk beneath the Oyster-bed is frequently perforated with numerous irregular tubes, running about 6 inches to a foot perpendicularly into the chalk, and filled with green sand from the superincumbent bed. This is particularly visible at Kembridge, Clay Hill, near Newbury, and at Reading.

The shells in this area are found in all stages of growth; many attain a large size. Some of the *Ostrea Belloracina* measure 5 or 6 inches by 4 and 5; the *Pectunculus* 1½ to 1¾ inch in both directions; the *Cyrena deperdita* and *cordata* have a breadth of 1½ inch; and the *C. cuneiformis* sometimes as much as 2 inches; whilst the *Melania inquinata* is often 2½ to 2¾ inches long, the *Cerithium variabile* nearly 2 inches, and the *Melanopsis* 1¼ to 1⅜ inch.

The brown epidermis of some specimens of *Cyrena* can sometimes be distinctly traced, and the ligament occasionally remains. Sometimes even the colouring of the shells has not entirely disappeared, and the fine marking on some of the small *Neritinæ* is often retained. The dried animal matter of the animal itself is sometimes preserved in small brown pieces in the interior of some of the shells. Some of the small seed-vessels and portions of leaves also occasionally retain their elasticity and traces of their brown colouring matter.

In the few pits between Upnor and Boughton, which exhibit sections of the lower part only of the " Woolwich and Reading series," I have not, any more than in the same beds at Upnor, been able to discover organic remains. At Boughton, where there is a change in the lithological structure of the Woolwich beds, it is accompanied at the same time by a complete alteration in the organic remains. All traces of the fluviatile shells of Woolwich are lost, and the equivalent beds, which are however imperfectly exposed, appear here to be unfossiliferous; but the light greenish sands on the level of the pebbly green sands and *Ostrea Bellovacina* beds of the central and western areas contain, with a few of the Woolwich forms, a new group of marine fossils in the state of fine siliceous casts. Several of the shells found here, such as the *Cucullæa crassatina, Cytherea Bellovacina,* and *Corbula (Arnouldi?),* are common to the underlying Thanet Sands; but there are others which are peculiar to these overlying beds, such as the fine *Cyprina scutellaria,* the *Pectunculus terebratularis,* the *Cardium Plumsteadiense,* and the *Corbula Regulbiensis.*

In the neighbourhood of Canterbury this division is unfossiliferous, but in the cliffs between Herne Bay and the Reculvers we again meet with the zone of silicified fossils (*ante,* p. 111).

Nearer the Reculvers these beds contain silicified wood, of which, however, better specimens have been found by the Rev. James Layton of Sandwich in the pits between Ash and Wodnesborough. The structure of this wood is in general coniferous, but some specimens show a remarkable form of dicotyledonous texture. No shells are found there. At Richborough the lower part of this group again presents a thin band of silicified fossils of the same species as those of Herne Bay and Boughton, and in a beautiful state of preservation with every marking retained. As at the two former places the characteristic shell is the *Corbula Regulbiensis*, which occurs aggregated in masses; the *Cucullæa crassatina* is also abundant, as likewise the large *Cyprina scutellaria**. Although silicified and hard, they are, when first found, extremely brittle; and perfect specimens, except of the *Corbula*, are difficult to be procured.

In Essex and Suffolk I have not been able to find any organic remains in the few sections exposed in this division, with the possible exception of an oyster at Kyson. Nor does the Rev. W. J. Clarke, who was well acquainted with Suffolk, mention the occurrence of any fossils in the numerous localities he describes†.

LIST OF THE ORGANIC REMAINS OF THE WOOLWICH AND READING SERIES‡.

[The second column gives their synonyms, and the third indicates whether their range is in the Western (W.), Central (C.), or Eastern (E.) areas. See the area-divisions in p. 78. The " n. sp." refer to the new species described by Mr. Morris, and figured in Pl. II. of this volume.]

Bivalves.

Arca depressa, *Sow.*	*A. striatularis,* Melleville?....	C.
Cardium Laytoni, *Mor.*, n. sp...	....	E.
—— Plumsteadiense, *Sow.* (*a*)..	*C.semigranulosum,* Desh. n. Sow.	C. E.
Corbula (Arnouldii, *Nyst*?) (*b*)..	....	E.
—— Regulbiensis, *Mor.*(*c*),n. sp.	....	E.
—— —— var. β. *Mor.*	....	C.
Cucullæa crassatina, *Lam.*	*C. decussata,* Park...........	E.
Cyprina Morrisii, *Sow.*	*Venus ovalis,* Sow. M. C. pl. 567. fig. 2, non fig. 1?	E.
—— scutellaria, *Desh.*	non *C. scutellaria,* Nyst	E.
Cyrena cordata (*d*), *Mor.*, n. sp.	an *C. obovata,*var. *a.* Sow. pars?	C.
—— cuneiformis, *Fér.*	*Cyclas deperdita,*Pk.text,nonfig.	C.
—— deperdita, *Sow.*	non *C. deperdita,* Desh. or Park.	C.
—— intermedia, *Mell.*	an *C. Deshayesii,* Héb.	C.
—— tellinella, *Desh.*	....	C.
Cytherea Bellovacina, *Desh.* (*e*).	*C. orbicularis,* Mor.	E.
Dreissena serrata, *Mell.*? (*f*)....	....	C.
Glycimeris Rutupiensis, *Mor.* ··	....	C.? E.
Lithodomus	....	E.
Modiola Mitchelli, *Mor.* (*g*),n. sp.	....	C.
—— dorsata, *Mor.*, n. sp.	....	C.
Nucula fragilis, *Desh.*	....	C.
Ostrea Bellovacina, *Desh.*......	*O. pulchra, edulina, undulata,* S.	W. C.
—— tenera, *Sow.*	*O. angusta & plicatella,* Desh.?	C.
Pholas?	....	C.

* Some specimens of this shell measure 4 inches by 3.
† The recent section at Chelmsford (Artesian well, Appendix) would seem to show that shells do there exist. I was, however, unable to see the specimens, or to learn exactly whether any had been kept. They would probably be crushed by the auger, as the bore-hole was very small.
‡ I have to express my obligations to Mr. Morris, Mr. Edwards, and M. Deshayes for their kind aid and assistance in the comparison of many of these fossils. To Mr. Morris I am further indebted for the description of the new species.

Pectunculus terebratularis,*Lk.*(*h*)	*P. Plumsteadiensis*, Sow.	C. E.
Psammobia?Condamini,*Mor.*,n.s.	....	C.
Sanguinolaria Edwardsii, *Mor.*...	....	E.
Teredina personata, *Desh.*	*Teredo antenautæ*, S., pars,f.4-8	C. E.
Teredo antenautæ, *Sow.*	*Ibid.* fig. 1–3	E.
Unio (Deshayesii,*Watelet* ?) (*i*)..	....	C.
Thracia oblata, *Sow.*	*Lutraria*, Sow.	E.

Univalves.

Ampullaria subdepressa,*Mor.*,n.s.	....	E.
Auricula pygmæa, *Mor.*, n. sp...		C.
Buccinum (Pseudoliva) fissura-	....	C.
tum, *Desh.* ? (*j*)		
Calyptræa trochiformis, *Lam.* ..	*Infundibulum echinulatum*,Sow.	C.
Cerithium Lunnii, *Mor.*, n. sp...	....	C.
—— gracile, *Mor.*, n. sp......		C.
—— Bowerbankii, *Mor.*, n. sp...		C.
—— variabile,*Desh.*,var. *c,f,&g.*	C. (*Potamides*) *funatum, inter-medium & funiculatum*, Sow.(*k*)	C.
Dentalium		E.
Fusus latus, *Sow.* (*l*)	*F. deceptus*, Desh. ; an *Buccinum granulosum*, Mell. ?	C.
—— gradatus, *Sow.* (*m*)	....	C.
—— planicostatus, *Mell.*?	....	C.
Hydrobia Parkinsoni (*n*),*Mor.*,n.s.	....	C.
—— Websteri, *Mor.*, n. sp.....		C.
Melania inquinata, *Def.*	*Cerithium melanoides*, Sow. ..	C.
Melanopsis ancillaroides(*o*), *Dh.*?	....	C.
—— buccinoides, *Fér.* (*p*).....	*M. fusiformis*, Sow.,pars, f. 3-5.	C.
Murex foliaceus, *Mell.*?		C.
Natica glaucinoides,*Sow.* (var.?)..	non *N. glaucinoides*, Desh.; an *N. labellata*, Lam.	C.
Neritina consobrina, *Fér.*		C.
—— globulus, *Def.*	*N. uniplicata*, Sow...........	C.
—— pisiformis, *Fér.*..........	or *N. ornata*, Mell. ?	C.
—— vicina, *Mell.*? (*q*)		C.
Paludina lenta, *S.*,var. β. *Mor.*(*r*)	.................'	C.
Patella		C.
Planorbis hemistoma, *Sow.*		C.
—— lævigatus, *Desh.* ?........		C.

Entomostraca*.

Cythere Wetherellii, *Jones.* Pl. III. fig. 9	C.
—— Kostelensis, *Reuss*, sp. Pl. III. fig. 10	C.
—— plicata, *Münst.* Pl. III. fig. 11	C.
—— angulatopora, *Reuss.* Pl. III. fig. 12	C.
—— (Cytheridea) Mulleri, *Münst.* Pl. III. fig. 7	W. C.
—— —— var. torosa, *Jones.* Pl. III. fig. 8	C.
Candona Richardsoni, *Jones.* Pl. III. fig. 13...............	C.

Foraminifera.

Globulina.....................................	W.
Nodosaria bacillum, *Defr.*	E.

* For the determination of this and the following group, I am entirely indebted to Mr. Rupert Jones.

Truncatulina ....   C.
Textularia ....   C.
Globigerina ....   C.

Pisces.

Edaphodon (not determinable) ....   E.
Lamna (*Odontaspis*) [L. Hopei and dubia, *Agas.*?] (*s*) ......   W. C. E.
Lepidosteus, n. sp. Pl. III. fig. 1........................   C.
Myliobates (not determinable) ....   E.
Small undeterminable teeth, scales, and vertebræ and other
    bones ....   C. E.

Miscellanea.

Lophiodon or Coryphodon, *Owen, Brit. Foss.Mam.* p.306.f.105   C.
Chelonia (fragments of carapace) ....   W. E.
Cancer (part of claw) ....   C.
Spicula of Sponge ....   E.
Serpula, n. sp. Pl. II. fig. 26...........................   C.
Microscopic Bryozoa (Lunulites urceolatus, fragments) ......   C.
Flustra ....   C. E.
Opercula (of Cerithium ?) ....   C.
Eggs of Molluscs ? ....   C.
Wood, coniferous ....   W. C. E.
—— dicotyledonous ....   E.
Impressions of leaves and seed-vessels (Pl. III. figs. 4–6, and
    Pl. IV.) ....   W. C. E.

NOTES.

(*a*) M. Deshayes figures a specimen from the "Sables Inférieurs" of Bracheux which he calls the *C. semigranulosum*, Sow., and gives as
synonymous the *C. Plumsteadiense* of the same author. M. Deshayes'
specimens must, however, be probably referred only to the latter
species of Sowerby; the first-named species of Sowerby is not therefore
identical with the species to which M. Deshayes gives that name.

(*b*) These occur only in casts, which on a previous occasion were referred
to the *C. globosa*, Sow.; but this shell is more equivalved and less
globose than the Barton species, and more resembles the French species, which is found in the "Argile plastique" of Rilly, and has been
described, but not figured, by Nyst.

(*c*) This shell was first referred to *C. revoluta*, Sow., of Barton, but it is
more equivalved and the beak is less incurved. In my paper on the
Thanet Sands it was considered as the *C. longirostris*, Desh.; but this
shell, which M. Deshayes quoted from the "Sables Inférieurs" of
Bracheux, was figured from a bad specimen, and the name has since
been restricted by this able conchologist to the species from the Grès
Moyens of Beauchamp. The former is therefore undescribed, and is
probably the same shell as that here described and named.

(*d*) With the exception of the *C. cuneiformis* and *tellinella*, which are well-
marked species, these *Cyrenæ* form a very perplexing group. The
other three species here given, although in many cases presenting well-
marked and distinct characters, pass commonly into forms so nearly
resembling one another and the *C. cuneiformis*, that I almost hesitate
to adopt the specific distinctions here given. They have, however, been
adopted after a long and careful comparison of a very large series.

(e) The artist had so badly represented the figure of the French species, that it was not until the specimens were compared that the mistake of naming it anew could be discovered.

(f) This shell is here in too imperfect a state to admit of a positive determination.

(g) There are two French species, the *Dreissena antiqua*, Mell., and *Modiola angularis*, Desh., which require comparison with this. They are both found in the "Sables Inférieurs," but I have not met with them; and although the figures and descriptions do not quite agree, I suspect a closer resemblance than is apparent.

(h) The *P. terebratularis* is a very variable shell. M. Deshayes has in his "Coquilles Fossiles" quoted it from Bracheux and from Etampes, but has since restricted it to the former locality, and therefore to the "Lower Tertiaries." This species apparently includes the *P. Plumsteadiensis* and *P. brevirostris* of Sowerby.

(i) This has been referred to the *U. Solandri*, but, as well as the crushed and imperfect state of the specimen will allow us to judge, incorrectly; it rather closely resembles the French species which has lately been figured by M. Watelet from the "Lignites" of the Soissonnais.

(j) This, which is a very rare shell at Woolwich, is referred with a doubt to a French species that it seems identical with, except that it is always very much smaller. This, however, may arise from the more freshwater conditions at this locality.

(k) These species of Sowerby, although now considered only as one, form, as do also his species of the *Ostrea*, well-marked varieties constant in most cases to different beds of the Woolwich and Reading series, and caused apparently by this difference of habitat.

(l) The *Buccinum ambiguum*, Desh., also resembles some varieties of this shell, to which I have also referred the *B. granulosum* with a doubt. Having seen M. Deshayes' specimen of the *Fusus deceptus*, I have little hesitation in identifying it with the Woolwich species.

(m) Sowerby gave originally four species of *Fusus* from Woolwich. Two of these have since been excluded, and upon comparing a large series of these other two species, I cannot feel satisfied that even they are distinct. The *F. gradatus* seems to me to be the young of the *F. latus*.

(n) Several very small univalves are figured by Deshayes and Melleville from the Lower Tertiaries of France. I cannot quite identify any of them with the Woolwich species, although I suspect that some of them, especially the *Melania tritacea*, Desh., and the *Paludina miliola* and *intermedia*, Mell., may prove to be the same. From the figures of Deshayes, the Woolwich species, however, seem to have a closer resemblance to some specimens from the Calcaire Lacustre of St. Ouen and Montmorency.

(o) M. Deshayes has specimens of this shell from the Lignites of the Soissonnais, and it appears to resemble some of the Woolwich specimens. It is difficult however to distinguish the species of this genus, and although at Woolwich there seems at first sight to be two or three species, it is doubtful whether they will not all prove varieties of the next species.

(p) This is a very variable shell, the fusiform variety being the specimens figured by Sowerby as the *M. fusiformis*. This latter must however, I think, be confined to the fluvio-marine series of the Isle of Wight.

(q) This and the preceding species require comparison with the French specimens, as the figures given of them are not sufficiently distinct.

(r) It is doubtful whether this may not be a different species; but in this, as in the other freshwater species, the distinction between the older and the newer forms is remarkably small, a fact which can be readily understood when it is considered how many of the Woolwich species were originally identified with species of the Upper Eocene fluvio-marine beds of the Isle of Wight. The representative forms of these two periods present, in fact, a remarkable and close analogy.

(*s*) Three varieties of the teeth of *Lamna* are found, two of them bearing a close resemblance to these two London clay (Sheppey) species, but they do not seem to me to be quite identical. They may, however, only be varieties.

In addition to the fossils of the foregoing list, the following species have been quoted from Woolwich upon the authority of the early numbers of the ' Mineral Conchology,' but, I believe, in error, which has been partially corrected in a later index.

Cyrena (Cyclas) obovata, var., Min. Con. pl. 162. figs. 4 to 6. Confined to the Middle and Upper Eocenes of Hampshire.

Fusus (Buccinum) labiatus, Min. Con. pl. 412. figs. 1, 2. Confined to the Middle and Upper Eocenes of Hampshire.

Melanopsis fusiformis, Min. Con. pl. 332. figs. 1 to 7. Confined to the Middle and Upper Eocenes of Hampshire.

Neritina concava, Min. Con. pl. 385. figs. 1 to 8. Confined to the Middle and Upper Eocenes of Hampshire.

Potamomya (Mya) plana, Min. Con. pl. 76. fig. 2. Confined to the Middle and Upper Eocenes of Hampshire. '

Fusus costatus β. (Murex rugosus, Park.), Min. Con. pl. 199. fig. 2. Con-fined to the Crag.

The Rev. H. M. De la Condamine has also given, in his paper before referred to, eight species of *shells* and one of *Lamna* from Woolwich and Blackheath not in the above list, and which, I think, he will now agree with me have been introduced by some error in the specific determinations which it is desirable to correct, in order to prevent, as is the case with the above, any confusion, or difficulty to subsequent observers.

The *Corbula revoluta*, Sow., has been quoted from Herne Bay. It should be confined to Barton and Hampshire.

§ 4. *Lithological Structure.*

It happens with this, as with the preceding chapter, that the descriptions of the several local sections embrace the mention of almost all the varieties of mineral character presented by this group, and render it therefore unnecessary to give more than a general summary, and to allude to a few special points of inquiry : of these may in particular be instanced the origin of the Druid sandstones of Marlborough Downs and Salisbury Plains, and of the Hertfordshire Pudding-stones.

Viewed as a whole, the Woolwich and Reading series consist, 1st, of mottled clays, tenacious, free from carbonate of lime, and with a prevailing red base; 2nd, of sharp light-coloured quartzose sand, more or less mixed with green sand and with flint-pebbles. These two component parts usually form distinct and separate beds, extremely irregular in their range and development; the clays prevailing almost to the exclusion of the sands in the Isle of Wight and in part of the Hampshire district, and the sands increasing as the group trends through Wiltshire, Berkshire, and Surrey, but thick-bedded mottled clays still preponderating, until, on the confines of Surrey and Kent, Middlesex, and Essex, the latter are rather abruptly displaced by the sands, which finally in East Kent prevail exclusively.   The two principal subordinate features are, 1st, the occurrence of rolled flint-pebbles, black, and worn perfectly smooth and rounded*, usually of a small size, $\frac{1}{2}$ to 2 inches in longest diameter, but occasionally attaining a length of 10 to 15 inches.   These pebbles are generally dispersed in layers or imbedded in the sand, but they are in few cases associated with the clay beds.   It is within the area wherein the change from mottled clays to sands takes place that the pebbles are developed in their greatest profusion, forming at those places thick and extensive beds of shingle.   To the eastward beyond this area the sands are still characterized by dispersed pebbles, whilst to the westward of it the pebbles are restricted to a thin bed, either just overlying the green-coated flints which repose on the chalk, or else intermingling with these flints.   2nd, Green sand, which is usually either disseminated in dispersed grains, or else occurs in small patches or seams, and is chiefly confined to the lower portions of this division, and at the base of which it forms, mixed with clay and per-oxide of iron, a thin and nearly constant layer.   In Kent this green sand exists in larger proportion, often constituting irregular beds of light green sands, which are never, however, persistent over any wide range, and are always subordinate to the light quartzose sands. These grains of green sand vary in size from a pin's point to a pin's head, the larger ones being botryoidal-shaped, of a malachite-green colour, and rather soft.   These green grains have usually been indiscriminately referred to Chlorite and Green Earth, but the physical characters of these grains differ so widely,—some being light green, soft, opake, and earthy, whilst others are very hard, of a dark green or nearly black colour, translucid, and show facets,—that I would suggest whether or not, in addition to the former of these minerals, there may not be, mixed with the common quartzose sand, debris of Hornblende and Pyroxenes† in this state of small grains.

As minerals of more local occurrence may be noticed, 1st, The peroxide of iron, occasionally giving an ochreous and ferruginous colour to the strata, and sometimes cementing the sands into thin tabular iron-sandstones.   2nd, The hydrated peroxide of iron, or limonite, in concretions, and occasionally forming ochres.   3rd, Iron pyrites, which is of comparatively rare occurrence except in the mixed green sands of Herne Bay.   4th, Carbonate of lime, which in this group must be considered as quite a subordinate mineral, being almost altogether restricted to the central area beneath and around London, occasionally acting as a cement to some of the sandstone conglomerates, and sometimes forming an extremely hard fine-grained concretionary rock.   5th, Carbonaceous clays, and thin bands or rather

---

* Some of these pebbles are shivered and broken *in situ* (usually by pressure). Others again have been broken before being rolled into their present position, presenting a fractured surface with the sharp edges worn off.

† I have not had time to proceed further in this inquiry, which is one of considerable interest in a theoretical point of view.

patches of lignite, are occasionally met with in the lower part of the mottled clays; but they occur more commonly in association with the fluviatile beds of Woolwich : they do not possess any importance, although occasionally expanding in some places to the thickness of a few feet, but are more often measureable by inches. The local sections and details (§ 3.) give some of the main points of its occurrence *.

It is at the base of this division that I should place the *Websterite* and *Hydrate of Alumina* found by Dr. Mantell at Castle Hill, Newhaven. I have since found the latter with the pebbles and flints in immediate contact with the chalk, at Northaw.

Small crystals of sulphate of lime occur occasionally in the clays and sands of the fluviatile group. A thin seam of clay found by Mr. De la Condamine at Counter Hill, showed on the faces of lamination a surface covered with very small sharp cavities, formed apparently by crystals of selenite having been dissolved out. I have not met with selenite in the mottled clays.

A singular fact was noticed a few years since in the 'Annales des Mines,' in connection with the mottled clays of the "Argile Plastique" of the Paris basin, viz. that they contained a very considerable proportion of gelatinous or soluble silica, *i. e.* silica in an active chemical state, and soluble in alkaline solutions without fusion†. I have recently tested the mottled clays from various places in the London district, and find that they also contain this gelatinous silica, which can be readily separated out by boiling in a solution of caustic potash. The proportion, however, is very variable. This peculiar condition of the silica has an important theoretical bearing.

§ 5. *Druid Sandstones.*

The position in the Tertiary series which should be assigned to the large blocks of white saccharoid sandstone found scattered over the surface of many parts of the chalk districts, and met with occasionally within the tertiary area itself, has long been and still remains an unsettled question. As these isolated blocks are always siliceous, not unfrequently exhibit traces of rootlet-like impressions, and occasionally contain round flint-pebbles and subangular slightly worn flints, they present, with the latter exception, a lithological structure very similar to that of the blocks found irregularly dispersed sometimes in the lower, but more especially in the upper division of the Bagshot Sands between Esher and Strathfieldsaye; and, as no other tertiary formation presents on first appearance so good a *primâ facie* right of possession, they were, in the absence of all distinct or-

---

* It is too impure for use. At Lewisham a heap of pyritous lignite which had been thrown on one side, caught fire, and burnt for several months. It was the occasional occurrence of lignite in these beds, here and at Blackheath, that gave rise to the popular belief of coal beds existing at the latter place.

† This was in 1846. The first notice of this peculiar condition of silica is, I believe, that by M. Sauvage in 1840 (Ann. des Mines), when he detected the presence of it in some of the beds of the lias and in some beds between the Chalk and the Gault.

ganisms to assist in the determination, generally referred to the age of those sands *. The weight of evidence is however, I think, against the origin usually assigned to them, although that evidence is circumstantial rather than direct.

In the first place, if they were derived from the Bagshot Sands, it is difficult to conceive why they should not be scattered as commonly over the generally broad belt of London clay intervening between the area of the Bagshot Sands and the Chalk, as they are over the area of the latter;—that connecting links should not have been left between the parent beds and the groups of greyweathers scattered over Marlborough Downs and the Chiltern Hills. But no such general phænomenon is exhibited within the London-clay area. It is further to be observed, that the Bagshot Sands (the lower division) themselves, although well developed between Strathfieldsaye and Newbury, do not in that district contain any large blocks of sandstone †. In Kent, over no part of which county do the Bagshot Sands extend, the Druid sandstone is abundant on many parts of the chalk hills. No fringe, in fact, of detached sandstone blocks skirts the Bagshot Sands, whereas wherever such scattered groups do occur they invariably subtend either the main body or detached outliers of the Lower Tertiaries.

On some of the high hills towards the borders of the extensive chalk downs forming Salisbury Plains, especially to the northward and eastward of Amesbury, or between that town, Bedwin, and Kingsclere, cappings of the lower tertiary sands and clays are not uncommon; whilst other hills, where no mass of tertiaries remain, show by the presence of numerous tertiary flint-pebbles on their summit the wreck of tertiary strata once spread over this area. The drift of the district also often abounds with these characteristic pebbles. At Marlborough the tertiary strata range up close to where the dispersed blocks of sandstone commence. A ridge of hills formed of these lower tertiaries on a base of chalk dominates over the platform of the latter formation for some miles in a direction W.N.W. from Newbury. As it trends westward the bed of sand immediately over the chalk expands, becomes extremely white and pure, and in one place, just below Wickham Church, contains at its base a few seams of pebbles and worn subangular flints. It is precisely the unconsolidated substance of the Druid sandstone; still I could not find, nor had the foreman who had worked twenty-one years in some adjoining pits ever found, a block of sandstone *in situ* in the sands. But then it must be considered how small an extent of this bed is opened out,—only two or three regularly worked pits in the distance of six miles,—and the extremely small proportion

---

* Not, however, universally so: by some geologists the origin of these blocks has been correctly referred to the "Plastic Clay Formation," but no proofs have yet been offered in support of the suggestion.

† So rare is it, in fact, to find any blocks of stone in that part of the country, that a small mass of about a foot square, lying on the gravel of Silchester Common, has been considered of sufficient importance to have a local name assigned to it—"The Nymph Stone."

this bears to the mass, in which these concretions are of a merely local and rare occurrence. Nevertheless on the slopes of this ridge, especially along its south-western flank, the number of blocks of Druid sandstone scattered over the surface of the ground just below the outcrop of the sands is very considerable; as they become more numerous they also become larger. These hills, if prolonged, would pass by Lambourne six miles further to the N.W., and it is on the downs about that village that the Druid sandstones are particularly numerous and large. That the tertiary strata ranged in that direction is proved by a few traces of them yet remaining *.

Again, in Buckinghamshire, Oxfordshire, and Hertfordshire, grey-weather sandstones and pudding-stones occur in districts throughout which are scattered numerous outliers of the Lower Tertiaries, once continuous over the whole area, and in the wreck of which, at their denudation, these blocks seem, as in Wiltshire, to have been left behind. So also with the large accumulations of sandstone blocks on the north downs above Maidstone.

If therefore we admit the distribution of the Druid sandstones to be in accordance with the range of the Lower London Tertiaries rather than with that of the Bagshot Sands, the next question is to ascertain what evidence there is of the occurrence *in situ* of similar masses of stone in the different groups of the former series.

1. With regard to the Thanet Sands :—Although often presenting favourable elements, and occasionally semi-indurated, they are rarely consolidated. At the Reculvers, however, they contain a bed of concretionary sandstone; but it has a calcareous cement, contains no pebbles, and exhibits frequently the impressions of shells ; whereas the erratic sandstones of Kent, Bucks, and Wiltshire are neither calcareous nor fossiliferous, and are not uncommonly sub-conglomerate. Further, the Thanet Sands do not range more than six to ten miles westward of London. It is therefore not probable that the Druid sandstones belong to beds of this age.

2. The Basement-bed of the London Clay presents a very small development westward of London, and although concretionary blocks are often found in it, they are all comparatively of so small a size, besides being generally calcareo-argillaceous, and almost invariably fossiliferous, that it is not in this direction we must look for the origin of these sandstones. But to the eastward of London this bed becomes more important, and at Boughton it contains a subordinate bed of a siliceous sandstone, often extremely hard, very local and very variable, and of a character which would harmonise perfectly well with some of the blocks on the slopes of the East Kent Chalk ranges.

3. My belief, however, is that the greater portion of the blocks known as Druid Sandstones, Greyweathers, Sarsen Stones, and Pudding-stones are derived from the middle division of the Lower London Tertiaries. It is very rarely that solidified portions of the strata are found *in situ*, but the same difficulty occurs in as great

* As, for instance, at Liquid Farm, five miles W.N.W. from Wickham.

a degree with the sandstones of the Bagshot Sands. As usual with concretionary masses, they occur in patches in particular districts, and are far from being a general accompaniment of the sands. In Hampshire I know only of one group of them which has the appearance of being *in situ*,—the one before referred to (p. 81) as occurring near Dorchester*. Still the case there is not clear. In the western part of the London tertiary district the middle division of the Lower Tertiaries always contains more or less extensive beds of quartzose sand, with patches or layers of pebbles in the lower part more especially of the group, while patches of subangular flints are also occasionally met with; consequently we have the elements necessary to produce the required results whenever circumstances, as might so easily happen, occurred to consolidate the materials. Although instances of this fact are not numerous, still they are in sufficient number to prove the probability of the supposition.

On the eastern slope of Bagshot Hill, near Hungerford, there is a spot from which blocks of sandstone and of sandstone conglomerate have been removed†. This pit, which is now abandoned, is so shallow as not to show the superposition of the beds: they appear, however, immediately to overlie the chalk. The case is clearer at Nettlebed Hill ; I have there seen, a few feet above the chalk, blocks of sandstone, some of large size, *in situ* in the sands interstratified with the mottled clay (see fig. 4. p. 89).

At Tiler's Hill near Chesham the white quartzose sand underlying the Basement-bed of the London clay contains a thin subordinate band of a soft saccharoid sandstone. Near Batler's Green, two and a half miles northward from Elstree, Herts, there existed a few years since a shallow pit, in which beneath the gravel there was exposed a surface of thick tabular pudding-stone overlying the chalk and apparently *in situ*. A bed perfectly identical in composition, *i. e.* consisting of a fine pure white quartzose sand full of black flint pebbles, but not consolidated, was opened a few years ago in a pit one and a half mile from Ware, on the London road : it was 3 feet thick, reposed directly on the chalk, and underlay some sandy mottled clays. Blocks of sandstone and of sandstone conglomerate are also found in the sands subordinate to the mottled clays beneath the London clay at Pinner (see p. 91). These cases are few and local, but so also is the distribution of the greyweathers themselves, and it is to be observed that the occurrence of the latter is exactly coincident with the development and preponderance of the sand beds of the mottled clay series. Thus around Reading, where mottled clays preponderate, there are few sandstone blocks on the surrounding chalk hills ; but in proceeding towards Newbury the clays give way to sands, which, three miles north of that town, constitute the main

* In Hampshire the Bracklesham series contains several solid seams, both in the Isle of Wight and the Isle of Purbeck, yet but few blocks are found scattered on the surface. The chief one is that known as the Agglestone, near Studland.

† I am indebted for a knowledge of this locality, and for much other information respecting Salisbury Plains and the Wiltshire Downs, to Mr. W. Cunnington of Devizes.

feature of this series. At Newbury the proportion of sands decreases, but these beds again become more important in proceeding from Newbury towards Marlborough. Now it is precisely in these directions that the blocks of greyweather sandstone set in and attain their greatest development*. On the hills above Goring sandstone blocks are not uncommon ; and I have here recently found the mottled clays, associated with a thick bed of white quartzose sand, ranging close to the edge of the chalk escarpment from Woodcot Common to near Combe End Farm. Crossing the gorge of the Thames the same beds are found capping the hills at Bassildon, and a trace of them apparently exists near Aldworth. In fact, throughout the chalk district of Wilts, Berks, Oxfordshire, Bucks, Herts, and Kent, the tertiary outliers are far more common than has been supposed. They distinctly show the former spread of the Lower Tertiaries, the Woolwich and Reading series especially, over the whole area, up even to the very edge of the chalk escarpment.

In the direction of High Wycombe and Nettlebed the sand beds are again in excess. On the chalk hills above Bradenham, three miles northward of the former town, sandstone blocks are very numerous, and, although enveloped in a ferruginous clay-drift, they are, I believe, nevertheless nearly *in situ*†. Around Hedgerley and Uxbridge, where mottled clays prevail, few sandstone blocks occur. In the neighbourhood of Hatfield, Hertford, and Ware, the sands of the Reading series, perfectly white and siliceous, are often, if I may use the expression, glutted with flint-pebbles ; it is over this area more particularly that the Hertfordshire pudding-stones are so abundant.

Beneath and also to the south and south-east of London, a very hard, light-coloured, fine-grained, calcareo-argillaceous rock, usually without fossils, is often present in the lower part of the Woolwich beds just under the shelly clays. This bed, however, rarely exceeds the limits of the fluviatile and estuarine clays, and forms therefore a mere local feature. At Gravesend we find in nearly the same position a thin tabular layer of hard siliceous sandstone. These agree with the numerous thin hard tabular pieces of sandstone found scattered over the surface of the ground around Apchurch near Sittingbourne. On the hill above Stifford Bridge, Essex, where the lower tertiaries were cut through, there are a few blocks of pudding-stone. In the neighbourhood of the conspicuous tertiary outlier at Cobham near Gravesend, large mammillated blocks of siliceous sandstone are common on the chalk hills. Blocks of a larger size, but more even-surfaced, abound on the downs above Maidstone ; they are also

---

* The remarkable and thick trail of sandstone blocks in the valley of rocks near Marlborough is well known. Many other valleys in that district, as those to the south of East and West Kennet, Dean, Clatford, and others, exhibit the same phænomena, although not on so large a scale. The hills on the sides and at the heads of these narrow vales are also strewed over with numerous detached blocks.

† At Walter's Ash and Napple Common ; they are equally abundant on Denner Hill, three miles west from Great Missenden.

numerous in many places between this spot and the downs above Folkestone, as near Charing. On the chalk hills sloping from this line of escarpment down to the Thames, such masses are likewise common.

It is possible that in Kent the upper and lower divisions of the Lower Tertiaries may have partially contributed to the supply of these dispersed sandstone blocks; but on the hills of Hertfordshire, Oxfordshire, and Wiltshire, and the extensive elevated chalk-platforms forming Salisbury Downs, where these masses are occasionally so numerous, I believe that they are all derived from the middle division of the Lower Tertiaries, outliers of which still remain to prove the former extension of these strata over those areas, for they have, with these few exceptions, been wholly removed by subsequent denudation*.

The absence of all organic remains, so peculiar a feature of the sands of the Woolwich and Reading group westward of London, strengthens the supposition of these equally unfossiliferous sandstones being derived from this source†.

With the large softer masses of saccharoid sandstone of Salisbury Plains and Marlborough Downs, there are however found a number of small blocks and pieces of a very fine-grained, hard, compact, siliceous sandstone generally of peculiar botryoidal forms, not conglomerate, and often with traces of long rootlet-like processes‡; but I have not seen such rock-specimens in the Lower Tertiaries§, nor have I been more successful in finding them in situ in the Bagshot series. Their age must be considered uncertain; at the same time the occurrence of specimens with these rootlet-like processes weighs certainly in favour of their origin from the Bagshot Sands, as we know that similar impressions exist, although very rarely, in the blocks of sandstone found in the Upper Bagshot Sands. But in the sands or the laminated clays associated with them such impressions are not met with, although, as in the Lower Tertiaries, impressions of plants and leaves have been found. These rootlet-like casts and impressions are, however, organisms too indistinct to be of any definite value as a proof of age.

As before observed, much weight must not be attached to the rarity

---

* It may be objected that no blocks of sandstone are now found scattered over the surface of Salisbury Plains. They are certainly scarce, but I have found a few in the valleys, although generally there hidden by the drift. Their very scarcity has, however, probably hastened the destruction of the few that have existed, and have been used for various economical purposes.

† At least the only exception is the occasional bed of the *Ostrea Bellovacina* and shark's teeth at the base of this series, but the concretionary masses and the white sands occur more in the body of the strata. Still, traces of these fossils may possibly be found in some of the blocks around Newbury, or in some of the Hertfordshire pudding-stones; but hitherto no such impressions have, I believe, been met with.

‡ They are common also in the flint-gravel of the valleys of the district.

§ That is to say, in the district westward of London. The fine-grained hard concretionary stone, before mentioned (p. 103) as occurring in the Woolwich series beneath or near London (Charlton), sometimes presents however a very similar appearance and fracture.

of concretionary sandstones in the sections and cuttings of the Lower Tertiaries. In the Bagshot Sands themselves they are confined to a comparatively small range of country, and even in that district I have never seen them in sand-pits or road-side cuttings. They are sought out specially at a few spots on the hills by dipping iron rods into the sands. Again, although at and near London the Lower Tertiaries so often contain subordinate concretionary or conglomerate rocks, how rarely do such masses show at their outcrop : at Sundridge only are some of these latter beds worked.

The flint-gravel which caps the hills around Newbury contains a few rather large specimens of the harder sandstones, but the gravel of that system of valleys which wind down from the chalk hills on the north-west of Newbury abounds with such blocks, together with a good many large blocks of the more saccharoid and softer stones. The course of this drift is towards, and not from, the area of the Bagshot Sands ; and as we have no proof of the extension of this formation over the Chalk Downs, whereas we know that detached outliers of the Lower Tertiary sands extend far over those hills, we should expect to find, in the drift, the debris derived from the latter and from the chalk, and not from the Bagshot Sands. Whence also, as well as from their association, I am inclined to consider that both descriptions of sandstones are derived from the Lower Tertiary sands.

Further, admitting the fact of an occasional and local consolidation of the sand beds of the Lower Tertiaries, we have an *à-priori* argument in favour of the whole group of the Druid Sandstones of Wilts, Hants, Bucks, and Kent, and of the Pudding-stones of Herts, being derived from this source, from the circumstance that the lithological structure of each variety is respectively in accordance with the mineral components forming the strata in the immediate vicinity of the places where these rock-blocks are found ; *i. e.* that the concretionary stone in each case represents the component parts of some portion of the adjacent " Woolwich and Reading series," with the difference that they are consolidated.

This conclusion is corroborated by the very definite and distinct proofs furnished by the cliffs of St. Marguerite near Dieppe. We there find the Woolwich fluviatile clays with the *Cyrena cuneiformis, Melania inquinata,* and *Cerithium variabile* underlaid by a bed of whitish quartzose sand reposing upon a very uneven surface of the chalk. The section is between one and two miles in length, although it is only near the lighthouse (le phare d'Ailly) that the fluviatile beds exist. These sands contain in several parts of the section subordinate blocks of a white saccharoid concretionary siliceous sandstone, which is worked to some extent, and affords masses frequently measuring many feet in length. These sandstones also often contain, like the Druid sandstones of Wilts, rolled flint-pebbles and subangular flints. As these beds are evidently a prolongation of the Woolwich beds on the Sussex-district type, the phænomena thus exhibited in the neighbourhood of Dieppe may fairly be admitted in collateral proof of the argument with respect to the origin in this

country also of the Druid Sandstones from beds of the age of the
"Woolwich and Reading series*."

§ 6. *Conclusion.*

The sectional diagrams, A, B, C, Pl. I., which, owing to the want of
some connecting links, were not completed until after the preceding
pages were written, confirm, in my mind, by the structural fitness of
their parts, the conviction, before expressed, and derived from lithological and palæontological evidence, of the independence† of the
"Middle division of the Lower London Tertiaries," with regard to
the "Thanet Sands,"—the latter forming a distinct and underlying
marine deposit; and that, notwithstanding the nearly total difference
of all its characters, the estuarine and freshwater group of fossiliferous
strata at Upnor and Woolwich must be regarded as strictly synchronous with the unfossiliferous mottled clays of Alum Bay, Reading,
and Hedgerley. Cases are common where such changes of condition,
as those displayed in this "Woolwich and Reading division," take
place in particular beds of a series; in this instance, however, the
alteration affects the whole depth of the group, not as a recurring
change at different periods, but as a maintained development at
different places. It shows an accumulation of materials not within
the range of a single river action, howsoever variable, but of contemporaneous strata deriving, in the same sea, supplies from different
and independent sources. Still, notwithstanding the variable character of the mass as a whole, there are two subordinate features, the
one mineral and the other palæontological, sufficiently well maintained,
although not constant, over both the Reading and the Woolwich
areas to afford a common base-line. It has been shown that the

* I find that M. Passy, in his ' Descrip. Géol. du Dép. de la Seine Inférieure '
(Rouen, 1832), takes the same view of the relation of the "Grey-weathers" of
Wiltshire and of the "Grès à silex pyromaques" of the Dieppe Cliffs, drawing
his conclusions, however, with respect to the former, simply from their lithological
resemblance to the latter (pages 127–131).

† At all events so far as the central and eastern areas are concerned. The only
point about which I feel slightly doubtful, is whether some of the thick pebble
beds under and around Shooter's Hill may not belong to the upper part of the
Woolwich series, rather than to the Basement of the London Clay, inasmuch as the
character of the former is so variable as often to render it lithologically undistinguishable from the latter, except when seen in actual superposition, and for this
extremely few opportunities occur. For the same reason the beds which at Upnor
and Herne Bay I have included in the "Basement-bed" may also possibly belong
to the upper section of the Woolwich series, in which case the Basement-bed
itself might be considered in this area to merge into the thin seam of sandy clay
(with fossils at Upnor and with a few pebbles at Herne) just at the base of the
great mass of the London Clay. It is also difficult to say positively whether some
lower portion of the Reading series may not possibly be synchronous with the
Thanet Sands. In the absence of sections which alone could clearly settle this
point, I have given the best conclusion I could arrive at upon collateral evidence.
I mention these doubts, which, however, do not affect the superposition and
grouping of the three divisions here proposed, although it would modify the exact
lines of separation, in order to direct attention to any new facts which may arise
to throw light upon those questions where I consider the evidence not quite
conclusive.

20 feet of pebbly light greenish sands overlying the Thanet Sands in West Kent, consist of a clear sharp quartzose sand mixed more or less with grains of green sand, flint pebbles, and argillaceous matter. Now, although the latter are almost always present, still the proportion of them becomes in places so small that their presence is not readily apparent, and a bed of sand, more or less pure and white, remains. The great development of pebbles in this bed takes place in the neighbourhood of London. As the beds range eastward they pass into sands, often apparently forming with the "Thanet Sands" one nearly undistinguishable mass; and in the same way as they range westward they occasionally put on, from this loss of the pebbles and green grains, almost exactly the characters presented by the Thanet Sands at Woolwich and Lewisham, and for which they have hitherto been mistaken. Still, on the whole, the presence at the base of the Woolwich and Reading series of slightly argillaceous sands, more or less mixed with green sand and flint pebbles, is a most permanent lithological character of this division. We have, further, some evidence, scanty though it is, of organic remains, the *Ostrea Bellovacina* and teeth of *Lamna* occurring at intervals at the base of the mottled-clay series of Reading, from Hungerford and Newbury to Headley, Hanwell, Northaw, and Hertford, and again beneath London (sections in Appendix), where the mottled clays of Reading become intercalated with the fossiliferous beds of Woolwich; and further eastward in the same position at the base of this series at Erith, where the Woolwich type alone obtains. This organic link does not extend further eastward, unless the *Ostrea* at Oakwell should, when better specimens are obtained, prove to belong to that species; but the teeth of *Lamna* are, however, met with. Under ordinary circumstances but little weight could be attached to the evidence of two such fossils, or of such common mineral characters; still, when we take into consideration the chances of their association, their conjoint evidence becomes of much greater value, although after all the aid of superposition is necessary. On these data taken together, the pebbly sands, with their zone of *O. Bellovacina*, may be considered as a sufficiently definite and well-marked horizon between the Woolwich and Reading series and the Thanet Sands. In the neighbourhood of London this lowest bed of the Woolwich series further shows, by the occasional presence of the *Cyrena cuneiformis, Melania inquinata*, and *Cerithium variabile*, a fauna distinct from that of the Thanet Sands; but in East Kent, where the change of condition between the two periods is not so marked, part of the marine fauna of the latter is continued upwards into the former deposit, many species of which may be particularly specified, the *Cucullæa crassatina, Sanguinolaria Edwardsii, Corbula Regulbiensis, Cyprina Morrisii, Thracia oblata, Cytherea Bellovacina, Ampullaria subdepressa*, and *Glycimeris Rutupiensis*, passing from the Thanet Sands into the Woolwich series. Other species, however, as the *Panopæa granulata, Pecten Prestvichii, Pholadomya cuneata* and *Koninckii, Scalaria Bowerbankii, Trophon subnodosum*, and *Leda substriata*, do not extend higher than the "Thanet Sands," whilst

K 2

several new species, including the fine large *Cyprina scutellaria*, the *Pectunculus terebratularis* and *Cardium Plumsteadiense*, and some peculiar fossil woods, make their first appearance in the Woolwich group. The *Corbula Regulbiensis*, which is comparatively rare in the Thanet Sands, becomes also most abundant in places.

This fauna is, in East Kent, confined to the lowest bed of the Woolwich series. The upper beds are unfossiliferous, with the exception of the rare occurrence of the small fragments of the *Myliobates, Edaphodon,* and *Chelonia.* As we approach London, however, the middle and upper members of this deposit become well marked by their organic remains. Of the marine fauna of Herne Bay, the *Corbula Regulbiensis, Nucula fragilis, Cardium Plumsteadiense,* and *Pectunculus terebratularis* (var. *Plumsteadiensis*), occur at Woolwich and Bromley,' whilst in addition to this group we have the remarkable local development of those estuarine and more freshwater forms,—the *Cyrena, Paludina, Melania, Melanopsis, Planorbis, Unio,* and *Neritina.* These latter forms prevail more especially in the centre of this division, in that portion of it so well exhibited at Woolwich, extending beneath London on one side, and stretching to Upnor on the other. Above these Woolwich clays in the same central area are beds with a more estuarine fauna at first, but showing as they pass upwards conditions still more freshwater than those which prevail in the beds beneath. To this upper part of the series belong the Paludina-limestone and the Unio bed at New Cross. As this series trends towards London all the members of it disappear and are replaced by mottled clays and sands, the Woolwich clays being alone prolonged, and forming beneath London a single fossiliferous zone distinctly intercalated between two masses of the mottled clays (see Well-sections, Appendix). This is shown in the sectional Diagrams A & C, Pl. I. ; but to the south of the line here intersected we find another zone of the *Cyrena, Melania,* and *Ostrea,* intercalated on a higher level with these mottled clays, and of which examples are found in the sections at Balham Hill, Wandsworth, and Mitcham (Appendix). It is only by connecting these beds by underground sections that the probable position of the well-known Sundridge, Bromley, and Chiselhurst beds may be inferred; for, owing to the want of surface-sections, no direct connection can be established between the beds of the Woolwich and Sundridge pits ; but if we pass round by London, Clapham, Wandsworth, Mitcham, and Croydon, we find this upper zone, at first only slightly developed, assuming as it trends southward and then south-eastward an increased importance, and eventually expanding and replacing the upper group of sands and mottled clays, whilst on the contrary the underlying lenticular mass of Woolwich clays thins out and is replaced by mottled clays, so that this division then presents a large development of mottled clays below, with shelly estuarine clays, limestones, and conglomerates above. I believe that the insulated shell-bed at Guildford belongs to this upper series. Here, as before mentioned, the traces of animal life are confined merely to a thin superposed layer. Beyond both to the westward and northward, the great bulk of the sands and mottled clays, which now prevail exclusively, are perfectly barren ; and the contrast which they afford with the common occurrence of organic remains in the field we have just quitted is very striking,— the more so from the circumstance of the unfossiliferous masses preponderating so largely, and the fossiliferous beds being confined to so comparatively small an area of the Woolwich and Reading series.

It is this Woolwich and Reading series which, of all the Lower Tertiaries, presents the greatest resemblance in France and England. The mottled clays of Paris and Montereau are not to be distinguished from those of Reading and Newbury, whilst the *Melania inquinata, Neritina globulus, Melanopsis buccinoides, Ostrea Bellovacina, Cerithium variabile,* and *Cyrena cuneiformis,* constitute at Epernay, Soissons, and Dieppe, as at Woolwich and Upnor, the common and characteristic species of the fluviatile and estuarine areas of this period.

The total number of Molluscs found in the "Woolwich and Reading series" amounts to 53, of which 25 are peculiar to it, whilst of the remaining 28 species 12 are found in the "Thanet Sands," 22 range up into the "Basement-bed of the London Clay," and 6 are common to the three divisions.   Again, taking these three divisions of the "Lower London Tertiaries" together, the species of fossil shells now enumerated from them amounts to as many as 82, of which 29 are found in the "Basement-bed of the London Clay," 23 in the "Thanet Sands," and 53, as mentioned above, in the Woolwich and Reading series*. Further, of these 82 species 27 range up into the London Clay, and 6 have a further extension upwards into the middle Eocenes, whilst 55 species are peculiar to these Lower London Tertiaries. A fauna of this class and of this extent (and which I believe is yet far from being fully worked out†), in addition to which there is to be noted a not inconsiderable list of *Entomostraca, Foraminifera,* and *Plants,* entitles, I consider, these Lower London Tertiaries to a more important and independent position than has hitherto been assigned to them.

---

* A further examination of some of the species enumerated in my lists of fossils of the Basement-bed of the London Clay and of the Thanet Sands, has shown the necessity of an alteration in the determination of some of the species which were then identified with known species of some of the more important overlying Eocene deposits; amongst these there will be found in the first-named list (Journ. Geol. Soc. vol. vi. p. 281, Table A.) the species given in the first column; the second column gives the corrections.

Corbula revoluta, *Sow.* —— longirostris, *Desh.*	*C. Regulbiensis* (see note *c*, p. 119).
Cyrena obovata, var. *Sow.*	*C. cordata* (note *d*, p. 119).

And in the second list (Journ. Geol. Soc. vol. viii. p. 248),—

Dentalium nitens, *Sow.*	*This identification is doubtful.*
Corbula, as above.	
Cytherea orbicularis, *Mor.*	*C. Bellovacina,* Desh.

† In addition to the above there are about 20 to 25 specimens of apparently new species, but not in a state sufficiently perfect to determine.

In my last paper on the Thanet Sands I showed the probability of the Wealden elevation having commenced at that early Tertiary period; and of a small island, without any important river, having existed somewhere in the central position of the present Weald. It was further shown that the Thanet Sands present in part of their range a worn and eroded upper surface, on which the Woolwich series reposes. Now as that surface was one of sand, the edge of which would have been softened even by a small and prolonged ordinary quiet action of the sea currents, which would also have produced an intermixture of the two beds, I conceive that where there is erosion and clear demarcation the change has been sudden and abrupt; but where on the contrary there is a passage in the beds, as for example at Herne Bay, we must suppose a point more distant from the centre of disturbance, and where the change both in lithological structure and in the fauna only became apparent subsequently, as the new order of things gradually prevailed over the preceding one. Where, therefore, we have phænomena of this description, and a distinct alteration, taken as a whole, in the lithological structure of the beds above and below such divisional lines, I cannot but think that, however slight those alterations may be, they indicate a change in the hydrographical condition of the then existing land and sea caused by movements sudden and powerful in proportion to the effects exhibited on the pre-existing sea-bed by the scouring power of the sea during the translation of its mass; whilst the permanent alterations in mineral composition show that such effects were not transitory or momentary, inasmuch as they led to maintained changes in the nature of the materials carried down from the land or worn from the cliffs, indicating in fact a different arrangement of the rivers and the coast lines. In this case the change is proved also by the alteration in the character of the organic remains, which in the lower sands (Thanet Sands) are marine, whilst the Woolwich series contains a superimposed group of estuarine and fluviatile shells.

That the pebbles were rolled from time to time into the position in which they are now found, and that they were not worn there, may be inferred from the fact of their association with delicate and friable shells which have remained uninjured amongst them; from Molluscs having bored undisturbed into the bed of mixed sand and pebbles; from *Ostreæ* and *Serpulæ* having so often attached themselves to, and grown upon, some of the pebbles; and from the circumstance that broken pebbles occasionally occur, the fractured surfaces of which only show worn edges, with no approach to a restoration of the pebble form *.

* The sand of the Woolwich Series I have heard attributed to the wear and destruction of the chalk-flints which produced the pebbles. That a certain quantity of sand resulted from such an action is inevitable, but that the whole mass was derived from that source cannot be. The grains of the sand consist usually of pure transparent quartz, worn but not rounded. The presence further of grains of Chlorite and other allied minerals shows that there were other sources of supply

The prevailing set of the currents or tide is shown by the prevailing dip of the layers of false stratification being northward, or from off the presumed island, at angles varying from 10° to 35°.

The irregularity of this river-accumulation is shown in the extreme irregularity of the beds, which constantly exhibit the shiftings and changes seen in the sand-banks of existing estuaries. Not only are the several members of the "Lower London Tertiaries" divided by irregular surfaces, but the Woolwich series itself often presents in its central area instances of its several beds being deposited upon slightly eroded surfaces one of another.

Further, the occurrence of *Lithodomus* in the eastern area, and of *Pholas* in the central area, shows the near proximity of a coast-line. The beautifully preserved plants of Reading also indicate neighbouring dry land.

Judging from all these phænomena I infer that the period of the Thanet Sands was brought to a close by a movement of elevation, which threw off the sea from the shores of the island we have alluded to, and swept down into the changed and shallower sea-bed the coarser sand and rounded shingle existing ready-formed on the coast-line. To such a movement I attribute the pebbly light green sands forming the base of the Woolwich and Reading series; the ordinary currents of the sea having, after the first movement of elevation, distributed the debris thus amassed and formed the beds on which the *Ostrea Bellovacina* lived. In the mean time the size of the island was necessarily increased by this movement of elevation, and its drainage having thereby become larger, and its streams and rivers more important, one of these rivers, still not a large one, must, during a slightly subsequent period of quiet, have brought down and accumulated the Woolwich shelly clays with their estuarine and fluviatile shells. This settled state of things was, however, not long-continued; renewed, but slow movements, probably of subsidence, must have taken place; the Woolwich river action must have ceased, or rather its direction changed; for that its debouchure was slightly altered, is indicated by the fact that the next fluviatile zone was not accumulated over the older beds, but on one side of them; instead of being chiefly at Upnor, Woolwich, and London, it took place from Bromley to Deptford, Wandsworth, and Guildford.

In the mean time in the more open sea of East Kent these slight changes were less felt, and the marine condition of the strata and their character as they existed at the "Thanet Sands" period remained for a time comparatively unaltered. To the westward, on the contrary, some new and large river-action appears to have been opened out from another land by the changes which led to the formation of the Woolwich and Reading series. The debris forming the mottled

than mere chalk cliffs, and that source was probably some of the subcretaceous arenaceous strata, which present a lithological base similar to that of the Lower Tertiary sands, although the materials are somewhat differently sorted and some few of the more soluble and finer portions are washed out.

clays resemble that which might be brought down from decomposing granitic or basaltic districts, probably from some land to the S.W., towards Brittany or the coast of Spain. The general aspect of a large proportion of the mottled dark red clays favours this view, which is further corroborated by the fact before alluded to of the presence of gelatinous silica, or silica in that condition in which we may presume it to be when derived directly from the decomposition of felspathic rocks, without having gone through any intermediate geological stage. The influence of such river-action was evidently greater in Hampshire than in Berkshire, the beds in the former county being of nearly double the thickness of those in the latter, and far more homogeneous. Compared to the Woolwich clays, the mass of materials forming the mottled clays is out of all proportion larger. Its arrangement is also very peculiar, its lines of bedding being almost always waved and curved, as though brought down and deposited by fits and starts, as by the freshets of a large river. The smaller mass of sands with which they are interstratified were probably brought down continuously by the Weald-Island rivers, chiefly from an area of Lower Greensand, spread by sea currents, and thus intercalated with the great mass of these mottled clays derived from this other more distant source. The almost total absence of carbonate of lime and the presence of the gelatinous silica are causes probably sufficient to account for the absence of organic remains wherever these mottled clays prevail.

After a time this Lower Tertiary period was brought to a close, and its islands, with their streams, whose action we have been studying, were submerged, by the great movement of subsidence, at first rapid,— and productive of the transport of the conglomerate and mixed strata forming the Basement-bed of the London clay over the whole of the varied surface of the Woolwich and Reading series,—and which subsidence was afterwards continued by that quiet and prolonged movement, which we have shown to be necessary for the accumulation of the like materials of, and transmission of a like fauna throughout, the great mass of the overlying London clay.

The reasons for believing that the temperature of the sea at the " Thanet Sands" period * was lower than that which prevailed during the period of the London Clay, apply in some measure, but probably less forcibly, to this intermediate epoch of the " Woolwich and Reading series." The general character both of the fauna and flora shows a preponderance of forms such as, on the whole, we might expect to meet with at present in more moderate climates than the one in which the more tropical-seeming vegetation and animals of the London Clay could have flourished. For a subject, however, of this problematical nature, the data are too limited to arrive at any very satisfactory or definite result. I merely state the general impression, rather than any sufficient conviction, I have received from the inquiry into this subject.

* Quart. Journ. Geol. Soc. vol. viii. p. 260.

NOTE.

The observations on the age and structure of the Tertiary series, from the Chalk up to the Fluvio-marine strata of Hampshire, which this paper completes, having been brought forward at intervals during a period of seven years, some changes have necessarily suggested themselves during the progress of the inquiry. On the main points connected with the Marine Eocene strata, I have nothing material to alter; but as in my first paper (Journ. Geol. Soc. vol. ii.) I retained the term "London Clay" to the clays of Barton, from its having been previously so applied, and termed the brown clays with organic remains (Strata 4–6) the "Bognor clays," and which I had occasion afterwards to show were the equivalents of the London Clay proper, I dropped the latter name with regard to the Barton clays, and retained it for those beds only which I had before called the "Bognor clays." This, I believe, has caused some uncertainty as to the arrangement which I proposed; I therefore have annexed a diagram, showing the relations of the London and Hampshire Tertiary systems, and the order of superposition of the different formations, according to the terms last employed (Pl. I. General section).

I had hoped to have been able to resume the examination which I commenced, in the lower part of the Tertiary series of the Isle of Wight, in 1839; but want of time and other engagements interfered with that intention. It was therefore with great pleasure that I found the inquiry with regard to the structure and age of the Fluvio-marine series taken up by Prof. E. Forbes. Having necessarily had occasion, in the course of the investigation of the Woolwich beds described in the preceding pages, to inquire into the range and character of the fossils of that group more particularly than in the indirect reference to its fossils made in my Isle of Wight paper, I found that some identities which I had given in proof of several species being common to the "Lower London Tertiaries" and to the Isle of Wight Fluvio-marine series, were wrong. This arose in some measure from errors of observation of my own, and from confounding together species differing in character, but which had the same specific name given to them by different authors; also from taking the localities of the species from the figures and descriptions in Sowerby's ' Mineral Conchology,' without being aware at the time of several corrections which that author had introduced in a supplementary list published at a later period; and partly from the range and identities given to some species in M. Deshayes's ' Coquilles Fossiles des Environs de Paris,' respecting which the author appears to have been wrongly informed. As the results at which Prof. Forbes has arrived are of very great interest and importance, I hasten to correct these mistakes, lest any partial argument adverse to his views might perchance be founded upon them.

In the paper above referred to I gave a list of 78 species of shells from the Fluvio-marine beds of Headon Hill; and I endeavoured to show that a certain number of these ranged downwards into Lower Tertiary beds; and that 27 species were found in the French Tertiaries. The following are the determinations which I believe to be wrong:—

1. *Limnea pyramidalis*, Brard. It must have been by mistake that I referred this species to the *L. cornea*, Brongn. They are different.

2. *Melanopsis ancillarioides*, Desh. This, again, is referred in error to the *M. buccinoides*, Fér. M. Deshayes, however, mentions (Coq. Foss. vol. ii. p. 21) that a variety of the latter, common in the "Argile plastique" of Epernay, is found in the Isle of Wight.

3. *Corbula nitida*, Sow. This is not the *C. nitida*, Desh., as the use of the same specific name led me to assume.

4. *Cerithium acutum*, Sow. Non *C. acutum*, Desh.

5. —— *ventricosum*, Sow. Non *C. ventricosum*, Desh.

6. —— *funatum*, Sow. *C. variabile*, Desh., figured by Sowerby from Newhaven and Hordwell, but since restricted to the former.

7. *Cytherea incrassata*, Desh., must, I believe, be considered synonymous with the *Venus incrassata*, Sow.

8. *Cyrena cuneiformis*, Fér. Quoted by M. Deshayes from Headon Hill; but the Isle of Wight species is certainly not identical with the Woolwich one. The latter appears to be the true *C. cuneiformis* of Férussac. The former is probably the *C. semistriata*, which again M. d'Archiac had stated he had found at Woolwich.

9. *Cyrena deperdita*, Sow. Non *C. deperdita*, Desh.

10. —— *obovata*, Sow. Barton; the var. figured from New Cross does not apparently belong to that species.

11. *Paludina lenta*, Sow. M. Deshayes gives it from the Isle of Wight and from the "Argile plastique" of Soissons. It appears, however, that though very closely resembling the Woolwich species, it may possibly be considered as a variety of that species.

12. *Potamomya plana*, Sow. Figured from Plumstead, but afterwards quoted only from the Hampshire series. M. d'Archiac, however, gives it from the "Argile plastique" of the Aisne, together with the *Tellina antiqua*, Sow.

13. *Fusus labiatus*, Sow. Quoted from both Hampshire and Woolwich; the latter reference was subsequently dropt.

With regard to the correlation of the Alum Bay and White Cliff Bay sections, Prof. E. Forbes informs me that he has reason to question my identification of Stratum No. 60 of the former locality with No. 36 of the latter. As far as I can judge, without revisiting the spot, his reasons appear to me to be well founded.

* I should also have given the *Cerithium margaritaceum*, Sow., which is the *C. involutum*, Lam.

APPENDIX.

Well-sections to follow, for reference, after the section at Park Hill, Croydon: *ante*, p. 99.

South to North sections,—from Croydon to Ware.

At Mitcham Mr. Nightingale kept the following careful record of his well, and preserved a series of specimens, but I found the shells generally too much crushed by the auger to be determinable.

Well-section, Nightingale's Factory, Mitcham, 1850.*

		Feet.
	Black mould	3½
	Gravel	0½
London Clay.	Blue clay	101
	o. Blue clay mixed with *shells*	2
	n. Rock (*septaria*)	3
	m. Blue sand with a small quantity of water	3
	l. Blue clay mixed with *shells*	3
	k. Black clay, very hard	1
	j. Blue clay	3
	i. Peat earth, very soft and open (*lignite*)	3
II. *Woolwich*	*h.* Bright blue clay	3
and Read-	*g.* Black clay mixed with white shells (*Cyrena*)	1
ing Series,	*f.* Slate-coloured marl mixed with yellow (*Mot-*	
46 feet.	*tled clay*)	3
	e. Yellow mixed with pink (*do.*)	4
	d. Red and pink (*do.*)	4
	c. Blue sand mixed with clay	5
	b. Green sand mixed with clay, galt, and light	
	blue sand	1
	a. Green hard sand mixed with black pebbles	
	and white galt	7
III. *Thanet*	*c.* Blue-drab coloured sand	22
Sands,	*b.* Darker sandy loam	15
38 feet.	*a.* Green-looking flints, black and brown inside:	
	a good spring of water	1
		189

Chalk, with layers of flints every 3 feet, and an abundance of soft water in every layer, finishing the well at 211 feet.

Well-section, Copper Mills, Garret, near Wandsworth.

(Mr. E. l'Anson, Jun.)

		Feet.
	Gravel	9
London Clay...	Grey clay	70
I. *Basement-bed of*	*b.* Indurated clay	1
the London Clay,	*a.* Rolled pebbles	0½
1½ feet.		
	u. Grey clay	4
II. *Woolwich and*	*t.* Yellow grey clay	2
Reading Series,	*s.* Blue clay	2
54 or 62½ feet.	*r.* Carbonaceous matter and clay	0½
	q. Shells	1
	p. Grey clay	2
	Carried forward	92

---

* For the section of a well at Streatham Common, see Trans. Geol. Soc. 2nd ser. vol. ii. pt. 1. p. 135.

			Feet.
		Brought forward	92
	o.	Sandy and water..............................	1
	n.	Yellow clay	2
	m.	Mottled grey and yellow clay..............	4
	l.	Sandy and water	2
	k.	Yellow mottled clay	3
	j.	Grey clay.....................................	3
II. *Woolwich and*	*i.*	Red clay	3
Reading Series,	*h.*	Mottled clay	1
54 or 62½ *feet.*	*g.*	Yellow clay	6
	f.	Mottled clay	4
	e.	Mottled clay	8
	d.	Dark blue clay................................	4
	c.	Septaria ?.....................................	1
	b.	Clay and gravel	1
	a.	Green sand and water........................	8

Chalk not reached.   143

a. II. may possibly be the upper part of the Thanet Sands.

The following section is given by Mr. Lapidge, in the 'Geologist,'
vol. ii. p. 20 :—

Well-section, Surrey County Lunatic Asylum, near Wandsworth.

			Feet.
London Clay,	*b.*	Yellow clay mixed with veins of sand	20
231 *feet.*	*a.*	London clay with large clay-stones	211
	r.	Sand with clay and *shells*	6½
	q.	Dark sand	4
	p.	Shelly rock	5
	o.	Brown sand.....................................	1½
	n.	Sand and clay	2
	m.	Mottled Potter's clay	4
	l.	Sand and clay	2
II. *Woolwich*	*k.*	Dark sand and *shells*	5
and Read-	*j.*	Pure light-coloured sand	1
ing Series,	*i.*	Dark sand	2
55 *feet.*	*h.*	Sand and clay	1
	g.	Pink and yellow mottled clay	4
	f.	Light brown and white clay	4
	e.	Dark red and white clay	4
	d.	Chalk and pebbles	1
	c.	Green sand	3
	b.	Variegated green and brown sand................	6
	a.	Green sand	4
	d.	Brown sand, wherein was water, which rose to within 36 feet of the surface...................	5
Thanet	*c.*	Fine dark grey sand	33
Sands,	*b.*	Sand and pebbles, from which the water rose to within 28 feet of the surface...................	2
40½ *feet.*	*a.*	A hard stratum (uncertain)	0½
		Chalk	1½
		Flints	4

347

The "chalk" is probably merely some calcareous bed overlying a
thick mass of the green-coated flints ("Flints"), below which would
be the true chalk, or else the figures are reversed.

Well-section, Balham Hill, near Clapham Common.

(Dr. Mitchell's MSS. vol. iv. p. 205*.)

		Feet.
	Mould	1
	Yellow clay	4
	Sand	4
	Gravel	6
London Clay.	b. Brown clay	6
	a. Blue clay or burl	233
	i. Oyster-shell rock	5
	h. Brown clay	13
	g. White clay	4
II. Woolwich and Reading Series, 53 ft.	f. Yellow clay	3
	e. Red clay	2
	d. Light blue clay	5
	c. Black clay	3
	b. Brown clay	13
	a. Pebble-stones	5
Thanet Sands.	Sand	40
		347

Well-section, York-mead, Lambeth.

(Parl. Report, "Supply of Water in the Metropolis," 1828, p. 111.)

		Feet.
	Made ground, gravel, and clay	30
	Stony blue clay (*London clay*)	139
I.?	Clay stone	0½
	Hard rock	1½
II.	Hard mixed clay and sand	20
	Shell and pebble stones	6
	Green soft sandstone came up in sand	14
		211

The complete suite of specimens preserved by Mr. A. K. Barclay enables me to give the following section in greater detail than usual. It establishes the important fact of the well-marked local occurrence of the *Ostrea Bellovacina* at the base of Group II. (*a, b.*), and shows clearly the Woolwich shell bed (*g*) placed between two considerable masses of mottled clays.

Well-section, Barclay and Perkins's Brewery, Southwark.

	Feet.
Made ground and silt with vegetable remains	20
Grey clayey sand with specks of phosphate of iron	1
Gravel	6½
Carried forward	27½

* Although the publications on Tertiary Geology of the late Dr. James Mitchell are not numerous, he was an indefatigable observer and collector in this field, and was ever ready to assist others unreservedly with his facts and profusely with his specimens, as I can testify from personal experience. On many points his views were often peculiar, and not in conformity with prevailing opinions; but his convictions were always honest and boldly expressed. He has left five folio MS. volumes of valuable rough notes on the Geology, Botany, and Wells of the neighbourhood of London. These are now in the possession of his nephew Mr. James Templeton of Exeter, who has been good enough to allow me the free use of them. This and several other well-sections are from this MS. work.

			Feet.
		Brought forward	27½
London *Clay.*	Brown and blue clay.	At 84 feet a thin layer of pebbles .... At 92 feet a layer of septaria .... At 96 feet a layer of septaria .... At 99 feet a layer of septaria .... At 99 feet a mass of wood pierced by Teredo	77¼
		j. Mottled clays. Red and light greenish at 100 feet ...... Light brown and grey at 112 feet ...... Very light-coloured mixed sand at 113 ft. Brown and light grey at 114 feet	22
		Brown and light grey at 128 feet......... Light greenish at 129 feet	3
		Brown at 130 feet............................ Greenish and sandy at 134 feet	4
		i. Light brown sand and grey clay	1
		h. Grey clay and vegetable matter	2
		g. Grey clay with a few shells (*Cyrena*?).....................	3
II.*Woolwich* *and Read-* *ing Series,* *62 feet.*		*f.* Mottled clays. Greenish, brown and grey at 141 feet... Red, full of race, at 146 feet .... Red and green at 147 feet .... Brown and greenish at 148 feet	8
		e. Sandy clays, partially mottled: Brown and greenish, with flint pebbles, at 149 feet................................. Do., with middle-sized pebbles, at 150 ft. Do., with larger-sized pebbles, at 152 ft. Very small pebbles, subangular, 154 ft.	7
		d. Clayey green sand with pebbles and wood	2 ?
		c. Green sand with larger pebbles	1
		b. Green sand, bright-coloured, a few pebbles, and *Ostrea.* „ „ large and worn *Ostrea* and a few pebbles	6
		a. Grey clayey sand, with a few *Ostrea Bellovacina* at 167 ft. „ „ darker and more argillaceous, and *Ostrea* more numerous at 169 feet	3
III. *Thanet* *Sands,* *36 feet.*		*b.* Grey sands, dark and greenish .... „ „ lighter..	35
		a. Green-coated flints in argillaceous green sand	1
			203
		Chalk..	100

Well-section, Fishmongers' Hall, north end of London Bridge.

(Sections of Borings published by the Metropolitan Commissioners of Sewers, 1849; Sheet 3.)

			Feet.
		Made ground, black boggy soil and peat ...	27
		Clay and sand....................................	7
		Gravel	14
London Clay.		Blue clay	129
II. *Woolwich* *and Reading* *Series, 60 ft.*	*d.* Mottled or coloured clay		20
	c. Shell rock		11
	b. Green sand....................................		5
	a. Fine sand mixed with pebbles		24
	Chalk.		237

If the chalk is correctly placed in this section, which seems doubtful, it must be a boss rising through the Thanet Sands.

Well-section, St. Mary's Woolnoth, Lombard Street.
(Dr. Mitchell's MSS. vol. v. p. 21.)

		Feet.
	Gravel .... } 164	
London Clay.	Blue clay	
II. *Woolwich and*	*c.* Sand..	2
Reading Series,	*b.* Sands and mottled clay	35
53 *feet.*	*a.* Black flints and sand	16
III. *Thanet Sands,*	*b.* Sand, greenish...............................	35
36 *feet.*	*a.* Flints	1

To the Chalk 253

The following well, of which, like that at Messrs. Barclays, specimens and particulars were carefully taken, is particularly interesting
from its confirming the same facts, and yet showing marked variations in the relative character of the beds *a* to *o.* II.

Well-section, Bank of England, 1851.

(From section published for private distribution, and from inspection of the specimens), Pl. I. Diag. A, Loc. sect. 20.

		Feet.
	Made ground	22
	Gravel	4
	London clay	111
	o. Light yellow mottled clay	2
	n. Light yellow mottled clay, sandy	6
	m. Red and brown mottled clay	2
	l. Light-coloured sand	5
	k. Light-coloured mottled sandy clay	1½
	j. Light blue and brown mottled clay	8
II. *Woolwich*	*i.* Carbonaceous clay and lignite	1¼
and Read-	*h.* Light grey sand	2
ing Series,	*g.* Light grey clay and shells (*Cyrena, Melania*)............	1
58 *feet.*	*f.* Dark grey clay and shells (*Cyrena, Melania, Ostrea*) .	2¼
	e. Hard light-coloured concretionary limestone	3
	d. Red, blue, and brown mottled clay	1½
	c. Flint-pebbles in clay	5
	b. Bright dark green sand and flint-pebbles	13½
	a. Dark green sand with shells (*Ostrea*)	4
III. *Thanet*	*b.* Light grey sands, the lower part darker and more ar- } 38	
Sands,	gillaceous...	
39 *feet.*	*a.* Bed of flints	1

234½

Chalk 100

334½

In the next section the Woolwich clay beds are probably represented by Stratum *f.* II.

Well-section, Shoreditch Workhouse. (Pl. I. Diag. C, Loc. sect. 6.)

(Mr. R. W. Mylne.)

	Feet.
Made earth	10
Gravel	8
London clay	58

Carried forward 76

Feet.

		Brought forward	76
I. *Basement-bed of the London Clay.*	*b.* Shelly rock		1
	a. Sand..		1
	j. Light clay		2
	i. Coloured clay (*Mottled clay*)		7
	h. Dark red clay (*ditto*)		3
	g. Bluish clay		3
II. *Woolwich and Reading Series,* 40 *feet.*	*f.* Black clay		7
	e. Sandy clay		3
	d. Oyster shells		3
	c. Pebbles..		2
	b. Green sand		9
	a. Pebbles in green sand		1
III. *Thanet Sands,* 39 *feet.*	*b.* Light sand with water...........................		38
	a. Flints		1

157

Chalk 100

263

Well-section, Hoxton.

(Mr. R. W. Mylne.)

Feet.

		Feet.
	Made earth and gravel	18
	London clay	69
II. *Woolwich and Reading Series,* 34 *feet.*	*c.* Mottled clay	16
	b. Pebbles, black and green, mixed with sand	10
	a. Green sand	8
III. *Thanet Sands.*	Black sand	30

To the Chalk........................ 151

Well-section, New City Prison, Holloway (*from inspection of specimens in the possession of Mr. Bunning*).

Feet.

			Feet.
	London Clay		135
	i. Mottled clay ....about		22
	h. Coloured sands	„	5
	g. Yellow sand	„	2
II. *Woolwich and Reading Series,* 61 *feet.*	*f.* Clayey green sand.........................	„	6
	e. Yellow and greenish sands	„	8
	d. Pebbles and green sand	„	6
	c. Sand and brown clay with traces of vegetable matter	„	7
	b. Dark green sand	„	6
	a. Sand with clay and pebbles	„	7
III. *Thanet Sands.*	Sands ?		12 ?
	Flints		1

217

Chalk 102

319

I could not exactly make out from the specimens where the Chalk begins in this section. The last Tertiary bed named is *a.* II., but as that seems to leave a space unoccupied, I have inserted " sands " with a doubt. At the Pentonville Prison the Mottled clay series is 55 feet thick and the Thanet Sands 35 feet.

Well-section, Hornsey.

(Mr. N. T. Wetherell.)

		Feet.
	Vegetable mould	2
	London clay	138
I. *Basement-bed of the London Clay?*	Clay and green sand	2 ?
II. & III. *Woolwich and Reading Series and Thanet Sands.*	Sand	8
	Wood or imperfect coal (*lignite*)	4
	Several beds of Plastic clay and sand, and sand. The last bed above the chalk consists of green sand and pebbles...............	71

To the Chalk 225

Well-section, Colney Hatch Lunatic Asylum.

(13th Report of the Committee of Visitors, 1850.)

		Feet.
London Clay.	*b.* Brown clay....................................	36
	a. Blue clay	98
I. *Basement-bed of the London Clay,* 3 *feet.*	*b.* Hard stone....................................	1
	? *a.* Green sand...................................	2
II. *Woolwich and Reading Series,* 27 *feet.*	*c.* Coloured clay..................................	8
	b. Coloured clay, various colours.............	13
	a. Black pebbles.................................	6
III. *Thanet Sands.*	Dark grey sand.................................	25

189

Chalk 141

330

Well-section, Winchmore Hill.

(Dr. Mitchell's MSS. vol. iv. p. 59.)

		Feet.
London Clay.	Blue clay	186
II. *Woolwich and Reading Series.*	*b.* Red clay	36
	a. Sands and gravel......................	8

To the Chalk 240

The preponderance of green sands in the place of the mottled clays, which are so well developed at Tottenham *, is a peculiarity in the following section. *a.* and *b.* II. may possibly belong to the Thanet sands.

Well-section, Waltham Cross.

(Mr. R. W. Mylne.)

	Feet.
Mould	2
Loam	4
Gravel	7
Gravel, very rough	3

Carried forward 16

---

* " Geol. England and Wales," note, p. 24.

		Feet.
	Brought forward	16
London Clay.	b. Blue clay	24
	a. Blue clay, mixed with dark sand	10
I. Basement-bed of the London Clay? 6 feet.	b. Blue clay, lighter-coloured, and sand ...	5
	a. Black pebbles	1
II. Woolwich and Reading Series. 51 feet.	i. Light green mottled sand..................	7
	h. White live sand............................	3
	g. Light green sand, slightly mottled	1
	f. Green sand, but darker.....................	3
	e. Green sand, mixed with flint-pebbles ...	3
	d. Dark bay green sand.......................	7
	c. Green sand and pebbles	1
	b Green sand, getting darker	16
	a. Green sand, very little difference	10
	Chalk not reached.	107

Well-section, Hoddesden Brewery.
(Mr. R. W. Mylne.)

		Feet.
	Gravel	20
Lower part of the London Clay and the Woolwich and Reading Series.	c. Loam and marly sands	45
	b. White sand	24
	a. Flints	1
		90
	Chalk	4

The sections in continuation northward of this line have been given in a preceding part of this paper (p. 92).

We will now take an East and West line, commencing near Esher where the principal changes take place in the structure of the Lower Tertiaries, and passing also through London to Chelmsford.

Well-section, Claremont.
(J. Day.)

		Feet.
Lower Bagshot Sands.	Sand	50
London Clay.	Blue clay	450
Woolwich and Reading Series, 60 feet.	c. Mottled clays	48
	b. Brown sand	10
	a. Green sand and flints	2
	To the Chalk	560

Well-section, Isleworth.
(Trans. Civ. Eng.)

		Feet.
	Gravel and sand	24
London Clay.	Blue clay...................................	216
Woolwich and Reading Series, 87 feet.	f. Clay, mottled light red, becoming darker as it deepens..................	68
	e. Blackish clay	3
	d. Yellow sand passing into light green	6
	c. Dark green clay	10
	Chalk not reached.	327

Well-section, Mortlake Brewery.
(Dr. Mitchell's MSS. vol. iv. p. 207.)

		Feet.
	Gravel	10
London Clay.	*b.* London clay (ash-coloured compost) ...	90
	a. Mottled red passing into red	109
	h. Green sand....................................	9
	g. Yellow sand	3
II. *Woolwich and*	*f.* Greenish sand and clay....................	17
Reading Series,	*e.* Purplish clay with lignite..................	4
58 *feet.*	*d.* Yellow sand ....,.....	2
	c. Light green sand	4
	b. Ash-coloured clay with *shells*	15
	a. Green sand....................................	4

267

Chalk 3

270

The term " Mottled clay" applied to Stratum *a.* II. is, I suspect, a wrong term. I have therefore grouped it as part of the London Clay, which gives a thickness to that formation agreeing with neighbouring sections.

Well-section, Griffin Brewery, Chiswick.
(Mr. R. W. Mylne.)

		Feet.
	Earth and gravel......	
	Sand and fine gravel	40
	Gravel and sand	
London Clay.	Blue clay	140
	e. Mottled clay	6
	d. Blue clay mixed with sand	9
II. *Woolwich and*	*c.* Brown and sandy mottled clays.............	15
Reading Series,	*b.* Bright red, yellow, pink and	
90 *feet.*	bluish mottled clays......	53
	a. Pebbles in bluish mottled clay	7
	e. Yellow sandy clay	1
III. *Thanet Sands,*	*d.* Variegated sand	2
29 *feet.*	*c.* Green and brown sand	23
	b. Hard green sand	
	a. Flints	3

299

Chalk 46

Well-section, Kensington Workhouse*.
(Mr. R. W. Mylne.)

		Feet.
	Made ground	8
	Gravel	3
	London clay	179
Woolwich and Reading	Mottled clays	38
Series and Thanet Sands.	Pebbles and sand...............	42

270

Chalk 100

* In this section, as in that at Notting Dale, the lower sands and pebbles of the Woolwich series have, I believe, been confounded with the Thanet Sands.

Well-section, Elliott's Brewery, Westminster.

(Mr. R. W. Mylne.)

		Feet.
London Clay.	Made ground and gravel	32
	Blue clay	140
II. *Woolwich and Reading Series,* 68 *feet.*	*j.* Mottled clay	6½
	i. Sand....................................	1
	h. Red and yellow clay (*mottled clay*)	12½
	g. Blue sand..............................	1½
	f. Red marl (*mottled clay*)	13½
	e. Blue clay and *shells*	10
	d. Yellow clay	3½
	c. Red clay (*mottled clay*)	7
	b. Yellow clay	3½
	a. Gravel, rock, and blue sand	8½
III. *Thanet Sands,* 31 *feet.*	*b.* Green sand	9½
	a. Running sand	22
		———
		271
	Chalk	127

Well-section, Thorne's Brewery, Westminster.

(Mr. R. W. Mylne.)

		Feet.
	Made earth, gravel, &c.	27½
	London clay	100
II. *Woolwich and Reading Series,* 66½ *feet.*	*c.* Sand and clay	11
	b. Coloured clay	49
	a. Sand and pebbles...........	6½
III. *Thanet Sands,* 36 *feet.*	*c.* Sand with water	14
	b. Sand...........................	20
	a. Flints	2
		———
		230
	Chalk	70

Well-section, front of the National Gallery, Trafalgar Square.

(The Illustrated London News for April 5, 1845.)

		Feet.
	Made ground	9
	Gravel....................................	5
	Shifting sand	7
	Gravel	2
	London clay	141
I. *Basement-bed L. C. ?*	Thin layer of shells	1
II. *Woolwich and Reading Series, 40 feet.*	*b.* Plastic clay (*mottled clay*)........	30
	a. Green sand, pebbles, &c.	11
III. *Thanet Sands*	Green sand	42
		———
		248
	Chalk	147

Well-section, Apothecaries' Hall, Blackfriars.

(Mr. R. W. Mylne.)

		Feet.
	Made ground	12
	London clay	114
		———
	Carried forward	126

			Feet.
		Brought forward......	126
II. *Woolwich and*	*c.*	Dark sand...........................	13
Reading Series,	*b.*	Mottled clay.......................	30
48 *feet.*	*a.*	Clay, sand, and pebbles	5
III. *Thanet Sands,*	*b.*	Green sand	20
44 *feet.*	*a.*	Light black sand	24

	218
Chalk	76

Well-section, Royal Mint, Tower Hill. (Pl. I. Diag. A, Loc. sect. 21, & C, Loc. sect. 7.)

(Sect. Bor. by Metrop. Comm. of Sewers, 1849, Sheet 4, and from examination of specimens.)

		Feet.
	Made ground	11
	Gravel and sand	13
London Clay.	Blue clay	94
	k. Light sand	4½
	j. Light-coloured sand	14
	i. Dark-coloured sand	4
	h. Mottled clay	5¼
II. *Woolwich and*	*g.* Loamy dark sand and clay	5
Reading Series,	*f.* Shelly blue clay (*Cyrena, Melania, Ostrea*)	3
55 *feet.*	*e.* White rocky soil, very hard	2½
	d. Green sand and pebbles, hard and dry	3¼
	c. Loamy green sand and black pebbles	5
	b. Green sand and pebbles	6
	a. Green sand and shells (*Ostrea*)	4
III. *Thanet Sands,*	Dark sand	15
20½ *feet.*	Flints	5½

To the Chalk	195½

Well-section, Truman, Hanbury and Co.'s, Shoreditch.
(Mr. R. W. Mylne.)

		Feet.
	Made ground	
	Clay	
	Gravel and sand	23¼
	Clay	
	London clay	79¼
	m. Light blue mottled	11
	l. Blue mottled	2
	k. Dark mottled.....................	6
	j. Rock	1½
	i. Bluish green	4
II. *Woolwich and*	*h.* Hard blue loam and *shells*	6
Reading Series,	*g.* Hard yellow clay and pebbles	5
53 *feet.*	*f.* Pebbles	4
	e. Green sand and black pebbles	2
	d. Shell rock	1½
	c. Green sand and pebbles	5
	b. Dark sand and pebbles	4
	a. Oyster-bed	1
III. *Thanet Sands.*	Dark grey sand and pebbles	43

	199
Chalk......................	201

In this and the following section the development of the pebble beds in the lower part of the Woolwich series is remarkable.

Well-section, Walton's Sugar-house, Angel Court, Whitechapel.
(Dr. Mitchell's MSS. vol. iv. p. 48.)

		Feet.
	Mould and soil	6
	Gravel	12
London Clay.	*b.* Yellow clay	3
	a. Blue clay	97
	p. Light green sand and some clay	6
	o. Blue clay and sand	2
	n. Dark brown clay	12
	m. Blue clay and sand	2
	l. Blue clay and sand with *shells*	2
	k. Hard sand	1
	j. Hard green sand and clay	1
II. *Woolwich and*	*i.* Red and grey clay	2
Reading Series,	*h.* Yellow clay with pebbles	4
69 *feet.*	*g.* Clay and gravel conglomerate, very hard, with large pebbles	9
	f. Sand, pebbles, and a little clay	6
	e. Yellow clay	1
	d. Green sand, very hard	2
	c. Loose sand, black pebbles	4
	b. Blue clay	3
	a. Sand and black pebbles	12
		187

At Osborne-street, near the above, chalk was found about 26 to 30 feet lower, through a bed of fine white sand (*Thanet Sands*).—Dr. M.

Stratum *p.* II. may possibly be the Basement-bed of the London Clay.

Well-section, Kirk and Dycks', Osborne-place, Whitechapel.
(Pl. I. Diag. A, Loc. sect. 22.)
(Dr. Mitchell's MSS. vol. iv. p. 50.)

		Feet.
	Mould and soil	6
	Yellow clay	6
	Gravel	12
London Clay.	*b.* Yellow clay	1
	a. Blue clay	95
	h. Yellow-red clay	6
	g. Sand	1
	f. Yellow-red clay	12
II. *Woolwich and*	*e.* Green sand	5
Reading Series,	*d.* Yellow-red clay	10
54 *feet.*	*c.* Sand	3
	b. Gravel rock, very hard	9
	a. Green sand and black pebbles	8
III. *Thanet Sands.*	Sand	16
		190

Chalk not reached.

Judging from some adjoining wells, I think that *d.* II. is wrongly described, and that it represents the Woolwich shell bed.

Well-section, City of London Union, Mile End Road.

(Mr. R. W. Mylne.)

		Feet.
	Made earth and vegetable earth	4
	Yellow dry earth	2
	Coarse gravel mixed with fine sand	15
	Fine gravel and sand....................................	14
London Clay.	? Mixture of clay, sand, and water	20½
	a. Hard dry blue clay	40
	k. Soft blue clay with fine silky running sand	12½
	j. Sandy clay, yellow-coloured, and small stones	2¾
	i. Hard yellow sand...................................	1
	h. Sandy clay, yellow and green	4
II. *Woolwich and Reading Series,* 41 *feet.*	*g.* Compact sandy clay	2
	f. Compact green clay.................................	1
	e. Compact yellow and green	2
	d. Hard yellow clay and large pebbles	7
	c. Green sand	1
	b. Black sand	2
	a. Black sand and small pebbles......................	6
III. *Thanet Sands,* 38½ *feet.*	*e.* Black sand, compact	4
	d. Black sand, less compact	5
	c. Black clay, sandy grit.............................	1
	b. Black sand mixed with black clay, and soft.........	27½
	a. Black flints, small	1
		175
	Chalk.................................	10

I feel very uncertain where I should draw the lines of division in this section. They must be considered as doubtful. I am almost inclined to carry Group II. down to *c.* III. inclusive.

Well-section, Bromley near Stratford. (Pl. I. Diag. A, Loc. sect. 23.)

("Geology of England and Wales," p. 45.)

		Feet.
	Loam, clay, gravel, and sand	18
	London clay	44
	Blue clay	2
Basement-bed of the London Clay, 5 *feet.*	*b.* Clay, sand, and *shells* mixed	1
	a. Gravel, sand, and *shells*	4
II. *Woolwich and Reading Series,* 51 *feet.*	*i.* Fine sand	4
	h. Blue and yellow clay	9
	g. Sand and *shells*, with large lumps of pyrites...	4
	f. Blue clay, with abundance of broken *shells*, some resembling *oysters*, and pyrites	9
	e. Solid limestone	1
	d. Black sand, passing into small round pebbles, like the Blackheath pebbles	}
	c. Black sand, veined	22
	b. Some small pebbles in the sand, which is still hard and compact	
	a. Blue clay, very hard and firm	2

Beneath this last bed are probably the *Thanet Sands.*   120

Well-section, South side of the Export Dock, West India Docks.

(Dr. Mitchell's MSS. vol. iii. p. 85.)

		Feet.
Made gravel (?)		15
Clay		5
Gravel		25
Thanet Sands ? { Clear sand..		30
{ Sand and *shells*		45
		120
Chalk		240

I give this section from its peculiarity. The occurrence of shells above the Chalk I have not had confirmed.

Well-section, Trinity Wharf, Blackwall.

(Mr. R. W. Mylne.)

			Feet.
	Made ground		18
	Gravel		45
	London clay*		68
II. *Woolwich and Reading Series,* 34 feet.	*d.* Grey sand		8
	c. Shells and iron pyrites		2
	b. Oyster-shells and sand		14
	a. Stiff green sand		10
III. *Thanet Sands,* 71½ feet.	*b.* Grey sand		65
	a. Stiff sand and clay		7
			237
	Chalk		10

Well-section, West Ham, Essex.

(Mr. R. W. Mylne.)

			Feet.
	Made ground		8
	Black gravel		9
	Peaty clay		16
II. *Woolwich and Reading Series,* 58 feet.	*g.* Pebbles		2
	f. Shelly		4
	e. Light brown sand		18
	d. Clay and *shells*		6
	c. Hard *shells*		5½
	b. Green sand		1½
	a. Pebbles		5
III. *Thanet Sands.*	Sand		57
			132
	Chalk		306

---

* In the section of this well, and of the one at Bromley, I feel considerable hesitation in retaining the designation of "London clay" here given by the well-digger; for I am rather induced to think, from the outcropping of the Woolwich conglomerate in the river at Blackwall and of the Basement-bed of the London clay at Stratford, that the London clay does not exist in the first-named localities. It certainly may be there, and be thrown out by a fault on a line near adjacent. I consider it however more probable that the mineral character of the stratum has led to some mistake, and that the bed here taken to be the London clay may be a peculiar condition and unusual development of the mottled clays, where they clash and mix with the upper part of the Woolwich clays and sands, losing their

For a small section of the Basement-bed and of the upper part of the Woolwich series at Stratford see Journ. Geol. Soc. vol. vi. p. 262.

The sections of wells which I have from Ilford, Romford, Brentwood, and adjacent districts give us no particulars of the Lower Tertiaries, as water was in all cases obtained almost directly after passing through the London clay. Some preliminary works for an artesian well by the Local Board of Health at Chelmsford have, however,

---

mottled character and passing into a brown micaceous sandy clay. An instance of this has recently come before me in the section of a trial boring made opposite Blackwall. Beneath 33 ft. of peat and gravel were 55 ft. of brown clay, which had been mistaken for the London clay. At first sight it certainly a good deal resembled it, but on a closer examination it presented characters decidedly differing from that clay, which is of a lighter brown, or else bluish, more homogeneous, and is not so micaceous. It is in all cases very necessary to guard against well-sections not recorded with sufficient care. Several of those collected by Dr. Mitchell are in all probability given wrong by the well-digger, as one near Waterloo Bridge (W.), which brings the London clay too near to the chalk.

W.	Feet.			Feet.
Gravel and sand	40		Whilst in another well at Finsbury the mottled clays are omitted altogether.	
Blue clay	110			
Red clay	10		Gravel and London clay	160
Sand	5		Sand and pebbles	10
To the Chalk	165		*To the Chalk*	170

The same fact is observable in some of the sections collected by the Commissioners of Sewers; as for instance—

Well-section, Goding's Brewery.	Feet.		*Well-section, Thorne's Brewery.*	Feet.
Made ground	15		Made ground and gravel	40
Gravel	15		Blue clay	162
Blue clay	160			
			To the Chalk	202
To the Chalk	190		(See p. 148.)	

Well-section near Westminster Bridge.		*Mortlake.*	*Barnes.*
	Feet.	Feet.	Feet.
Made ground and gravel	27	10	18
Blue clay	160	180	180
To the Chalk	187	190	198

Some mistake is evidently made in these sections in carrying the London clay down to the chalk. In some others too great an extension has apparently been given to the beds of flint pebbles (called gravel), as they appear to occupy the place of the Thanet Sands as well as their own:—

Well-section, Bermondsey.	Feet.		*Well-section, Seager's, Milbank.*	Feet.
Bog earth and peat	9		Made ground	22¼
Silt	3		Gravel	3
Quick sand	20		Blue clay	93
Blue clay	60		Blue rock	2
Gravel	110		Sand and gravel	77¼
	202		*To the Chalk*	198

recently afforded a section of part of the beds beneath the London clay at that place.

Trial bore at Chelmsford.

(Specification paper.)

		Feet.
Drift.	Dark mould	3
	Yellow clay	1
	Gravel	15
	Sand (dark)	51
London Clay.	b. London clay	100
	a. London clay and silver sand	50
II. Woolwich and Reading Series?	Dark sand	12½
	Clay-slate (?)	0¾
	Clay and sand	4
	Clay-slate (?)	0½
	Dark sand, with fine clay at intervals	9½
	Clay, sand, and shells	2½
	Clay and shells	0¼
	Pebbles	1½
	Sand (spring)	4½

256

As I have not had the opportunity of seeing the specimens, I am unable to say positively to what part of the Lower Tertiaries these beds may belong: it is probable, however, that those beneath the London Clay down to the "Pebbles" inclusive may belong to the Woolwich series, and that the "Sand (spring)" may be the top of the Thanet Sands. The beds called "clay-slate" are, I presume, hard laminated clay or shale.

I have also recently been furnished by Mr. A. C. Veley of Braintree with the following section of a well at Halsted.

Well-section, White Hart, Halsted.

(Letter from the Rev. W. Clements.)

		Feet.
	A layer of sand and gravel	7
	A bed of yellowish clay	8
	The London clay	89
II. Woolwich and Reading Series.	A layer of yellow sand passing into brown clay	7
	A bed of plastic clay	19
	A greenish sand	15
III. Thanet Sands.	Several layers of sand gradually passing from a light colour to nearly a black, about	25
	Chalk	30

About 200

The Rev. W. B. Clarke also gives sections of two wells at Harwich, in which the mottled clays appear, but no fossils. (Trans. Geol. Soc. 2nd ser. vol. v. pp. 369, 370.)

Notes on some Miscellaneous FOSSILS *from the* "WOOLWICH *and* READING SERIES."

CORBULA ARNOULDII, Nyst. PL. II. fig. 3.

Described, but not figured, by M. Nyst in his "Descr. des Coquilles fossiles des Terr. Tert. de la Belgique," p. 67. This is a not uncommon shell in the Lignites of Rilly in Champagne. The French specimens in my possession are rather larger than the English species; and, further, as these latter are merely casts, they can only be referred with a doubt to this foreign species. From Oakwells, near Boughton.

CYRENA INTERMEDIA, Melleville. PL. II. figs. 10, 11.

Melleville, in his "Mém. sur les Sables Tert. Inf. du Bassin de Paris," figures and describes a *Cyrena* from Châlons-sur-Vesle, which, although rather larger, bears a close resemblance to a small and elegant shell common in the upper beds at and around Woolwich. The specimen here figured is referred with a doubt to this French species, which latter appears from the figure to be slightly more rounded.

AMPULLARIA (NATICA) SUBDEPRESSA, Morris. PL. II. fig. 16.

In my paper on the Thanet Sands, Mr. Morris briefly described a new species of *Ampullaria* under the above specific appellation; but it was not figured, owing to the imperfect condition of the specimen. Having better specimens from the Woolwich series and also from the Basement-bed of the London Clay, the shell in question is here figured. (For description, see Quart. Journ. Geol. Soc. vol. viii. p. 267†.) Richborough.

PATELLA. PL. II. fig. 24.

This is a single specimen found attached to a fragment of an Oyster at Sundridge Park by Mr. Lunn. It does not seem to agree with any of the French patelliform shells; but, owing to the want of the exterior shell, no exact specific determination can be made.

DENTALIUM. PL. II. fig. 25.

In the memoir on the "Thanet Sands" (Quart. Journ. Geol. Soc. vol. viii. p. 248), the *Dentalium*, apparently the same species as this, was considered to be the *D. nitens*. This determination, however, seems to me to be very doubtful. I should rather refer this species from Herne Bay to an undescribed form from the "Lower Tertiary Sands" of Beauvais. The specimens are too imperfect for exact determination.

† In a paper by M. Watelet on the "Sables Tertiaires des environs de Soissons" (Soc. Hist. Archéol. et Scient. de Soissons, 1853), which I have just received, is a fossil bearing a very close resemblance to this English species figured: it is, however, in a much better state of preservation. M. Watelet has named it *Natica infundibulum*.—[J. P., Jun., January 1854.]

SERPULA.　PL. II. fig. 26.

This is a very common fossil at Sundridge Park, although it rarely occurs elsewhere in the Woolwich series; but, although abundant, its characters are too indistinct for a specific name to be satisfactorily applied. It is a fine, thin, convoluted species. The specimen figured is part of a mass attached to an Oyster.

FIR-CONE.　PL. III. fig. 3.

This beautiful specimen, the cast of a Fir-cone in a ferruginous sandstone nodule, is from the Woolwich series of the Reculver Cliffs. It presents distinct differences from the Fir-cones of the London Clay, and from that figured by Mr. Dixon from Bracklesham (Dixon, Foss. Sussex, pl. 9. figs. 3, 4). The specimen from the Reculvers is a true and well-marked Fir-cone, belonging apparently to some species of *Abies*.

SEED-VESSEL (PL. III. fig. 4), and other VEGETABLE REMAINS. (PL. III. fig. 5).

These fossils from the Planorbis-bed at Counter Hill are figured rather for reference and record. At present no specific determination can be attempted. They differ from described specimens.

Two Dicotyledonous leaves have been found by Mr. De la Condamine in the Paludina-bed of the same locality.

FERN-LEAF.　PL. III. fig. 6.

One of the recent discoveries by the Rev. Mr. De la Condamine at Counter Hill. This Fern is probably an *Asplenium*; the leaflets occur in some numbers, and are associated with fragments of Monocotyledonous leaves (especially *Phyllites* "r," Pl. IV. figs. 22, 23), and one or more Dicotyledonous leaves.

REMAINS OF FISHES.

*Vertebra of Lepidosteus**.　PL. III. fig. 1.

This specimen was discovered by the Rev. Mr. De la Condamine at Upnor, and I am indebted to Prof. Owen for the following observations on this interesting fossil :—

"The body of an anterior abdominal vertebra of a large species of *Lepidosteus*, a genus of Ganoid Fishes now peculiar to the rivers and lakes of North America. The specimen is fossilized; similar, but smaller, fossil specimens have been discovered in the Eocene Tertiary deposits of Hampshire."—[Oct. 15, 1852.]

---

* The dark enamelled scales of the *Lepidosteus* have since been found by the Rev. H. De la Condamine at Counter Hill, and by Mr. Rosser at Woolwich : in both places in the upper beds of the Woolwich series. From the former locality Mr. De la Condamine has also obtained, in the Paludina-bed, another vertebra, belonging to a much smaller species of *Lepidosteus* than the above-described.

Fish Vertebræ.

The vertebræ of *Lamnæ* are not rare in the "Lower Tertiary Sands," and with them occur in rather greater abundance the vertebræ of some osseous fish, one of which is here figured (PL. III. fig. 2); many of them are, however, of a much smaller size.

Fish-scales. PL. III. figs. 2*, 2**.

These are the large scales of some Cycloid? fishes, to which possibly the last-mentioned vertebræ may also be referred.   With these are found smaller scales of similar character, and a few very small conical teeth belonging probably to the same class of fishes.   Localities : Woolwich and Sundridge.

Cycloid scales and fish-bones occur also at Counter Hill, in the Paludina-bed.

BIRD REMAINS.

A very interesting specimen of a small, irregularly cylindrical bone, about half an inch in length, discovered by the Rev. H. M. De la Condamine at Counter Hill, whilst these pages were passing through the press, has been determined by Prof. Owen, who has kindly examined it, to be *the first phalangeal bone of the foot of a bird.* It is the only such specimen found. [J. P., Jun., April 10, 1854.]

Descriptions of some NEW SPECIES *of* SHELLS *from the* "WOOLWICH AND READING SERIES." By JOHN MORRIS, F.G.S.

CARDIUM LAYTONI, n. sp.   PL. II. figs. 1, 2.

Testâ trigonali, inæquilaterali, posticè subangulatâ, obliquatâ, costatâ; costis numerosis, planulatis; margine dentato; umbonibus incurvis, approximatis.

A trigonal, inequilateral, and somewhat oblique shell, with the posterior portion slightly angulated; the surface is marked with numerous flattened ribs and linear interspaces, which become more distinct and separated on the posterior angulated side; the margins are strongly dentated.   This shell is distinguished from *C. Plumsteadiense* by its smaller size, more uniform marking, and the posterior side not being so much produced or angular.

The specimen figured was found at Richborough by the Rev. J. Layton, of Sandwich, after whom the species is named.

CORBULA REGULBIENSIS, n. sp.   PL. II. figs. 4, 5.

Testâ ovato-transversâ, subgibbosâ, rostratâ; striis tenuissimis irregularibus ornatâ.

—————— ——————————, ——, var. β.   PL. II. fig. 6.

Testâ irregulari, vix rostratâ.

An ovate and somewhat quadrangular shell, with the posterior margin but very slightly produced, except in the variety from Herne

Bay, which is generally so. The surface is covered with irregular fine laminæ, slightly raised; the umbones very small, and approximate.

This species has been identified with an undescribed form from Bracheux, given to Mr. Prestwich by M. Deshayes, but which is not published. Named after the locality (the Reculvers) where this species is most common.

From Mr. Prestwich's collection.

CYRENA CORDATA, n. sp.   PL. II. figs. 7, 8, 9.

Testâ subtrigonali, crassâ, gibbosâ, rugosâ; umbonibus prominentibus, antico rotundato, postico subrostrato, depresso, attenuato.

The general form of this shell is trigonal; the beaks are prominent and incurved; the ventricose character of this shell towards the umbones gives it, when viewed anteriorly, a cordiform appearance (whence the name); the posterior side is attenuated and slightly truncate. The surface of the shell towards the anterior side is very rugose by the lines of growth.

This species is intermediate to *C. cuneiformis* and *C. deperdita*, and also resembles in its cordate form the *C. antiqua* of the Paris basin; it does not, however, possess the depressed character of the posterior cardinal edge.

From Mr. Lunn's collection.

MODIOLA MITCHELLI, n. sp.   PL. II. figs. 12, 13.

Testâ tenui, lævi, subtrigonâ, anticè obtusâ, posticè dilatatâ; cardine marginali recto.

A somewhat trigonal, depressed, and dilated shell, with the umbones obtuse, the dorsal line straight, and the byssal margin nearly straight, or but very slightly curved; the surface nearly smooth, or faintly marked by lines of growth.

This species is near to *Dreissena antiqua*, Mell., but the dorsal margin is more produced, and the general contour of the shell more spathulate.

Not rare in the upper part of the Woolwich series at New Cross, Deptford, Lee, and Blackheath. It is rarely found perfect. Named after the late Dr. Mitchell, who obtained the best-preserved specimens of this shell at New Cross, during the cutting of the Croydon railway.

MODIOLA DORSATA, n. sp.   PL. II. fig. 14.

A rare species—the specimen is hardly sufficiently perfect for an exact determination of its characters. It differs from the preceding species in the umbo not being so terminal, and the form being less spathulate and more compressed.

From Sundridge. Mr. Prestwich's collection.

PSAMMOBIA? CONDAMINI, n. sp.   PL. II. fig. 15.

Testâ ovato-transversâ, inæquilaterali, depressâ, subinæquivalvi, concentricè et irregulariter striatâ; margine antico rotundato, postico rostrato, attenuato, sinuato; margine postico subincurvato, declivi.

An ovate and somewhat spathulate-form shell, inequilateral, the surface marked with concentric irregular striæ; anterior margin rounded, posterior extremity produced and sinuated, posterior dorsal margin somewhat incurved.

This shell, which is referred with some doubt to the genus *Psammobia*, from its association with fluviatile forms, appears to be readily distinguished from the other Eocene species by the more spathulate form and the position of the umbones being nearer to the anterior margin.

This interesting form was found by the Rev. H. De la Condamine, in the clay bed at Counter Hill, Deptford.

AURICULA (CONOVULUS) PYGMÆA, n. sp.   PL. II. fig. 17.

A few small shells, apparently belonging to this genus, have been found by Mr. Rosser in the upper beds at Woolwich.

The shells are conical, and consist of four or five somewhat depressed volutions, and an ovate aperture with one fold in the columellar lip, and another towards the base.

CERITHIUM BOWERBANKII, n. sp.   PL. II. fig. 18.

Testâ turritâ, brevi; anfractibus subplanis, longitudinaliter nodoso-costatis; costis obliquis, transversim 3–4-plicatis; suturâ subprofundâ.

A turrited shell with nine or ten somewhat depressed volutions, with six to eight nodose costæ, which are obliquely arranged in longitudinal rows, and crossed transversely by three or four transverse obtuse ridges.

Rare in the upper beds of the Woolwich series. From Mr. Bowerbank's collection.

CERITHIUM GRACILE, n. sp.   PL. II. fig. 19.

Testâ elongatâ, gracili; anfractibus depressis costatis; costis parvis subobliquis; suturâ lineâ ornatâ.

An elegant and slender shell with numerous volutions, furnished with eight or nine small oblique costæ; suture slightly depressed and marked with a fine line.

Rare in the clays and fossiliferous sands of Woolwich. From the Rev. Mr. De la Condamine's collection.

CERITHIUM LUNNII, n. sp.   PL. II. fig. 20.

Testâ turritâ, brevi; anfractibus 7, transversim bicarinatis; interstitiis longitudinaliter striatis.

A small conical shell of about seven carinated volutions; the two principal obtuse carinæ occur on the body of each volution, with a smaller one near to the suture: the intermediate spaces are longitudinally striated.

A rare shell. It occurs with the last species. From Mr. Lunn's collection.

HYDROBIA PARKINSONI, n. sp.   PL. II. fig. 21.

Testâ ovato-conicâ, lævi; anfractibus 5 rotundatis, ultimo ventricoso; aperturâ obliquâ, ovatâ; suturâ subprofundâ.

A very small conical shell, with five or six rounded and smooth
volutions; the last volution is somewhat ventricose, with an ovate
aperture.

This species much resembles *Paludina intermedia*, Melleville, but
that shell is smaller, more obtuse, and the form of the aperture
different.

Common in the Woolwich beds from Guildford to Upnor. Named
after Mr. J. Parkinson.

From Mr. Prestwich's collection.

HYDROBIA WEBSTERI, n. sp.   PL. II. fig. 22.

This species much resembles the preceding, but is very slightly
larger, and has a more expanded and rounded mouth, which gives it
a more elegant appearance. It is a rarer form, and occurs in the
same beds.

Named, like the preceding species, after a well-known investigator
of the geology of our Tertiary districts.

PALUDINA LENTA, Sow., var. β. Mor.   PL. II. fig. 23.

Testâ ovato-conicâ, lævi; anfractibus 5–6 subrotundatis; apice obtuso;
aperturâ subovatâ.

A smooth conical shell, with five or six rounded volutions, the
apex obtuse, and the aperture somewhat ovate. This form, which
is difficult to distinguish from the *P. lenta*, Sow., is also considered
by M. Deshayes to occur in the Soissons (Lower Eocene) beds, and
to be the same as that found in the Isle of Wight.

Common in the Woolwich beds at Peckham, New Cross, and
Counter Hill.

Notes on the ENTOMOSTRACA *of the* WOOLWICH *and* READING
SERIES. By T. RUPERT JONES, Esq., F.G.S.

1. CYTHERIDEA* MULLERI, Münster, sp. PL. III. fig. 7. Bosquet,
   *Entomostracés fossiles des terrains tertiaires de la France et
   de la Belgique*, p. 39. pl. 2. fig. 4 a–f.

The valves of individuals of this species have been collected in great
number by Mr. Rosser in the Woolwich beds; both in the shelly
clays (of the middle of the series), and in the pebbly sand above the
clays. I have also found them in some plenty in clay with remains
of oyster shells from Woolwich, and I have met with rare specimens
in the "Oyster-bed" at Clay Hill, Shaw, near Newbury.

Generally the English specimens slightly differ from M. Bosquet's

* Cytheridea (*Bosquet*) is a subgenus of Cythere. (*Müller*), a minute bivalved
Crustacean inhabiting salt and brackish waters.

figures in almost wholly wanting the longitudinal parallel furrows on the ventral surface, which are continued transversely and concentrically across the anterior half of the valve; faint traces only of the concentric furrows being occasionally seen, though irregular transverse furrows full of pittings are conspicuous in old specimens. One such transverse furrow, immediately posterior to the "lucid spots" near the centre of the valve, is always present, even in young specimens. I have not yet met with well-preserved individuals retaining the setæ of the surface.

Varieties of *Cytheridea Mulleri* occur throughout the Tertiary formations; being found in Hesse, Austria, Bohemia, Westphalia, France, Belgium, and the Netherlands, in the *Eocene*; in Touraine (*Miocene*); and in the Netherlands (*Pliocene*). M. Bosquet also records this species as recent,—living in the Zuyderzee, Holland. In England varieties of this species occur in the Coralline Crag, the Barton Clay, and the tertiary sands of Coldwell Bay.

2. CYTHERIDEA MULLERI, Münster, sp.; var. TOROSA, Jones. PL. III. fig. 8.

The variety differs from the typical *C. Mulleri* in having the surface of the valves raised up into 1–7 irregular lumps or bosses. Of these knobs, which are often but ill-defined, sometimes seven can be counted on one valve. The spots most usually occupied, when the bosses are but few, are the posterior part of the valve and the central part immediately in advance of the place of the "lucid spots."

This variety has some resemblance to the *C. tribullata*, figured and described by Dr. A. E. Reuss, Haidinger's Verhandlungen, vol. iii. p. 60. pl. 9. fig. 10, one specimen of which (since lost) I have found in the Barton Clay. In general form *C. torosa* resembles that variety of *C. Mulleri*, in which the posterior extremity is contracted and acuminate (var. *acuminata*, Bosquet ?).

Found plentifully together with the typical form in the above-mentioned Woolwich deposits by Mr. Rosser.

3. CYTHERE WETHERELLII, Jones. PL. III. fig. 9 *a*, 9 *b*.

This elegant little species of *Cythere* proper has valves of an ovate shape, contracted posteriorly, compressed on the ventral surface, and with a somewhat triangular indentation at about the middle of the dorsal part. The profile of either valve is almost a parallelogram. The surface of the valves is ornamented by a delicate reticulation, the meshes of which are formed by slightly raised anastomosing borders.

I found several specimens of *C. Wetherellii* in clay with oyster-shell fragments from Woolwich.

The name borne by this new species is well known to the students of Tertiary Geology.

4. CYTHERE KOSTELENSIS, Reuss, sp. *Haidinger's Verhandlungen*, vol. iii. p. 68. pl. 9. fig. 22. PL. III. fig. 10.

Two specimens of a minute oblong *Cythere* from amongst Mr.

Note on the FOSSIL PLANTS *from* READING.
By J. D. HOOKER, M.D., F.R.S., G.S. &c.

THE fossils collected by Mr. Prestwich may be all safely assumed to represent a vegetation differing in no important respect from that at present inhabiting the north temperate zone ; but none of them afford sufficient data for approximating to the generic affinities of the plants to which they belonged*. After a careful collation of the specimens with many existing plants comprised in the present floras of Europe, Northern Asia, and North America, I find no characters by which they may be allied to those of one of these countries more than another. Indeed I feel satisfied that similar forms of existing plants might be associated by natural causes in any of these countries, but that they would not necessarily belong to the same species, or even genera, in all.

The total absence of any remains indicative of a tropical vegetation is important ; for although forms of foliage precisely similar to these leaves from Reading are even more abundant in some tropical countries than in temperate ones, it is legitimate to suppose that had the association resulted from a tropical vegetation, some more direct evidences of their origin would have been forthcoming.

I do not see that any objection can be urged to the assumption that the climate of the epoch during which these plants flourished was a temperate one, experiencing summer heat and winter cold, and that it was not colder than that which now prevails in England ; for the large size and membranous appearance of many of the leaves, which, like those of the maple, lime, poplar, &c., are annual, indicate some duration of summer warmth ; and the leaf-buds (figured 24, 25, and 26) are similar to those of various trees which lie dormant for a considerable period of the year. It may also be remarked that there are no appearances of articulations at the base of the leaves, such as would suggest the probability of any of them belonging to Leguminous or other plants with compound foliage, which in the present distribution of vegetation in the north temperate zone indicate a warmer mean temperature than England now enjoys.

The absence of any traces of Coniferous† or other gymnospermous vegetation, and of ferns, is a point of considerable interest ; for in all

---

* These important observations by Dr. Hooker on the probable temperature of this period were made perfectly independently of my own, for, when they were written, he had not read the previous part of this paper, published in the last Part of the Journal, p. 136, nor have I, until after the printing of the above, had any communication with him on the subject of these plants. The conclusions, therefore, to which we have both arrived, upon independent evidence, respecting the apparently moderate climate prevailing here at this old Eocene period, and the absence of those tropical forms which abound in the succeeding London Clay period, furnish strong corroborative proof of the truth of this singular fact. In my former paper on the Thanet Sands I had arrived at the same conclusion respecting the temperature of the sea in which this oldest of our Tertiary deposits was accumulated (Quart. Journ. vol. viii. p. 260).—[J. P., Jun., April 15, 1854.]

† Coniferous wood, however, is present in the Woolwich series of East Kent, and a Fern at Counter Hill.—[J. P., Jun.]

beds of an earlier epoch presenting as many species as are preserved
in this, ferns especially predominate. It must, however, be borne in
mind, that in the temperate floras of many parts of the northern
hemisphere, neither ferns nor gymnosperms are usually associated in
any great numbers with large-leaved dicotyledonous trees. In Japan,
I believe that Coniferæ and large-leaved Dicotyledons are associated,
as also in some parts of America; in England ferns generally accompany similar forms of foliage to the Reading fossils; whereas in Si-
beria, where broad-leaved dicotyledonous trees are abundant, ferns are
extremely rare; as is also the case, I believe, in many parts of North
America.

There is no foliage resembling that of grasses, sedges, or rushes,
among the Reading specimens, nor any appearance of organs of
fructification.

With regard to the individual fossils of these beds; all, except
figs. 22 and 23, are decidedly Dicotyledonous and Exogenous, 'and
none present structural or physiological characters of importance,
either in texture, form, or nervation. Figs. 22 and 23, from having
parallel veins, may be assumed to be monocotyledons; of these, 22
is too anomalous-looking for me to hazard even a conjecture as to the
appearance or nature of the plant to which it belonged; while there
are few natural orders amongst Monocotyledons to which 23 might
not be referred.

Though the leaves preserved in the Reading beds are all of the
very commonest forms in the vegetable kingdom (of Dicotyledonous
plants), I do not find that they exactly resemble those of any living
English species; and indeed even were the resemblance so close that
I could not distinguish them from existing forms, I should not consider myself warranted in drawing any conclusions therefrom; because, in the first place, the normal or typical form of leaf in any
species can seldom be decided by one specimen or at one epoch of
growth; secondly, because very similar leaves may belong to very
different species; thirdly, because the top, base, margin, and stalk of
a leaf are all absolutely essential for identification of the species to
which it belongs, and these are not all present in any of the Reading
specimens; and fourthly, because in these, as in all fossil leaves, the
important characters of texture, pubescence, and colour are necessarily
obliterated.

It would be very easy to produce from an herbarium leaves so
similar to 1, 2, 6, 12, 13, 14, 18, &c., as to deceive the inexperienced
into instituting crude affinities; but after a very careful comparison
of these fossil leaves with those of willows, poplars, oaks, maples,
Myricæ, Rhamni, and such familiar genera as must suggest themselves to every one, I find that while I cannot advance beyond plau-
sible suggestions, nor give better reasons for such affinities than those
presented by outline, I can adduce a copious list of far less familiar
genera belonging to widely different natural orders, to which there
are as good grounds to refer these leaves, as to the genera I have
enumerated. It must indeed be evident to any one acquainted with
the real value, in a systematic point of view, of characters derived

from foliage, that it merely requires a *leading idea* to suggest affinities when imperfect remains of foliage are alone at the naturalist's disposal. I have no hesitation in saying, that were I assured from collateral evidence of the flora of the Reading beds being intimately allied to that of India, I should find no difficulty in producing the allied living representatives; and the same may be said of the vegetation of many other parts of the globe : it requires, however, some general acquaintance with the plants inhabiting different parts of the world, to appreciate the fallacious nature of the evidence afforded by leaves; these being of all organs the least important for the higher purposes of classification : a fact rendered familiar to the botanist by the habitual practice of naming a species of one genus from the similarity of its foliage to that of some other plant often in a totally different natural order.

There are two points to which I may allude, as being of practical importance to be borne in mind in examining questions of this nature. One is the extreme difficulty found in identifying the imperfect remains of existing plants, although we may be familiar with the flora to which they belong; and the other is, that when the clue to specific identity is lost, and a false identification is made, it is generally very wide indeed of the truth. My attention has been particularly drawn to these facts in foreign countries, when examining recent deposits in silt; and, though I am quite ready to admit that the power of identification in such cases depends as much upon a degree of skill or tact, which differs in amount with every individual, as upon absolute botanical knowledge, still I think that no one who has not resorted to an *experimentum crucis* of this sort can form a just idea of the real difficulties of the task, of the number of species he may make of different leaves of the same plant, of the false affinities he may draw, and the false conclusions to which he may be led.

Had the fossils of the Reading beds been presented to me in a recent state, and without my knowing their native place, I do not believe I should have been able to approximate with any tolerable degree of certainty to their affinities one with another, or to their position in the vegetable kingdom; and as I further do not think that they are even generically recognizable, I cannot deem it advisable to give them generic and specific names. The excellent plate which accompanies Mr. Prestwich's memoir serves all the purposes of a description, as the fossils possess no botanical characters of importance not represented in the lithograph (Pl. IV.).

It will not, I hope, be inferred, that, in refraining from naming and defining these vegetable remains, I am undervaluing their importance in a geological or botanical point of view. On the contrary, I think that giving them a fictitious value of this kind (which requires neither skill nor knowledge) is not only a perversion of the true aim and object of botanical science, but is calculated to mislead both geologists and botanists, besides swelling those already unmanageable catalogues of names for unintelligible fragments of vegetables, miscalled systems of fossil plants. Both in a geological and botanical point of view the Reading fossils are of first-rate interest and importance, as presenting us with an association of forms so entirely analogous to those now existing, as to leave no grounds for assuming that the now prevalent forms of foliage amongst Dicotyledonous plants did not predominate before the glacial epoch, posterior to which all the existing British plants, except the alpines, were introduced into our island, as has been shown by Professor E. Forbes in his Essay on the Flora and Fauna of the British Islands. I need hardly add, that the vegetation of the Reading beds presents no affinities whatever with that of the London clay.

Observations on the Specimens.—Fig. 1. is a very common form of leaf amongst various classes of Dicotyledonous plants, but does not exactly resemble any living plant with which I am acquainted. I assume that the scar at its cordate base represents the point of insertion on the stem, and that the leaf was therefore sessile.

Fig. 2. resembles the foliage of many species of European, North American, or North Asiatic Maples, but may be compared with equal propriety to the foliage of so very many other genera and natural orders that I cannot attach the smallest importance to the resemblance.

Figs. 3–8. I can suggest no resemblances for them that are worth recording. Figs. 3 and 15 possibly belong to the same species.

Fig. 11. resembles a fragment of fern-frond, but equally well represents a portion of the pinnatifid leaf of a composite or umbelliferous plant, and may indeed be referred to very many other natural orders.

Figs. 12, 13, 14. are very common forms of Dicotyledonous leaves that do not suggest any particular analogies to me.

Figs. 16–21. are quite unsuggestive to me. Of them, 18 may be a portion of a pinnatifid leaf, or may be a fragment of the midrib, &c. of a large entire leaf.

Fig. 23. I have alluded to as probably indicative of a Monocotyledonous vegetation.

Figs. 24–26. are finely-preserved buds of a Dicotyledonous shrub or tree, but of what natural family it is impossible to say. Poplars, Ericeæ, and many other orders have similar ones.

Fig. 27. I can make nothing of.

Fig. 28. I am equally at a loss to understand. Seeds have been suggested by one friend, and an insect's gall by another.

Fig. 22. Were I assured that this was what it appears, a petiole with two leaflets or lobes of a fan-shaped leaf, it would be curious; but I have been so often deceived on the one hand by appearances assumed by fragments of foliage, &c. thrown into accidental juxtaposition, and on the other by the false analogies that imperfect specimens suggest, that I cannot venture to give any opinion about it.

EXPLANATION OF PLATES I. II. III. IV.

PLATE I.

I. GENERAL SECTION. Gives a general view of the Tertiary series in their range from the Isle of Wight to the Isle of Thanet, chiefly for the purpose of showing the correlation of the Middle and Lower Eocene deposits of the Hampshire district with those of the London district, and also to give the position and relation of the Lower London Tertiaries, of which latter beds the succeeding diagrams give enlarged representations.

II. DIAGRAMS. These give the structure as determined from a number of actual (local) sections of the Lower London Tertiaries, and more particularly of the middle division thereof, or the Woolwich and Reading Series. This latter, in Diagram A, is divided horizontally into three areas—the western one (W.) unfossiliferous, the central one (C.) fluviatile and estuarine, and the eastern one (E.) marine. In terming the first unfossiliferous, this is used as a comparative term; for a few rare fossiliferous beds do occur, as the one containing the *Ostrea Bellovacina*, which is not unfrequently found at the base of the series, but in no other part of it; whilst a few feet higher in the series the rich but local bed of fossil plants at Reading is placed. Apart from these exceptions, the great mass spread through this area contains no trace of organic remains. The horizontal extent of the fluviatile beds is well-marked by the lenticular dark-coloured mass in the central area. The marine character of C in the eastern area is apparent at a few localities only; a large portion of the mass contains no fossils. The numbers refer to sections actually observed; of these the following are described or mentioned in the text of this or of preceding volumes :—

DIAGRAM A.

	Loc.	Sect.	Page		Loc.	Sect.	Page
Hungerford		1	85	Royal Mint		21	149
Pebble Hill		2	85	Whitechapel		22	150
Newbury		3	87	Bromley, nr. Stratford		23	151
Red Hill		4	87	Charlton		24	103
Reading (Bath road)		5	88	Woolwich		25	102
Sonning Hill		7	89	E. of Bexley		29	107
Twyford, Berks		8	89	E. of Green St. Green		31	107
Starveall		11	90	Gravesend		32	107
Penlands		12	90	Shorne		33	107
Hedgerley		13	vi. 268	Upnor		34	107
Uxbridge		14	91	Otterham Wharf		35	109
Hanwell		15	94	Near Faversham		36–7	109
Castlebear Hill		16	94	N.W. of Boughton		38–9	109
Twyford, Middlesex		17	95	Boughton		40	109
Bayswater		18	96	N.W. of Canterbury		42	110
Trafalgar Square		19	148	E. of Herne Bay		43	111
Bank of England		20	143				

In addition to the foregoing sections there are the following, which are not described in the previous pages, and of which explanations are hardly necessary, as they are either described elsewhere, or else the dotted lines show the beds they traverse and the relative thickness thereof :—

Loc. Sect.

    6 ...... Katesgrove pit, Reading.   Dr. Buckland in Trans. Geol. Soc. ser. 2. vol. iv. p. 276.

  10 ...... Section at the brick-field on the hill between Maidenhead and Marlow.

  26 ...... Experimental pit sunk on the S. side of Plumstead Heath.

  27 ...... Well on Bexley Heath.

  28 ...... Old pit on the hill W. of Crayford. (This is drawn too near 29.)

  30 ...... Section on the sides of the lane leading into Darent Wood from Darent.

  41 ...... Well-section on Boughton Hill.

DIAGRAM B.

Loc. Sect.	Page	Loc. Sect.	Page
Chesham 1 90		Chobham ... 5... vol. iii.pl,14.f.10.	
Hedgerley......... 3 ......vol. vi. 268		Guildford ... 6... ....vol. vi. 260	

To these we have to add the following—

Loc. Sect.
>   2 .... Brick-field at Oak End near Chalfont.
>   4 .... Well-section.

DIAGRAM C.

Loc. Sect. Page		Loc. Sect. Page	
4 miles N. of Ware 1 92		Royal Mint 7 149	
1 mile E.S.E. of Hertford... 2 92		New Cross, Naval School*. 8 105	
Chalk pits near Northaw ... 3 92		New Cross, Railway 9 104	
Winchmore Hill 4 145		Sundridge Park................13 100	
Colney Hatch 5 145		Hayes Common................18 99	
Shoreditch.................... 6 143		Keston Common 19 99	

The following are the additional sections not described in the text:—

Loc. Sect.
>   10 ...... Lewisham (see Buckland in Trans. Geol. Soc. ser. 2. vol. iv. p. 287).
>   11 ...... Belmont near Chiselhurst.
>   12 ...... Section in brick-field on the hill half a mile N.W. of Chiselhurst
>   Common.
>   14 ...... Section of the shaft at the chalk-pits on the S. side of Chiselhurst
>   Common.
>   15 ...... Several small sections near Widmore and Leaves Green.
>   16 ...... Small cuttings on the road-side between Bromley and Hayes.
>   17 ...... Pits on the N. side of Hayes Common.

In these diagrams the local sections are not always taken on an exact straight line of section; where no sections offered on those lines, sections at short distances to the right or left of them have been taken. In looking at the diagrams, it is necessary to imagine that the unfossiliferous portion of A should be a mottled dark red, blue, and greenish colour, with subordinate beds of light yellow, which colours gradually pass, in the fluviatile area, into green at base, with grey, blue, red, and yellow above, which again give way in the marine area to a nearly uniform mass of very light green, assimilating greatly to the general tone of the underlying Thanet sands. The prevailing colour of the Basement-bed of the London clay should be ochreous of different depths of colouring, from very light yellow to deep ferruginous. It was intended originally to have coloured these Diagrams.

[Erratum, p. 142, in column of figures line 15 from bottom, for 100 feet read 164 feet.]

PLATE II.

Fossil Shells from the Woolwich Beds.

Fig.
>   1. Inside. } Cardium Laytoni, *Morris.* Richborough.
>   2. Outside.
>   3 a. Nat. size. } Siliceous cast of Corbula Arnouldii, *Nyst.* Oakwells.
>   3 b. Enlarged.
>   4. Perfect. } Corbula Regulbiensis, *Morris.* Reculvers.
>   5. Outside.
>   6. Outside......Corbula Regulbiensis, var. β, *Morris.* New Cross.
>   7. Outside. }
>   8. Inside. } Cyrena cordata, *Morris.* Deptford.
>   9. End view.

* *Local Sections* 8 and 9 should be placed near together in the Diagram.

Fig. 10. Exterior. } Cyrena intermedia, *Melleville.* Woolwich.
    11. Interior. }
    12. Exterior. } Modiola Mitchelli, *Morris.* New Cross.
    13. Profile. }
    14. Cast (imperfect) of Modiola dorsata, *Morris.* Sundridge.
    15. Exterior of Psammobia Condamini, *Morris.* Counter Hill.
    16. Side view of Ampullaria subdepressa, *Morris.* Woolwich.
    17 *a.* Nat. size. } Auricula pygmæa, *Morris.* Woolwich.
    17 *b.* Enlarged. }
    18. Cerithium Bowerbanki, *Morris.* Woolwich.
    19. —— gracile, *Morris.* Woolwich.
    20. —— Lunnii, *Morris.* Woolwich.
    21 *a.* Nat. size. } Hydrobia Parkinsoni, *Morris.* Woolwich.
    21 *b.* Enlarged. }
    22 *a.* Nat. size. } Hydrobia Websteri, *Morris.* Woolwich.
    22 *b.* Enlarged. }
    23. Paludina lenta (*Sow.*), var. β, *Morris.* New Cross.
    24. Patella. Sundridge Park.
    25. Dentalium. Herne Bay.
    26. Serpula. Sundridge Park.

PLATE III.

Remains of Fishes.

Fig. 1 *a.* Posterior }
    1 *b.* Anterior } aspect of an abdominal Vertebra of Lepidosteus. Upnor.
    1 *c.* Lateral }
    2 *a.* Inferior } aspect of a Vertebra of a Fish. Woolwich.
    2 *b.* Terminal }
    2*. } Cycloid? scales (imperfect). Woolwich.
    2**. }

Remains of Plants.

    3. Impression, in sandstone nodule, of the Cone of an Abies. Reculver Cliffs.
    4. Seed-vessel. Counter Hill.
    5. Vegetable remains ;—possibly compressed seed-vessels. Counter Hill.
    6. Leaflet of a Fern, like Asplenium. Counter Hill.

Entomostraca, from Woolwich.

    7. Cytheridea Mulleri, *Münster,* sp. : left carapace-valve.
    8. Cytheridea Mulleri, var. torosa, *Jones* : right carapace-valve.
    9 *a.* } Cythere Wetherelli, *Jones.* Left valve and the dorsal edge of the
    9 *b.* } right valve.
    10 *a.* } Cythere Kostelensis, *Reuss,* sp. Perfect specimen, showing its left
    10 *b.* } valve and the dorsal aspect of both valves.
    11. Cythereis plicata, *Rœmer,* sp. Left valve.
    12. Cythereis angulatopora, *Reuss,* sp. Left valve (imperfect).
    13 *a.* } Candona Richardsoni, *Jones.* Left valve, and the dorsal edge of the
    13 *b.* } right valve.

PLATE IV.

Impressions of Fossil Leaves from a Bed of Clay in the Railway Cutting near Reading (*vide supra*, p. 88, Plate I. Diagram A. Local Section 5 ; and p. 163).

[Notes on the relative abundance of the several forms in the specimens of the clay in Mr. Prestwich's collection.]

Fig. 1............... Phyllites... (*a.*) Single specimen, occurring with "*s*" in a group of "*b*."

2............... Phyllites... (*b.*) Abundant: occurs in groups; together with "*a*," "*c*," "*d*," "*e*," "*f*," "*g*," "*j*," large specimens of "*p*," "*r*," "*s*," "*u*," and large stem-like bodies.

3............... Phyllites... (*c.*) ⎫ Rare. Single specimens of "*c*," "*d*," and "*e*" occur on a small piece of clay, with

4............... Phyllites... (*d.*) ⎬ leaves of "*b*." A leaf similar to "*d*" occurs also with "*l*"; and another, but

5............... Phyllites... (*e.*) ⎭ with a long peduncle, occurs with "*p*."

6, 7, 8......... Phyllites... (*f.*) Abundant. In groups; together with "*b*," "*g*," "*k*," "*p*," "*q*," "*s*," and stem-like bodies.

9, 9*, 9**, 10. Phyllites... (*g.*) Abundant. In a compressed mass; and with "*b*," "*f*," "*j*," and "*s*." Nearly allied to "*b*."

11............... Phyllites... (*h.*) Rare (unique). With "*p*" and small stem-like markings.

12............... Phyllites... (*i.*) Single specimen, in very sandy clay.

13............... Phyllites... (*j.*) Abundant: in groups, with "*b*," "*g*," "*k*," "*p*," and stem-like bodies.

14............... Phyllites... (*k.*) Rare. Occurs with "*f*," "*j*," "*p*," and stem-like impressions.

15............... Phyllites... (*l.*) Rare. With a leaf resembling "*d*," large specimen of "*p*," and obscure grass-like impressions.

16, 16*......... Phyllites... (*m.*) Rare (two specimens): with "*p*."

17............... Phyllites... (*n.*) Single specimen: with "*p*."

18............... Phyllites... (*o.*) Single specimen; with traces of stem-markings similar to itself.

19, 20, 20* ... Phyllites... (*p.*) Abundant. Occurs scattered through very many portions of the clay; several leaflets often retaining their relative positions, as in fig. 20. A form similar to fig. 19, but larger, is also very common. Leaves of "*p*" occur with "*b*," "*d*," "*f*," "*h*," "*j*," "*k*," "*l*," "*m*," "*r*," "*s*," with a leaf like "*n*," and with obscure grass-like markings.

21............... Phyllites... (*q.*) Single specimen: with "*f*."

22, 23 .... Phyllites... (*r.*) Abundant in some pieces of the clay. (The relation of the leaf to the stem in fig. 22 is very obscure.)

24, 25, 26...... (Buds) ... (*s.*) Common; occurring with "*a*," "*b*," "*f*," "*g*," "*p*" and large "*p*," "*v*," and with leaves like "*e*" and "*j*"; but most commonly associated with "*b*" and "*g*." (The stem in fig. 24 is not connected with the bud.)

27............... (Stem) ... (*t.*) A ferruginous body in sandy clay.

28............... (Seeds ?)... (*u.*) Two specimens occur; with "*b*" and stem-like impressions.

29............... Phyllites... (*v.*) Single specimen, occurring with "*s*."

[*Note.*—The most abundant leaves are "*b*," "*g*," and "*p*"; less abundant, but also found in groups, are "*f*" and "*j*." Fragments of "*r*," and the buds "*s*," are not uncommon. Ferruginous relics of pieces of wood are also met with in these clays.]

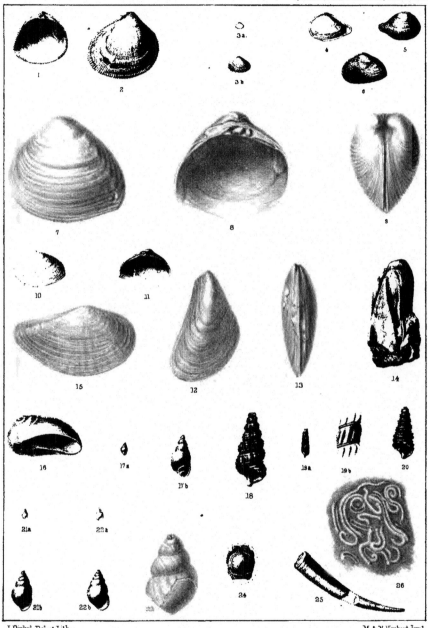

J. Dinkel, Del. et Lith. M & N Hanhart Imp.t

FOSSILS FROM THE "WOOLWICH AND READING SERIES".

G. West Lith

Ford & West Imp

FOSSILS FROM THE WOOLWICH AND READING SERIES.

Ford & West Imp.

ON

THE STRUCTURE

OF THE

STRATA BETWEEN THE LONDON CLAY AND THE CHALK

IN THE

LONDON AND HAMPSHIRE

TERTIARY SYSTEMS.

BY

JOSEPH PRESTWICH, Jun., Esq., F.G.S.

[*From the* QUARTERLY JOURNAL OF THE GEOLOGICAL SOCIETY OF LONDON
for August 1852, VOL. VIII.]

LONDON:
PRINTED BY TAYLOR AND FRANCIS,
RED LION COURT, FLEET STREET.
1852.

On the STRUCTURE *of the* STRATA *between the* LONDON CLAY *and the* CHALK *in the* LONDON *and* HAMPSHIRE TERTIARY SYSTEMS. By JOSEPH PRESTWICH, Jun., Esq., F.G.S.

Part III.*—THE THANET SANDS.

[Plates XV. XVI.]

(Part II. is deferred until a later period for reasons assigned in the subjoined note.)

THE first part of this paper, containing a description of that portion of the Lower Tertiaries immediately under the London clay, and which I termed the *"Basement Bed of the London Clay,"* was read before the Society in January 1850†. On that occasion my object was to show, that over the whole of the south of England tertiary area, a stratum forming a distinct and constant geological horizon clearly separated the London clay from the group of strata beneath it. The variable and interesting set of deposits between the Chalk and the London clay, including the "Basement Bed" of the latter, form the group hitherto called "the Plastic Clay Formation," which has been described " as composed of an indefinite number of sand, clay, and pebble beds, *irregularly alternating,*" and as being "members of one great series of nearly contemporaneous deposits," and essentially of fresh and brackish water origin. A careful examination of these strata has led me to believe, on the contrary, that a regular and definite order of superposition does exist, and that, instead of one series of alternating and intercalated strata, the conditions of structure and changes in the fauna show that there are five well-marked and distinct groups. Three, however, of these groups are apparently synchronous. Therefore the number of consecutive and separate divisions of the Lower Tertiaries may be reduced to three‡.

The term "Plastic Clay Formation" was originally given to this series in conformity with the divisions introduced into the French tertiaries by Cuvier and Brongniart, and was deemed applicable in consequence of the prevalence of variegated plastic clays at many

* The difficulty of obtaining, in the very variable strata of the "Lower Tertiaries," a series of sections that would, to my mind, satisfactorily establish their division into certain well-marked and persistent groups, has caused a longer delay than I could have wished in bringing this inquiry to a conclusion; and even now I find it advisable to describe the lowest member of the series before the central one, that should in natural order have followed next, the better to detach out of the series this latter more complex group, the description of which I must postpone to a future period. [J. P., Jun.]

† Quart. Journ. Geol. Soc. vol. vi. p. 252.

‡ It is true that certain characters and fossils pervade the whole series, and it may be thought unnecessary to establish divisions on features not more distinctive than those which guide us in these papers; but if not standing out in the strong relief indicating more important geological changes, they are, though small in degree, definite in form, and exhibit the more delicate shadings, stamped as it were by the diurnal occurrences of the time. They may be less impressive than the greater changes, but, as they are equally a part of the progress of the period, and depict the more gradual and lesser alterations in the configuration of the surface and in the distribution of life, they are full of interest and indispensable in filling up those details of the scene, which are so necessary to enable us to trace accurately each successive step in the history of the time.

places around London, and, again, more especially near Poole in Dorsetshire. But in the London district these clays are restricted to the western portion of the tertiary area, and occur but in one division of the series; whilst the Poole clays belong, not to the beds beneath the "London Clay," but form part of the "Bagshot Sands" above it. It is to be observed also, that these subordinate clays which give the name to this formation are the unfossiliferous portion of the series, and consequently they present only a mineral designation, whilst the palæontological type has been taken from the local and subordinate fluvio-marine group of Woolwich, Bromley, and adjacent districts, which, owing to its more favourable exhibition and rich store of organic remains, has attracted a larger share of attention than its relative development would warrant, and its characters have come to be considered the ruling, instead of the subordinate, although important, feature of the "Plastic Clay Formation." For out of nearly 3000 square miles over which the "lower tertiaries" are spread, these fluviatile and estuarine beds occupy really an area of only about 200 miles, nor is their vertical development relatively more important. In fact, so far from the more fluviatile conditions prevailing in the lower tertiaries, this series exhibits, on the contrary, throughout a great part of its range, proofs of a distinctly marine origin, whilst in another part the absence of fossils renders the question of origin uncertain. With regard also to their mineral structure, the conjoint use of the terms "London Clay Formation" and "Plastic Clay Formation" is apt to convey a wrong idea, inasmuch as they might be supposed to be two argillaceous deposits, or at least in some measure related in lithological characters, whereas they are, as is well known, totally dissimilar, the one formation being strictly argillaceous, and the other mainly arenaceous but with subordinate clays and conglomerates.

For these reasons therefore it seems desirable to change the name of this part of the Tertiary series, or at all events to restrict the present one to that portion of the series in which the plastic clays predominate; but still this name indicates a physical character so essentially a part of the ordinary properties of clays, that even in this more limited division their strongly marked *mottled* appearance would afford a less general and better designation. I therefore propose for the present merely to call the series between the London clay and the Chalk "The Lower London Tertiaries," and to subdivide them into the following groups in descending order :—

The Lower London Tertiaries.
1. *The Basement Bed of the London Clay.*
2*. *The Woolwich and the Mottled Clays, Sands, and Pebble Beds.*
3. *The Thanet Sands.*

* The order of subdivision of this part of the series will be given in the next and concluding part of this Paper.

With reference to the French tertiaries, M. d'Archiac has discontinued the use of the term "Formation d'Argile plastique," and named the series of strata beneath Calcaire Grossier, the "Sables inférieurs," subdividing them into six groups. In his extremely valuable 'Histoire des Progrès de la Géologie de 1834 à 1845' (note, p. 598), he observes, "Quelques géologues, trop préoccupés du rôle que joue l'argile plastique dont on trouve des amas plus ou moins étendus, mais

The sands which in Kent immediately overlie the chalk are here formed into a separate division, as I believe them to be entirely of marine origin, and distinct from the sands incumbent on the chalk at Hertford, Reading, Newbury, and elsewhere westward of London, but with which these Kent sands have been hitherto considered synchronous.   If such were the case, then certainly the mottled plastic clays and light-coloured sands lying between the chalk and the London clay at Reading might be regarded as the equivalent of the whole group of strata reposing upon the chalk at Woolwich and Upnor; but it can, I think, be proved that the Reading and Hertford beds are higher in the series than the Kentish sands, and that it is from the gradual thinning-out of the latter, as they range westward, and not by actual synchronous deposition, that this mottled clay group reposes immediately upon the chalk in Berkshire, and occupies therefore relatively to that formation the same position as the thick mass of lower sands in Kent *.

The grounds for this opinion will probably be better understood from the description of the several groups rather than by a prior enumeration of abstract reasons.   As before mentioned, I purpose commencing in this instance, as more convenient for the general argument, with the lowest beds, viz.—

"THE THANET SANDS†."

I have used this term in consequence of these sands being best exhibited, and marked by organic remains, in part of the Isle of Thanet

ordinairement discontinus, vers la base et vers le haut de ce groupe, ont désigné celui-ci sous le nom de *groupe de l'argile plastique*; mais cette expression, assez juste lorsqu'on ne considère que les environs de Paris, devient au contraire tout à fait fausse lorsqu'on embrasse la totalité du bassin. On ne tarde pas à reconnaître en effet que l'argile plastique proprement dite n'est qu'un accident de quelques mètres d'épaisseur subordonné à la partie inférieure d'une masse sablonneuse qui en a 80 et même davantage." These observations will apply to a certain extent to the English series; but the beds of mottled clay are in this country far more largely developed and hold a more important place in the Lower Eocene strata than M. d'Archiac describes them to occupy in France.

* Such is the difficulty of obtaining clear sections between the west of Kent and Berkshire, that even now it would not be safe to pronounce as a certainty that the whole of the Lower Tertiaries of the former county were of more recent origin than the Thanet Sands. It is possible that a small portion of the lowest beds may be synchronous with the latter. This, however, would only modify the divisions here proposed, and would not affect their general correctness.

† The only accounts we have of this lowermost bed are short abstracts of papers by Mr. Morris, Proc. Geol. Soc. vol. ii. p. 595, "On the Coast section from Ramsgate to Pegwell Bay;" and again at p. 450, "On the Strata usually termed Plastic Clay," wherein he describes the Woolwich and Upnor beds, and gives their relation to the Bognor and Herne Bay strata. In the same volume both Dr. Mitchell (p. 7) and Mr. Richardson (pp. 78 and 222) give some account of the cliffs at the Reculvers and Herne Bay, but these descriptions are very general. Brief notices of these sands, as forming part of the Plastic Clay series, occur also in Phillips and Conybeare's 'Geology of England' (pp. 37–51), and in papers by Mr. Webster (Trans. Geol. Soc. vol. ii. p. 196), by Dr. Buckland (Trans. Geol. Soc. vol. iv. p. 284), and by the Rev. H. M. De la Condamine (Quart. Journ. Geol. Soc. vol. vi. p. 440).

and in the immediately adjacent districts. It is these beds which form the cliffs at Pegwell Bay near Ramsgate (see section No. 1, Pl. XV.). They range inland from this point to Minster, but, although distinctly overlying the chalk, their position relatively to the other members of the "Lower Tertiaries" is not seen, as no beds higher in the series occur in this district. They are also well developed on the west bank of the Stour at the old Roman station of Richborough, and again on the side of the road in descending from Woodnesborough church towards Sandwich. The actual section at the former place, together with its relation to the strata at the latter place, and to the outcrop of the chalk, is shown in section No. 2, Pl. XV.

The Thanet Sands extend over nearly the whole of the district included between Sandwich, Canterbury, and the Reculvers, but are frequently overlaid by the middle division of the lower tertiaries, as in the section at Richborough. The higher beds of the lower tertiaries are here also wanting. The relation, however, of the lower divisions to the whole series can be studied in unbroken sequence in the cliffs between the Reculvers and Herne Bay, where the several members of the "Lower London Tertiaries" pass beneath the "London Clay" (see section No. 3, Pl. XV.). Further, not only is the co-relation of the several groups well exhibited in these districts, but each division has its distinct lithological character and fauna, and they are all under similar marine conditions, whereas, as these beds range westward, the frequent absence of fossils and the close similarity, in many cases, of lithological characters often render it difficult to determine the lines of separation of the different groups, except where the middle division contains subordinate fluviatile beds. In fact, in assuming that these Thanet Sands of the Reculvers and Richborough are the same as those which underlie the more fluviatile beds of the central group at Upnor and Woolwich (see sections 4 and 5, Pl. XV.), and repose immediately upon the chalk throughout Kent, Essex, and part of Surrey,—that they are distinct from the sands which alternate with the mottled clays incumbent on the chalk in West Surrey, Hertfordshire, Buckinghamshire, and Berkshire, and that the latter form a separate group,—it must be observed that neither mineral characters nor organic remains alone suffice to determine the question; for the proofs depend upon general structure and superposition, upon unity in the general design, and upon certain constant characters and conditions.

The following sections which I have given elsewhere[*], and for the use of which I am indebted to Mr. Van Voorst, will serve to illustrate the relative position and importance of the several divisions of the "Lower Tertiaries" in their range from east to west.

These sections are on a vertical scale of 50 feet to 1 inch.

[*] "A Geological Inquiry respecting the Water-bearing Strata of the country around London," 1851. 8vo. John Van Voorst, London.

Fig. 1.—*Section of the Cliff a mile and a half east of Herne Bay.*

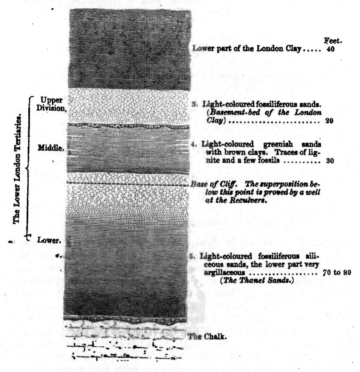

The Lower London Tertiaries.

Upper Division.

Middle.

Lower.

Feet.

Lower part of the London Clay..... 40

3. Light-coloured fossiliferous sands.
(*Basement-bed of the London Clay*) 20

4. Light-coloured greenish sands
with brown clays. Traces of lignite and a few fossils 30

Base of Cliff. The superposition below this point is proved by a well at the Reculvers.

5. Light-coloured fossiliferous siliceous sands, the lower part very argillaceous .... 70 to 80
(*The Thanet Sands.*)

The Chalk.

Fig. 2.—*General section of the strata beneath London.*

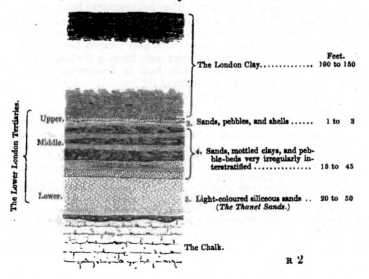

The Lower London Tertiaries.

Upper.

Middle.

Lower.

Feet.

The London Clay.............. 100 to 150

3. Sands, pebbles, and shells ...... 1 to 3

4. Sands, mottled clays, and pebble-beds very irregularly interstratified .... 15 to 45

5. Light-coloured siliceous sands .. 20 to 50
(*The Thanet Sands.*)

The Chalk.

Fig. 3.—*Section at the Brick-field, west of Hedgerley, six miles north of Windsor.*

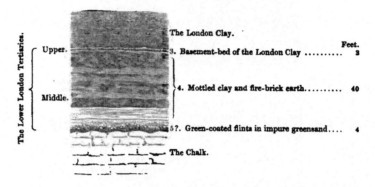

1. *Range and General Physical Characters.*

From the north-east of Kent, the Thanet Sands range past Canterbury, Faversham, Sittingbourne, to Chatham, occupying the lower grounds sloping down towards the Swale and the Medway, and occasionally capping the tops of the chalk hills for a short distance inland. Crossing the Medway, they form a broader zone by Upnor and Cobham, thence in detached outliers by Gravesend, Swanscombe, and Dartford. Here they stretch further south, spreading over a tract of country extending between the valleys of the Darent and the Cray, and thence by Farnborough to Addington and Croydon in one direction, and to Erith, Woolwich, and Deptford in the other. Throughout these districts these sands are with few exceptions very fertile, and their usually well-wooded surface * contrasts strongly with the more open chalk tracts. They form extensive hop grounds, and a large proportion of the well-known fruit orchards of North Kent are situated on this deposit†. Dipping under the London clay at Deptford and Lewisham, these sands pass beneath London, and become available in another important way, forming the large water reservoir to numerous artesian wells, both in London and in the districts immediately north and south of it‡.

At the Reculvers, the Thanet Sands appear to be about 70 to 80 feet thick, though only 25 feet of them are exposed in the cliff section; but a well, which was sunk at the village, reached the chalk after passing through a continuation of these sands for a further depth of

---

* Taken in conjunction with the upper divisions of the Lower Tertiaries.

† In the north-east of Kent these Thanet sands, with a slight covering of drift loam, form some of the most valuable arable land of the county.

‡ In London, owing to the large drain upon this source, the water no longer rises to the surface; but at a distance of four or five miles on either side of the Thames, as at Tooting, Garrett, Clapton, and Waltham Abbey, it still continues to overflow, although with rather diminished power (see work before referred to, p. 238, note).

about 50 to 60 feet. In some parts of the neighbourhood of Canterbury they cannot be much less than 80 to 90 feet thick. They then apparently maintain a tolerably uniform thickness of from 60 to 70 feet, as far as Chatham, Upnor (Sect. No. 4, Pl. XV.), and Gravesend. At Bexley Heath they have been ascertained to vary in thickness from 45 to 55 feet, and at Woolwich I find that they are 60 feet thick. Beneath London their thickness averages from 30 to 40 feet. They then become more rapidly thinner as they trend underground further westward, being only 20 feet thick at Wandsworth, 17 feet at Isleworth, 7 feet at Twickenham, and 3 feet at Chobham, beyond which they thin out, although I believe that originally they probably had a range westward co-extensive in some measure with the green-coated flints overlying the chalk. Along their south line of outcrop westward of London, they are exposed at Croydon and Carshalton, and disappear, I think, somewhere about Ewell or Epsom *, but the sections are too few and imperfect to determine this point. To the north of London the Thanet Sands do not range so far as Hertford, for there, and also at Northaw, as I shall afterwards show, the sands and conglomerates which repose immediately upon the chalk belong to the middle division of the Lower Tertiaries. (See figs. 1, 2, & 3.)

In North Essex the zone of outcrop of these sands usually occurs on the slope of hills, and they therefore form a very narrow belt, which is further frequently so obscured by drift, that they do not constitute any marked feature in this district. Owing to this cause and the want of sections, their structure there remains uncertain †. Their thickness may be from 30 to 50 feet. In South Essex, however, they are well exhibited in the line of country between Purfleet, Grays, and East Tilbury; and are as fully and similarly developed there as in the opposite part of Kent.

[Besides the localities mentioned elsewhere in the text, the following are some other places at which sections of the *Thanet Sands* are exposed—Harbledown and Whitehall westward of Canterbury; around Boughton near Faversham; on the N.W. of Shottenden Hill, four miles S.E. from Faversham; and again in the lanes traversing Bysing Wood, one mile W. from Faversham; the hill between Key Street and Newington Street, near Sittingbourne; Ottersham Quay, near Rainham; and in the lane leading from Lower Rainham to Rainham, and that between Tweedale and Gillingham; road between Stroud and Gad's Hill, and west slope of Gad's Hill; lane leading from the high-road to Shorne Ridgeway, and also the one leading

---

* In the brick-field at Nonsuch Park, near Ewell, the " Mottled Clays " are well exhibited, and evidently descend very near to the chalk, but the section is imperfect. In the railway-cutting at Epsom I found the " Thanet Sands " reduced to a thickness of 14 feet. At Headley-on-the-Hill, the mottled clays with an underlying band of *Ostrea Bellovacina* repose immediately on the chalk, without the intervention of the Thanet sands. At Fetcham, a few miles west from Epsom, a bed of sand 25 to 30 feet thick overlies the chalk, but I believe it to belong to the " Mottled Clay " series, as it is underlaid by the bed of *Ostrea Bellovacina*.

† The country is so obscure on the borders of Herts and Essex, that I cannot well determine where the " Thanet Sands " end and are succeeded by the " Mottled Clay" group. This latter, however, is in full force at Ware, and again near Bishop Stortford, but its structure is here very variable, frequently passing into sands difficult, without better sections, to distinguish from the " Thanet Sands," which, judging from several small sections, probably commence somewhere near this latter point.

to Shorne, and from Gad's Hill to Higham; several lane cuttings between Cobham, Ifield, and Thong; south side of Windmill Hill, near Gravesend; especially the lane leading from Betsham to Stone, on the S.W. side of Swanscombe Wood, near Greenhithe; the lane leading from Darent to Darent Wood, just where it enters the wood, and the lane leading from Bexley to Baldwin's Park; lane leading up the hill N. of the Abbey Wood Station; the lanes and roads in the neighbourhood of North Cray, St. Paul's Cray, and Orpington; the lane just east of Kevingdown near St. Mary's Cray; pit on the Bromley road just below the windmill at Chiselhurst; lane sections and pits at Grays, Little Thurrock, Chadwell, and West Tilbury; pits at Charlton; others on the hill between Lewisham and New Cross; and pit in Coombe Lane, Croydon.]

2. *Lithological Character.*

The mineral structure of this deposit is very simple. It consists essentially of a base of fine light-coloured quartzose sand, mixed, in its lower beds more especially, with more or less argillaceous matter, but never passing into distinct clays. It also contains a small proportion of dark green grains*, which sometimes give to these beds, otherwise on the whole of a very light yellow or stone colour, an extremely slight ash-green tinge; but in the stratum, 2 to 6 feet thick, immediately lying upon the chalk, they so predominate as to form an impure argillaceous greyish greensand, very constant in its position and characters. Examined through a microscope, the grains of sand appear colourless and subangular, worn, but not rounded. In the upper part of this deposit they form a loose unadhering mass made up almost entirely of pure quartzose grains, but in descending, these bright transparent grains appear mixed with an opaque whitish argillaceous powder. The argillaceous matter is usually light-coloured, and does not therefore colour the sands, merely giving a certain amount of cohesion, so that when dry the beds are sometimes semi-indurated. In some places, however, the clay with which the sands are mixed is darker-coloured, as in the lower beds at Pegwell Bay† and Herne Bay. A peculiarity of these clayey sands is the very marked difference of colour which some of them exhibit when wet and dry—a difference greater than usual. In places, beds, which when wet are of a rather deep dark grey colour, not only become many shades lighter when dry, but actually seem to lose all colour, and turn so white as to resemble chalk at a distance. The top of this deposit is also occasionally coloured ochreous by the peroxide of iron, as at Richborough, Herne Bay, and at Boston Common near Plumstead. With these exceptions the general colour and appearance of the lower sands is remarkably uniform, hardly varying throughout Essex, and in Kent from Faversham to Greenwich. It rarely forms very distinct strata, excepting always its basement-bed, but exists as a thickly bedded mass of fine sand (in great part nearly white), except where, in the N.E. of Kent, it becomes, in its lower beds especially, darker and more argillaceous, and shows a well-defined stratification.

* It is, however, the middle group of the "Lower London Tertiaries" that is more particularly marked by the presence of green sands; they form one of its distinctive characters.

† It is this bed which probably helps to form the good anchorage-ground of the Downs, which are opposite to Pegwell Bay.

The upper part of these sands near London, and throughout the greater part of Kent, appears to be almost perfectly free from carbonate of lime, and in the middle and lower parts usually mere traces of it are present.   A rough analysis of six specimens from various localities yielded only from 1 to 2 per cent.   At Herne Bay and Pegwell Bay, however, carbonate of lime is present in greater abundance, so as to be readily detected by the ordinary tests.   It forms, a few feet from the top of the deposit, at these places, a tabular bed of large, hard, flat, concretionary masses, effervescing strongly with dilute acid.   At Wingham, near Canterbury, these beds form a considerable thickness of semi-indurated fossiliferous marls.   As this division approaches London, the carbonate of lime almost entirely disappears *: owing to this cause, and the perfect permeability of the strata, even the carbonate of lime of the shells, of whose existence we have some evidence, has been entirely removed.

A distinctive feature of this division is, that it never contains layers or beds of those rounded black flint-pebbles so common in the overlying divisions, nor does it ever exhibit subordinate beds of those mottled clays which so well mark the middle division.   A few rounded flint-pebbles, some few even as large as a cannon-ball, have been occasionally found in the mass of the lower sands, but they are usually dispersed singly, and are of very rare occurrence.

Mica is sparingly disseminated in the sands.   At Pegwell Bay, however, it occurs in a thin band of sandstone, in quantity sufficient to divide it into fine laminæ.   The peroxide of iron slightly tinges some of the beds, and forms occasionally small nodular sandy concretions and casts of the interior of the shells.   It is sometimes present in the form of veins traversing the sands diagonally, and also in patches as stains in the sands, but it never forms solid masses or layers of ferruginous sandstone.   With the exception of the calcareous sandstones of Pegwell Bay and the Reculvers, the Thanet Sands very rarely, if ever, contain blocks or layers of concretionary sandstone. At Erith, such masses of flat, tabular, very hard sandstone have, it is true, been found near the top of the pit †; and in the lane leading from Gad's Hill to Shorne Ridgeway, a block of this description was to be seen, apparently in situ, a short time since in a cutting through either the upper part of these sands or the lower part of the middle division.   These sands may possibly have furnished some of the large masses of sandstone which so commonly occur in the drift on the edge of the chalk downs in Kent, but I believe that the bulk of them were derived from the next division of these Lower Tertiaries, and more especially from the "Basement-bed of the London Clay."

Small grains of selenite are, according to Mr. De la Condamine, frequently mixed in some abundance with these sands in the neighbourhood of Blackheath.

A very marked feature of the "Thanet Sands" is the constant occurrence at the very base of the deposit, and immediately reposing on

* At Faversham even the few fossils which are preserved are almost all in a silicified condition, and only traces of carbonate of lime are present.

† It is uncertain, however, whether these do not belong to the middle division.

the chalk, of a layer of flints of all sizes, just as they occur in the underlying chalk, from which in fact they appear to have removed comparatively without wear or fracture; for they are almost as perfect as the undisturbed flints, but present this difference, that instead of their usual white or black coating, these flints are almost invariably of a deep bright olive-green colour externally; the white outer coating, which is often very thick, seems removed (as though by an acid), and the flint then stained green. So strong is the colour, although it forms a mere film, that flints removed by denudation from this bed, subjected to great wear and many changes, and imbedded in fresh beds, whether of the Tertiaries or the Drift, can always be recognized by the peculiar green colour which they invariably retain. The colour in fact seems to be not a mere stain, but an actual alteration in the structure of the flint, arising apparently from its having entered into a chemical combination with the iron of the mud or silt in which they became imbedded, forming in consequence a true silicate of iron. There is frequently a thick inner brown stain of the peroxide of iron, but as in the silicate the iron is usually in the state of the protoxide, it would almost appear as though the flints had been imbedded at the sea-bottom in a ferruginous mud, and that then some cause, productive of an action on the silica, and a decomposition or deoxidization of the mineral containing the iron, acted simultaneously on the two, and brought them, in presence, into a state in which they would readily combine. To this however I merely direct attention; it is a subject which needs a special inquiry. If it should prove to be, as I anticipate from the few experiments I have made, a true chemical combination, it will be a curious fact, for almost all the minerals in which the silicate of iron is a main ingredient, as the chlorites, amphiboles, pyroxenes, &c., belong to rocks of igneous or metamorphic origin. Its formation by moist means seems to be the exceptional case; but should the view here suggested be correct, it will show that there may be cases in which sedimentary beds of greensand may have derived their characters from changes subsequent to their deposition, as well as by the more usual direct disintegration of the unstratified and metamorphic rocks.

There is on the whole in the Thanet Sands a uniformity and breadth of character entirely wanting in the overlying division of the Lower Tertiaries, which deposit is on the contrary extremely variable in its structure, showing rapid changes within short distances and great variety of lithological composition. This well-maintained regularity in the one, whilst the accompanying overlying beds undergo at the same time considerable alteration, is in fact one of the features which serves to mark the two divisions, notwithstanding that the middle group, in its many phases, occasionally puts on characters so resembling the lower ones as to render it difficult to distinguish them apart. This fact will, however, be brought out more clearly in describing hereafter the next or middle division of the Lower Tertiaries.

For a more particular account of the lithological characters of this deposit at a few given places, see the descriptions of sections, p. 250, and Explanation of Plate, p. 261.

3. *Organic Remains.*—The fauna of this division of the Tertiary series is both limited in its species and confined in its range. In a few localities only are its fossils at all abundant, and they occur in patches and irregular layers, in which, although the number of individuals is sometimes great, the species are always few. Nevertheless they form a well-marked and distinct group, a large proportion of which is peculiar to this deposit. This scarcity of organic remains is in part attributable probably to the mineral character of the strata, for these being almost entirely composed of fine siliceous sands, with an admixture of clay and carbonate of lime only (apart from a few exceptional cases) in very small and variable proportions, they are generally very porous and permeable. It is these beds which, as before mentioned, constitute the main water-bearing strata beneath the London Clay. They everywhere admit of the passage of water, with which they are invariably charged when below a certain level. The consequence of this is, that the substance of the shells has been almost always removed, or, where it remains, it is generally in an extremely friable state. Where the sands are sufficiently argillaceous, the casts of the shells often remain; but where this is not the case, even traces of them are of very rare occurrence. Where, however, in addition to the clay, carbonate of lime is present in appreciable quantity, then the shells are preserved in considerable numbers, but they are generally very tender and difficult to remove.

By these observations I do not mean to imply that the "Thanet Sands" may have been originally equally fossiliferous in West as in East Kent, for it is probable that the causes which have favoured the preservation of the shells when dead, may also have tended to their development when living. That it is at the same time a true cause to a certain extent, is evident from the fact that in a few exceptional cases, which we shall hereafter mention, where the fossil has by chance been brought into a condition to be uninfluenced by the action of water, then a few isolated proofs of the existence of animal life, in areas otherwise barren, have been preserved.

At the south end of the section at Richborough, the fossils are numerous and perfect. A few yards further north, and still on the same level, the external casts only are found. Many of these are in a beautiful state of preservation, but are exceedingly soft and friable. At the other end of the section the impressions are scarce, and the shells still more so. At Pegwell Bay and Herne Bay the Thanet Sands happen to be more argillaceous and calcareous than usual, and there the shells are more numerous and more regularly distributed, whilst the irregular calcareous concretions and the few layers of semi-indurated marls have served in both places to preserve the organic remains. In the upper bed, however, of loose incoherent yellow sand at Herne Bay, the irregularity in the occurrence of the fossils is again observable. At their highest level, near the Reculvers, they are full of friable shells, which become scarcer, and finally disappear, although numerous impressions remain, as the bed trends westward and dips beneath the central beds of the Lower Tertiaries.

A peculiar condition of the fossils sometimes occurs at Richborough and the Reculvers; in some of those cases where the shell has been removed, the animal matter has resisted decomposition and forms an earthy brown semi-elastic film covering the internal cast. In burning it gives off ammonia in abundance. Judging from the same test, animal matter is often traceable in the blackish green mud-like sediment in which the green-coated flints are imbedded.

On the side of the road on Woodnesborough Hill, about one furlong N.N.E. of the church, I found a few years ago fragments of numerous shells in the sands 30 to 40 feet above the chalk. In the lanes 1 and 1½ mile W. of Ash, leading down the south slope of the hill, along which the road from Sandwich to Canterbury passes, I have found casts of the *Cyprina Morrisii*; and again at Wingham, nearer to Canterbury, there is a considerable thickness of the Thanet Sands in a semi-indurated state and containing numerous impressions of shells. The road just out of the village, and leading to Preston Street, cuts through these beds, whilst on the top of the hill the sands of the central division of the Lower Tertiaries are largely quarried. In a field just below the cottages 1¼ mile 13° W. of N. from Wingham Church is a bank of the Thanet Sands full of casts of shells; and again on the sides of the lane leading up E. from the small valley halfway between Upper Hoath and Beaksbourne Street, and just two miles 22° S. of E. from Canterbury Cathedral, is an excellent section of the Thanet Sands in their semi-indurated condition and abounding in fossils, but all in a state of casts both internal and external. On the high-road about 1½ mile W. from Canterbury I have also found traces of casts of shells.

In all these places, the characteristic and by far the most abundant shell is the *Cyprina Morrisii*. The *Cucullæa crassatina*, one or two species of *Artemis* or *Cytherea* (including the *C. orbicularis* of Edwards), the *Thracia oblata*, *Pholadomya cuneata*, *Corbula longirostris*, a small *Leda*, and *Ampullaria subdepressa*, are far from uncommon. Other species are comparatively scarce.

A large number of the bivalve shells have been drilled by Zoophagous molluscs, but the proportion of shells belonging to this latter class preserved in these strata is very small.

Westward of this district the organic remains of the Thanet Sands become exceedingly rare. Some years since Mr. Crowe found the *Cucullæa crassatina*, and, I believe, a few other shells, but all in the state of siliceous casts, in the lower part of the Thanet Sands between Faversham and Boughton*, but the section no longer exists. I have carefully examined numerous sections between Faversham, Sittingbourne, Chatham, Upnor, and in many parts of the north-west of Kent, without being able to find more than slight indications of fossils, and even these indistinct traces are uncommon†. I have met

---

* It is said to have been in a field near the brook in Nash Park. If so, it could not have been many feet above the chalk.

† Since writing the above, I have found in a bank bordering the lane, one furlong due S. from Oakwell Farm, which is, by the Ordnance Map, exactly 2¼ miles due W. from Faversham Church, a seam full of shells in the state of semi-opaque siliceous casts. The *Cyprina*, *Cucullæa*, and a *Cytherea* are common. The silicification

such traces between Tweedale and Gillingham ; and at the ballast-pits at Erith* the casts of bivalve shells are occasionally found. Mr. Morris states that the cast of the *Pholadomya* has been met with in the lower sands at Woolwich. Mr. Taylor confirms this fact, inasmuch as he has found impressions of shells in the sands at the large ballast-pit near the Charlton station, and amongst them an indisputable cast of a *Pholadomya*. In the various sections of these sands which I have examined in Essex, I have never been able to find any organic remains.

There are, however, some very curious oviform bodies occasionally met with in considerable abundance in the lower part of the Thanet Sands. I first noticed them in Pegwell Bay, and afterwards at Shottenden Hill ; more recently I have found them in still greater quantities at Bexley†, and in a pit one mile nearly due W. from West Tilbury Church. They form short quill-like tubes, consisting of an aggregation of egg-shaped bodies about the size of cress-seed (see Pl. XVI. fig. 11). There is no organic structure visible, but this is apparently owing to the organic matter being removed and replaced by an infiltration of argillaceous matter from the surrounding matrix. Is it possible that these bodies may be the eggs of Gasteropodous Molluscs ?

Throughout Kent the traces of vegetables in a very fragmentary state are not uncommon. They are generally mere small indistinct impressions in the soft sand, or sometimes equally indistinct fragments of carbonaceous matter, but they never occur in the connected form and to the extent which they do in the overlying group. At Grays and Woolwich long tubular fucoidal-looking casts are not uncommon ; and east of Herne Bay the large flat tabular masses of calcareous sandstone are often covered with long vermiform impressions and casts, apparently of *Fuci* or of spongiform bodies.

In the determination of the species of Molluscs in the accompanying list, Mr. Edwards and Mr. Morris have been so good as to assist, and the latter to undertake the description of the new species. I give columns of the three principal fossiliferous localities, but, as before mentioned, there are other localities in which many of the species are found. To Mr. T. Rupert Jones I am indebted for an examination of several specimens of the Thanet Sands for Foraminifera. He found them only in a few specimens, and then but rarely ‡. The chief locality where they occur is Pegwell Bay.

At Richborough small bones and scales of fishes occasionally occur, but I could not meet with any specimen sufficiently perfect to determine the species. Teeth of the *Lamna* are also found in several places.

is not very perfect, some portion of the shell being generally wanting. Very beautiful casts, in clear transparent quartz, of a very small *Corbula*, are, however, perfect in form and very abundant. Sponge *spicula* are also abundant.—*May* 1852.

* Mr. Morris informs me that teeth of the Shark have been found in the Thanet Sands at Erith. I have just found there a large *Cyprina*.—[July 1852.]

† In the lane leading towards Dartford Heath.

‡ Mr. Jones has also been enabled to add to my list a few Foraminifera and one Entomostracan, that he had previously collected from the Thanet Sands of Pegwell Bay.

Organic Remains of the Thanet Sands.

c Common. r Rare. cc Very common. rr Very rare. ccc Very abundant.	Richborough.	Pegwell Bay.	The Reculvers.	Highest vertical range in the English marine Tertiaries.
UNIVALVES.				
Ampullaria subdepressa, *Morris* (a.)... c	*	*	*	
Calyptræa trochiformis, *Lam.* ? .... rr	...	*	...	Barton Clay.
Chemnitzia or Eulima, a very small species .... rr	...	*		
Dentalium nitens, *Sow.* (a*.) .... r	*	*	*	Barton Clay.
Fusus, one or two species .... r	...	*	*	
Rostellaria or Aporrhais.................. rr	*			
Scalaria Bowerbankii, *Mor.* pl. 16. fig. 9 (a†.) .... rr	...	***	*	
——, a smaller species (b.) .... rr	*			
Trophon subnodosum, *Mor.* pl. 16. fig. 10. .... rr	...	...	*	
BIVALVES.				
Arca, one, or probably two, small species (c.) .... r	*			
Astarte tenera, *Mor.* pl. 16. fig. 6 (d.) r	*	...	*	Basement-bed L. Clay.
Cardium, large species .... rr	...	*		
Corbula globosa, *Sow.* ? c	*	*	*	Barton Clay.
—— longirostris, *Desh.* (e.) c	*	*	*	Bracklesham Clay.
Crassatella .... rr				
Cyprina Morrisii, *Sow.* ccc	*	*	*	Basement-bed L. Clay.
——, a rather larger species (f.) c	*	*	*	
Cytherea orbicularis, *Mor.* pl. 16. fig. 5. c	...	*	*	
——, a rather smaller species (g.) ... r	*	*	*	Basement-bed L. Clay.
——, a very small species.............. cc	*	*		
Cucullæa crassatina, *Lam.* (h.) c	*	*	*	Mid. Div. L. L. Tert.
Glycimeris Rutupiensis, *Mor.* pl. 16. fig. 2. .... r	...	...	*	Mid. Div. L. L. Tert.
Leda substriata, *Mor.* pl. 16. fig. 7. ... c	*	*		
Lucina (i.) .... r	...	*		
Modiola .... r	...	*	*	
Nucula Bowerbankii, *Sow.*.............. c	*	*	...	London Clay.
—— fragilis, *Desh.* (j.).................. c	*	*	*	
—— margaritacea, *Lam.* ?.............. c	...	*	*	Barton Clay.
Ostrea, a very small species .... r	*	*		
——, a large species .... rr				
Panopæa granulata, *Mor.* pl. 16. fig. 3 (k.) r	...	*	*	
Pecten Prestvichii, *Mor.* pl. 16. fig. 8. rr	*	...	*	
Pholadomya cuneata, *Sow.* c	...	*		
—— Koninckii, *Nyst* (?) (l.) c	*	*	*	
Pinna .... r	*	*		
Ringicula turgida .... rr	...	...	...	Barton Clay.
Sanguinolaria Edvardsii, *Mor.* pl. 16. fig. 1. c	...	*	*	
Saxicava compressa, *Edw. MSS.* ? (m.) rr	...	*		
Thracia oblata, *Sow.* cc	*	*	*	London Clay.
ENTOMOSTRACA.				
Cythereis, nov. sp. .... rr	...	*		

c Common. r Rare. cc Very common. rr Very rare. ccc Very abundant.	Rich-borough.	Pegwell Bay.	The Reculvers.	
FORAMINIFERA.				
Nodosaria bacillum, *Defr.* .... r	...	*	...	Occurs in the L. Clay.
Cristellaria platypleura, *Jones* c	...	*		
—— Wetherellii, *Jones* c	...	*	...	Occurs in the L. Clay.
Rosalina Mariæ, *Jones* .... rr	...	*		
—— Beccarii ?, *Linn. sp.* .... rr	...	*		
Polymorphina ampulla, *Jones* .... rr	...	*		
——, sp. .... rr	...	*		
MISCELLANEA.				
Scales and small bones of Fishes ...... rr	*	*	*	
Traces apparently of Crustaceans ...... rr	...	*		
Traces of carbonized plants and fragmentary vegetable impressions cc	*	*	*	
Long tubular casts, probably fucoidal or spongiform c	*	*	*	
Sponge spicula.				
Oviform bodies, filling tubular cavities.				

(*a.*) This was first referred to the *Natica labellata*, which is quoted by M. d'Archiac as occurring in his "Sables Inférieurs," but not in the lower stage of it. M. Melleville also gives it from his lowest division of these sands near Rheims.

(*a*.*) The only species of *Dentalium* given by Nyst, from the "Système Landenien," is the *D. strangulatum*.

(*a†.*) This very much resembles a species brought by Sir Charles Lyell from the Lower Tertiary sands ("Système or Terrain Landenien" of Dumont) of Folx-les-Caves in Belgium, but the specimen is a cast, and not sufficiently perfect for positive identification.

(*b.*) The specimen is very imperfect, and may be the young of the preceding fine specimen, which is in the collection of Mr. Bowerbank. M. Nyst, on the authority of Galeotti, quotes the *Scalaria acuta?*, Sow., which is a Barton species, from the "Terrain Landenien" of Folx-les-Caves.

(*c.*) One of these much resembles the *Arca depressa*, Sow., which occurs in the Woolwich clay beds.

(*d.*) M. Nyst figures a specimen from the "Terrain Landenien" of Folx-les-Caves, and names it *A. inæquilateralis.* It closely resembles the English species.

(*e.*) M. Melleville gives this species amongst the fossils of his lowest division of the "Sables Inférieurs."

(*f.*) It is doubtful whether this be not the species figured by M. Deshayes as the *C. scutellaria*, a species mentioned both by M. D'Archiac and M. Melleville as of not uncommon occurrence in the lowest division of their "Sables Inférieurs." The figure given by Nyst of a specimen from some of the much more recent Tertiaries of Belgium is probably not Deshayes's species.

(*g.*) One of these species may possibly prove to be the *Cytherea Bellovacina*, Desh., which Deshayes states to be common in parts of the "Sables Inférieurs" of the North of France. M. Melleville also gives it.

(*h.*) This is also a characteristic species of the "Sables Inférieurs" of the North of France. M. d'Archiac places it in his 3rd division (reckoning upwards from the chalk); M. Melleville in his lowest.

(*i.*) M. Nyst figures a specimen (*L. Galeottiana*) which a good deal resembles the smaller Pegwell Bay species. Amongst other deposits in which it is found, he mentions the "Terrain Landenien."

(*j.*) This occurs in the "Sables Inférieurs" of Beauvais.

(*k.*) The *Panopæa* occurs in the "Système Landenien" of Belgium, and in the "Sables Inférieurs" of France.

(*l.*) This is apparently the *P. Koninckii* of Nyst, who figures it as a characteristic shell of the "Terrain Landenien." The *P. margaritacea* is also mentioned by Nyst as a fossil of the "Terrain Landenien," and by D'Archiac and Melleville as from the "Sables Inférieurs."

(*m.*) Resembles the *Saxicava Grignonensis* of Deshayes.

We have therefore in the Thanet Sands 39 species of Testacea, of which 24 are determined. Of these only 6 are common to the whole of the Eocene series, and 2 more range as high as the London Clay. Of the remaining 16 peculiar to the *Lower Tertiary strata*, 3 extend into the "Basement-bed" of the London Clay, and 2 to the level of the Woolwich group, whilst as many as 11, or nearly one half of the whole, are peculiar to the Thanet Sands. The distinction is not to be attributed to different conditions of the waters, for although at Woolwich this has necessarily operated by excluding the more marine species and introducing in their place others of fluviatile and æstuarine origin, still in, and adjoining, the Isle of Thanet, both the middle and upper divisions of the Lower London Tertiaries are marine, and consequently the conditions in this respect of the three groups are equal, and still the difference of fauna holds good.

Annexed are the detailed sections of the two localities where the Thanet Sands are most fossiliferous (the Reculvers excepted). Their relation to the other parts of the Lower London Tertiaries is shown in sections 1, 2, & 3, Pl. XV.

Fig. 4.—*Section of part of the Cliff at Pegwell Bay, near Ramsgate.* (*s* in Section 1, Pl. XV.)

Feet.

1. Drift of light-coloured brick-earth, with a thin irregular seam of gravel (angular and small round flints), mixed with broken fragments of the shells of the underlying beds, at its base 4–6
2. Light yellow slightly clayey sand with shells in layers and patches; " *a*," tabular masses of fissile micaceous calcareous sandstone, with few shells,—a very small *Corbula* often occurs in great abundance; " *b*," small calcareous concretions, in which the *Pholadomya Koninckii* is not uncommon; " *c*," large concretionary blocks, often very argillaceous; their lower surface frequently presents masses of shells, especially the *Cyprina Morrisii.* Traces of Plants occur both in " *b* " and " *c*." 16
3. Grey clayey sands, rather dark when wet, but lighter-coloured when dry (the upper part especially looking at a distance almost like chalk),—the lower part is more argillaceous and darker; " *d*," a seam of grey clay with shells in patches; " *e*," a thin layer of impure greensand full of very friable shells. Several shells, especially the *Pholadomya cuneata*, a *Nucula*, and the small *Cytherea*, together with frequent traces of plants, are dispersed in some abundance and in a good state of preservation throughout this bed, " 3 "... 15

Fig. 5.—*Section of the Sand-pit by the side of the Railway at Richborough Castle, near Sandwich.*

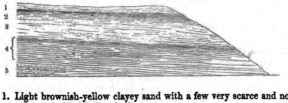

		Feet.
	1. Light brownish-yellow clayey sand with a few very scarce and not determinable bivalve shells	3
Middle division of the Lower Tertiaries.	2. Very sandy light brownish-grey clay full of small, rough, twig-like fragments or pieces of iron sandstone, with cores of yellow sand, and having the appearance of vegetable origin,—contains a very few and very small black flint-pebbles	2½
	3. Very light and loose ash-green sand, rather fine,—in some places coarser, with one thin seam of shells (*Corbula*, *Glycimeris*, and *Cyprina*). The lower part contains an occasionally ochreous layer. A few small round flint-pebbles are dispersed throughout. The lower part of this stratum has taken up part of the underlying bed, and the line of separation is, therefore, not very sharply marked	8
The Thanet Sands.	4. Rather bright ochreous clayey sand, passing down into a light brownish yellow colour, in some parts with seams of sandy clay. Casts of shells are common in this bed, but more particularly in the lower and more argillaceous part of it	7
	5. Light yellow loamy sand with shells in irregular layers and patches on the left hand of section. They are very abundant—in some places in fragments, in other places whole and perfect, but extremely friable	4

Beyond this a bed of hard semi-indurated sand, 3 feet thick, with a few shells, rises. Argillaceous beds, not well exhibited, succeed.

The surface on the top of this section consists of about 1 foot of earth, with a few pebbles, chiefly the rounded ones. The hill rises at the back about 10 feet higher, but no section is exposed. Small round flint-pebbles are numerous on the surface of the hill.

4. *Conclusion.*

From the facts brought forward in the preceding pages, but which, with regard to the middle division of the Lower London Tertiaries, will be described more in full hereafter, it appears that while this latter group exhibits on the same horizon, a fauna at one place marine, at another æstuarine, and at last passing into one chiefly fluviatile, the Thanet Sands maintain within the same area a uniform marine character. In its range westward the fossils are certainly few, but still the occurrence of the *Pholadomya*, which is never found in the Woolwich clays and conglomerates, or in the sands interstratified with the mottled clays, but is, as before mentioned, met with in the sands beneath the shelly fluviatile beds at Woolwich and Charlton, affords an unmistakeable proof of the different conditions under which the two divisions were formed. Taking therefore these facts, in conjunction with the persistent lithological character of the lower deposit, and the irregularity in this respect of the other group, we are, I think, justified in maintaining over the whole area the divisions which we have found more evident and marked further eastward, and in assigning to the lower one a distinct and separate place in the Eocene series.

Bearing upon this question is another point of physical structure, the details of which will be given at length in my next paper, but which I may briefly allude to here. It has been mentioned that the upper part of the Thanet Sands is usually light-coloured and very uniform in texture, whilst in many places the lowest bed of the overlying division consists of rounded black flint-pebbles imbedded in a coarse green sand. When their mineral characters are thus perfectly distinct, the worn and indented line of junction of the two groups is often very marked. Sometimes it seems as if the mud and pebbles of the upper bed had been driven and *splashed* into the soft upper surface of the underlying "Thanet Sands." All the phænomena point in the same direction, and, taken generally, go to prove a change of conditions between the two periods. In the one case we have a deposit, littoral probably, but distinctly marine, and in the other a variable accumulation of coeval marine, æstuarine, and fluviatile strata.

At the same time it is to be observed, that when, as frequently happens, neither division contains any fossils, if some of the other distinctive features are wanting, and the upper group becomes more arenaceous, lighter in colour, and the conglomerates more diffused, the separation of the two groups is sometimes extremely difficult, for they seem to pass one into the other and to form a series, the upper part of which is hardly distinguishable in general appearance from the lower *. It is only when the characters of one or the other become, as it were, more concentrated, that the separation is clearly marked.

There is an objection to these subdivisions which may at once strike those who have been accustomed to view the " Plastic Clay Formation" as a whole and as a series of recurring strata, arising from the occurrence at the base of the "Thanet Sands" of Woolwich and Upnor, as well as of the " Mottled Clays" of Reading and Newbury, of the layer of argillaceous greensand with the rough greencoated flints, reposing throughout the range of both divisions immediately upon the chalk, and presenting throughout very similar mineral characters. This common character has always been considered an argument in favour of the synchronism of the two groups. At the same time it did not escape observation that the *Ostrea Bellovacina* was never found in this bed in Kent, whereas it was common at Reading and Newbury ; but as even elsewhere in the latter district the occurrence of this fossil was by no means a constant character, its absence altogether in the former district was naturally not con-

---

* Even at the Reculver Cliff, notwithstanding the occurrence of organic remains, this is particularly the case, owing apparently to the materials of the upper bed of the Thanet Sands, having become mixed up with the lower part of the overlying division.

sidered very material*. It seems to me, however, that the oysters
are not part of the flint bed, but were deposited upon it—sometimes,
where little sand intervened, in contact with, or even partly amongst,
the flints—at other times, and which is more commonly the case, as
a separate and distinct layer overlying the flints. I believe that this
oyster bed belongs to the lowest part of the central division of the
" Lower Tertiaries." It has already been observed that this part of
that group often consists of coarse argillaceous green sands mixed with
more or fewer round flint-pebbles ; therefore when this stratum comes
into contact with the one containing the green-coated flints, the similarity of the matrix in either case is such as to render it difficult to
draw any line of demarcation between them. Now with the oysters
are almost always associated small rounded flints, which do not occur
with the green flints beneath the " Thanet Sands," and the two forms
of the flints exhibit the results of physical causes so entirely distinct
that they cannot possibly be the result of the same agency : the enormous wear necessary to produce so perfect a form as the ordinary
round flint-pebble could never have left the great, massive, angular,
green-coated flints as it were unscathed ; nor could the powerful but
transient action necessary to uproot these flints from the chalk have
sufficed to wear down and give finish to the more perfectly rounded
pebbles. These latter, after having been worn down elsewhere, must
have been spread over the former at a subsequent period, and mingled
with the *Ostrea Bellovacina* which was then living on the spot.

Still it is evident, from the peculiar and distinctive character of
these large angular flints lying on the chalk throughout the tertiary
area, that their accumulation is attributable to one and the same
cause—that their uprooting and dispersion must have been contemporaneous over the whole district. After this they were, in the instance of the Kentish area, covered by a thick deposit of sands, which
did not extend into the Berkshire area† (fig. 1 & 3, *supra*), or else
they have been subsequently denuded throughout the latter district
and this basement-bed alone left, and re-covered immediately by the
lower beds of the upper series, into the composition of which coarse
green sands so often largely enter, forming therefore with the green-
coated flint-bed a consecutive mineral series, not distinguishable from
one another when viewed as a local phænomenon‡. This thinning

---

* At the same time the *Ostrea Bellovacina* was known to occur at Woolwich,
in the upper and middle beds ; at Bromley in some intermediate beds ; and at
Northaw and Hertford in beds immediately upon the chalk and under a considerable thickness of sands—facts supposed to show the irregular dispersion of
this shell throughout the whole series, as well as the irregular grouping and distribution of the strata.

† The green-coated flints extend into the Hampshire tertiary district. Therefore the sea of the earliest tertiary time may have extended over all this area,
although the accumulation of strata was afterwards interrupted, or the Thanet
Sands have been denuded.

‡ Since writing the above, I am however informed by Mr. Lunn that he has
found, in the green-flint bed immediately over the chalk at Charlton, remains of
shells, apparently oysters, but in too fragmentary a condition for exact determination ; also that the workmen showed him a large and perfect specimen of an
oyster which they said came from this bed. This, however, is an exceptional case,

out of the Thanet Sands westward of London, and the rise of the "Ostrea Bellovacina" bed of Reading from the surface of the Chalk to the zone of the Woolwich fluviatile series at London, are points which are not clearly exhibited in open sections, but which are better made out by the sections afforded by the wells to the westward of London.

Although the Thanet Sands are limited in their range westward to about the parallel of Windsor, yet with regard to their range eastward it is probable that they attain a more important development in the north of France and Belgium than in England. I have seen them in the neighbourhood of Calais, where they underlie the London clay, and from the description of M. Galeotti* and Omalius D'Halloy†, it is probable that the beds overlying the chalk at Tournay belong to this same age. The *Pholadomya, Panopæa, Astarte,* and *Cucullæa* are there found in beds of nearly the same mineral characters, but their associates are species which do not occur in England. There is, however, apparently some error in the lists of these shells. When the results of M. Dumont's admirable researches are better known, the comparison of these lower tertiaries will be readily made. He has already published a sketch of the co-relations of the Belgian with the French and English tertiaries‡, but as it is unaccompanied by sections and without lists of organic remains, I cannot judge of its accuracy. In his visit to this country last summer, he pointed out to me the many characters common to these Thanet sands and to his "Landenian System," which occupies the same position in the Belgian series §.

The recent visit of Sir Charles Lyell to Belgium will, I have no doubt, remove the uncertainty which we feel respecting the organic remains, and throw light on the relations of the English with the Belgian tertiaries,—a point of much interest, as these two series are evidently much more closely related than the English are with the French series.

The lower tertiary beds in France have been described by M. Elie

as I have never myself found any traces of shells in this bed in the numerous sections of it I have examined throughout Kent, nor can I hear of their having been observed by others. It is, however, quite possible that the *Ostrea Bellovacina,* or some other large species of oyster, may occur in the Thanet sands, as several species of shells are common to this and the overlying group. I have, in fact, recently found a fragment of a large oyster in the lower part of these sands, near Faversham, but it is evidently not the *O. Bellovacina.*

* Mém. de l'Acad. de Bruxelles, vol. xii. 1837, and also his separate work on the geology of Brabant.

† Coup d'œil sur la Géologie de la Belgique, 1842.

‡ Rapport sur les travaux de la Carte Géol. de la Belgique, 1839, in the Bull. de l'Acad. Roy. de Bruxelles, vol. vi. p. 11. *Ibid.* vol. xvi. 1849. "Sur la position géologique de l'Argile Rupelienne, et sur le synchronisme des Formations tertiaires de la Belgique, de l'Angleterre, et du Nord de la France," *Ibid.* vol. xviii. No. 8, 1851.

§ Since writing this paper I have visited the "Système Landenien," in the neighbourhood of Mons and Tournay, and perfectly agree with M. Dumont in considering it synchronous with the "Thanet sands." His determination of the order of superposition of the Belgian tertiaries seems as skilful as, there is every reason to believe, it is accurate. I had not, however, an opportunity of examining any but the lower divisions of the Tertiary series.—*May* 1852.

de Beaumont *. He particularly notices the chloritic sands in the north of France as constantly reposing upon the chalk and forming numerous detached outliers, and discusses their relations to the lignites of the Soissonnais and to the Calcaire grossier. M. D'Archiac has since distinguished these sands under the designation of the " Glauconie inférieure," constituting the sixth or lowest division of his " Sables inférieurs," which include all the beds between the Calcaire grossier and the Chalk †. It is with this group that the Thanet Sands appear to me to bear the closest resemblance, although there are some anomalies in the evidence afforded by organic remains. The only fossils quoted by M. D'Archiac from these sands are casts of the *Cyprina scutellaria,* a *Serpula,* a species of *Sponge,* bones of *Emydes* and of a small carnivore (*Palæocion primævus,* Blainv.) ; whereas amongst the shells which he mentions as characterizing his fourth division of the "Sables inférieurs" (Grès et Sables coquilliers) are the *Cucullæa crassatina* and *Corbula longirostris,* the former one of the most characteristic species of the Thanet sands. With them are associated the *Ostrea Bellovacina,* two species of *Venericardia, Nucula fragilis, Cyprina scutellaria,* &c. These two divisions are separated by the " Lignites and Argile plastique."

Some marine beds, far more fossiliferous than the above, have been described by M. Melleville‡ and M. Hébert § in the departments of the Aisne and the Marne. M. Hébert considers that this deposit is synchronous with the sands of Bracheux and Abbecourt, and that they both underlie the lignites and repose immediately upon the chalk, except where the "Sables de Rilly" and the " Calcaire pisolitique" intervene. M. d'Archiac on the contrary is of opinion that these beds, equally with those of Bracheux, &c., are higher in the series, and above the " Lignites and Argile plastique ||."

In this uncertainty, and pending a fuller description of the fossils of these lower marine tertiaries in France, it would be premature to conclude with which one or more of these beds the "Thanet Sands" are the exact equivalent, although I have no doubt of its including the "Glauconie inférieure" of the more northern parts of France, but where unfortunately this stratum is comparatively unfossiliferous¶.

Neither the "Glauconie inférieure" nor the lower marine sands range to the south of the parallel of Paris.

---

* " Sur l'Etendue du Système Tertiaire inférieur dans le Nord de la France," Mém. Soc. Géol. de France, vol. i. p. 107, 1833.

† Bull. Soc. Géol. de France, vol. vi. p. 240, 1835; *Ibid.* vol. x. p. 173, 1839 ; and Hist. des Progrès de la Géologie, vol. ii. p. 599, 1848.

‡ Bull. Soc. Géol. de France, vol. ix. p. 214, 1838. Ann. des Sciences Géol. vol. ii. p. 7, 1845.

§ Bull. Soc. Géol., 2nd series, vol. v. p. 388, 1848 ; vol. vi. p. 695 *et seq.*, 1849 ; and vol. vii. p. 338, 1850.

|| Hist. des Progrès de la Géol. vol. ii. p. 607.

¶ Several other local works may be consulted with advantage on this subject ; amongst them are those of M. Buteux on the Department of the Somme, and M. Graves on the Department of the Oise.

General considerations respecting the distribution of land and water in the English Tertiary area at the commencement of the Eocene period.—In no part of the tertiary area of the south of England is there any indication of a passage either in mineral structure or in organic remains between the Chalk and the Tertiary series. With regard to the physical conditions, the change is most marked and abrupt. Extensive and deep wear of the chalk evidently took place before the commencement of the lowest Eocene deposits. In the neighbourhood of Calais, at St. Vallery-sur-Somme, Pegwell Bay, Upnor, Woolwich, Stortford, and thence to Reading, Newbury, Salisbury, Newhaven, and Alum Bay, the chalk invariably presents a worn though not very irregular surface, and is strewed over, as before mentioned, with those peculiar green-coated flints. This mass of flints, although generally not above 1 to 2 feet thick, in itself indicates a wide destruction of the chalk. But independently of this, another denudation had probably previously worn down a very large mass of the chalk along the southern boundary of the London tertiary area. In this direction all the upper beds, and a large portion of the middle beds of the chalk, have been removed; and it is probably owing to this cause that the chalk, which has been ascertained to be above 1000 feet thick at Saffron Walden, and is apparently about 800 to 900 feet thick at Luton and along its northern line of escarpment, becomes apparently gradually thinner as it ranges towards London, and eventually becomes reduced at the edge of the escarpment overlooking the Weald to a thickness not exceeding on the average 400 feet *. The following diagram (fig. 6), which gives the general representative section, independently of the exact conformation of the surface, from Saffron Walden to the chalk-escarpment above Godstone, exhibits the structure of the chalk here referred to :—

Fig. 6.—*Diagram to illustrate the thinning out of the Chalk in the direction of the axis of the Weald.*

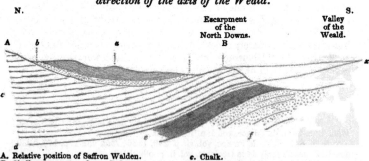

N.   S.

Escarpment   Valley
of the   of the
North Downs.   Weald.
B

A. Relative position of Saffron Walden.
B. Chalk escarpment above Godstone, surmounted with a patch of the Lower Tertiary beds.
a. London Clay.
b. Lower Tertiaries.

c. Chalk.
d. Upper Greensand.
e. Gault.
f. Lower Greensand and Wealden.
x. Point at which the present upper and under surfaces of the Chalk, if they were prolonged, would converge.

* At Bushey near Watford the chalk-marl was reached at a depth of less than 400 feet beneath the tertiaries, and at London the lower chalk without flints commences at about 250 feet below the surface of the chalk, which is here, as well

It therefore appears that the chalk was extensively denuded before, or at the commencement of, the deposition of the oldest tertiaries, and that this denudation was stronger towards the south than the north; consequently the chalk, to have been brought within the action of these denuding forces, must have had its surface more exposed in one direction than in the other, and have undergone, even at this early period, in order to have become so exposed, an elevation to the south of the tertiary area and about parallel with the escarpment of the North Downs. The phænomena in the Hampshire tertiary district seem to be very similar; although, from the complete denudation of the South Downs, tertiary outliers, like those on the North Downs, are wanting, still there are indications of the lower tertiary beds having spread over the chalk. It follows therefore that if the ratio of decrease in the thickness of the chalk were continued from Hertfordshire, then beneath the London tertiaries, and across the North Downs, to the Wealden area (before its denudation), it is probable that, before reaching the centre (x) of the latter district, the chalk had either thinned out altogether or else existed merely as a thin crust; and consequently that an elevation of the lower cretaceous and Wealden series, intermediate between the London and Hampshire tertiary districts, or in fact in the position of the present Weald, had already taken place before any of the tertiary beds were deposited.

It may be objected that the elevation of this central Wealden mass already existed before the chalk was deposited,—that it was a shoal in the old chalk sea,—and even that the cretaceous series formed originally but a thin covering over this part of the old sea-bed, and only attained their full development as the water became deeper towards the north. If this however were the case, there would be an overlapping in some part of the series, and we should further have the lower cretaceous beds (1 & 2, fig. 7) wrapping round this shoal with a thickness gradually increasing as we receded from it into deeper water, so that on the edge of the shoal itself the lower beds would be necessarily very thin or wanting, whilst we should have in the upper beds of the chalk near this centre (a) indications of a littoral zone.

But we find both the Gault and Upper Greensand on the whole as well developed in Kent and Sussex (y, fig. 8) as in Cambridgeshire and Bedfordshire (x). Nevertheless there is a change in the Lower Chalk —the Clunch of the latter counties is evidently a far thicker and more important rock than the Lower Chalk of the former counties. It is therefore not improbable that there was a slow and quiet movement of elevation in Kent, or of depression in Cambridgeshire, and whose commencement might date from changes that took place at the end

known, covered by 100 to 200 feet of tertiary strata. From Croydon and Epsom, towards Merstham and Dorking, there is evidence indicating that the chalk is probably not more than 400 to 500 feet thick, whilst on the summit of the North Downs overlooking Godstone, Reigate, and Dorking there are outliers of the *lower tertiary beds*, which reach to the very edge of the escarpment overlooking the *greensand district*; and from measurement of the chalk between the upper greensand and the base of these tertiaries, I find that at Dorking and Reigate the chalk is not above 400 to 450 feet thick, whilst above Godstone *it does not exceed a thickness of* 300 *feet*.

Fig. 7.—*Diagram showing the conditions that would have resulted from the deposition of the Cretaceous Beds on the edge of a shoal formed by the previous elevation of the Weald.*

a. Elevated mass of the Weald.   1 & 2. Lower Cretaceous strata, thinning out to the south,
b. Cretaceous beds.   whilst the Upper strata overlap successively
                                         upon the Wealden rocks.

Fig. 8.—*Diagram showing the relative thickness of the Lower Cretaceous beds, and the denudation of the Chalk, over the Weald.*

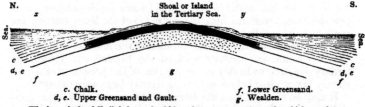

c. Chalk.   f. Lower Greensand.
d, e. Upper Greensand and Gault.   g. Wealden.

[The lower beds of Chalk below *x* should have been represented as rather thicker and the Lower Greensand rather thinner.]

of the Upper Greensand period and at the dawn of that of the Chalk; still it was not of that extent to prevent the extension over the southern area of an important mass of lower chalk and of the middle chalk with flints.   Neither the upper nor the lower chalk, however, possess that great development which they do in Herts and Cambridgeshire—the one apparently having been removed by denudation, and the other originally deposited in a thicker mass.

On either alternative, of a depression in Cambridgeshire or an elevation in Kent, the result would still be the same, in that we should have the chalk surface relatively higher and nearer to the sea-level in the latter than in the former county.   This would favour the wearing down of the chalk by the action of the sea over the present area of the Weald, and as we see reason to believe that the chalk within that area was removed or reduced to a thin shell, it is probable that some of the underlying beds of the green-sand or even of the Wealden might have become exposed to the denuding action.   See fig. 8.

There is no appearance, however, in the Lower Tertiaries of debris derived from any large mass of clay such as the Wealden, whereas the light-coloured sands, with traces of greensand and occasionally of carbonate of lime, forming the Thanet Sands, have a mineral character perfectly harmonising with a reconstruction out of the Upper Greensand chiefly, with the Gault and upper part of the Lower Greensand partially.   It would thus seem that only these portions of the lower cretaceous series had, together with the Chalk, at that time been raised to the surface, and furnished materials for the Thanet Sands.

Again, we find in the next or middle division of the Lower London Tertiaries an enormous accumulation of round flint-pebbles, which, generally speaking, could not have been rolled and worn into their present shape on the spots in which they are now found. They were, I believe, formed during the deposition of the Thanet Sands, and afterwards spread out by other operations on the surface of these sands and incorporated with the strata formed during the period of the Woolwich and Mottled Clay series which immediately followed.

From the foregoing considerations it is probable that there was some extent of dry land, possibly an island, somewhere intermediate between a line drawn on the north from Farnham towards Canterbury, and on the south between Winchester and Newhaven, and extending eastward into the north of France *; and that the long-continued wear on its coast accumulated on the shores extensive banks of pebbles, whilst the finer sediment produced at the same time, in conjunction with the debris brought down by the operation of streams, formed at a distance from the land the strata of this oldest Eocene epoch †. Diagram fig. 8 illustrates this hypothetical view.

One reason for believing that this land formed an island is, that had the land stretched far east and west it must have reached beyond the chalk-district, and it is more than probable that the currents and tides of the sea would then have drifted the shore-pebbles from the older rocks in one of these directions, and mixed them up with those derived from the flints of the chalk, along some parts at all events of the line of coast; whereas in an island the cliffs of which consisted exclusively of chalk or of soft beds of greensand (if without drift-gravel), the flints would form the only material capable of resisting long wear and of furnishing the beach-shingle ‡. On this view alone can I account

---

* In his memoir " Sur l'Etendue du Système Tertiaire inférieure " in the north of France, M. Elie de Beaumont arrives also at the same conclusion respecting the existence of an island in the position of the present Wealden and Boulonnais during the formation of the Lower Tertiaries period, and gives a sketch of the geography of that period. (Mém. Soc. Géol. de France, vol. i. p. 111, and pl. 7. fig. 5.)

† The extent of this land, however, I believe to have been small compared with that of the period of the Woolwich fluviatile and æstuarine deposits, for all the remains of plants are in a very fragmentary state and not in any mass, as though large rivers were wanting and the land were drained merely by small streams and torrents; in confirmation of which view it is to be observed also that there are no distinct river-deposits with fluviatile shells in the Thanet sands, which fact shows that the materials were either derived from the wear of the coast or from small streams which would not effect the uniformity of character of the marine deposit. This might require an immense period of time, but of this we have evidence in those really wonderful accumulations of rounded flint-pebbles before mentioned. Further, we know that the Thanet sands are spread much more widely over the chalk than are the fluviatile series, in consequence probably of a further elevation of the land and the conversion into dry land of part of the adjacent sea-bottom at the latter period.

‡ There is, I am aware, some difficulty in determining the origin of these round flint-pebbles. They are evidently chalk-flints, but they present some characters rather distinct from those of the ordinary chalk-flints of the neighbourhood of London. The fossils found in them are very scarce and not very conclusive. Mr. Flower, who has examined with great care large numbers of these pebbles, considers them derived from some more distant locality, as their organisms

for the remarkable freedom from all admixture of pebbles of the older rocks* in the enormous flint-pebble beds of the Lower Tertiaries. It is to be observed also that we have no chert-pebbles, which may arise from its more splintery structure, or from the sea not having encroached so far on the land as to have reached the cherty beds of the lower greensand.

Thus the changes in the remarkable area of the Weald appear to date back to a period possibly far anterior to that even of the lowest tertiaries. While, however, I am inclined to extend the action of the subterranean forces acting along that axis to an epoch antecedent to that at present assigned to it, I at the same time consider, with many other geologists, that the chief disturbances are of comparatively recent date. I cannot think that that denudation of the Weald which tended to give it the present form, or even its main features, was coeval with a gradual elevation during the London Clay period, and that the debris of the Wealden clays drifted out during this prolonged denudation supplied the materials for this more important eocene deposit. The denudation, or denudations, resulting in the present peculiar structure of the Weald, I would rather place in the newer pliocene and the post-pliocene periods†. Still, as before mentioned, I believe that a portion of the Weald was elevated at the commencement of the tertiary period, and that there was a long-continued and gradual action of the sea on that coast (during probably a very slight progressive subsidence), unaccompanied by the operation of any large rivers from the land; for the spread of the Thanet Sands appears to have been effected more by marine currents and tidal action than by river transport, if we can judge by the facts stated above, that no distinct fluviatile beds have yet been found in them, and that their marine character is preserved over their entire area. Small streams must necessarily have existed, but none of power sufficient to accumulate distinct and independent groups of strata.

The changes, therefore, which took place in the Weald during this tertiary period were, I conceive, confined to the planing down of the chalk and part of the greensand, whereby a large mass of strata was removed from this area,—an operation which must have greatly facilitated the further changes which, at a later period, ended in producing the existing striking configuration of the surface.

These views with respect to the distribution of land and water at this geological epoch are in some measure corroborated by the evidence of organic remains, for it is curious that the fauna of the Thanet Sands seems to indicate that the temperature of the sea in this district was rather lower than at the subsequent period of the London Clay. We cannot of course argue conclusively upon this point, but, merely viewing the question generally, the limited number of

differ from those of chalk-flints around London. I hope he will shortly make public the result of his researches on this subject.

* Except a very few quartz-pebbles which may have come out of the chalk.

† I do not here enter into the general question of the elevation of the Weald, as that will form part of a paper on the "Drift" of the South of England, which I hope at a future period to lay before the Society.

species, the prevalence of *Cyprina, Astarte, Glycimeris,* and *Thracia* in these strata, combined with the absence of such genera as *Pyrula, Cancellaria, Voluta, Conus, Mitra,* and *Pleurotoma,* of the numerous large Cephalopods, and other animal and vegetable products of a presumed warmer climate, which abound in the London Clay, rather tend to point out the *probability* of a lower temperature in the sea of the Thanet Sands,—a fact in unison with the physical evidence of a sea open apparently to the north, and an island presenting a barrier to the south, and extending probably from the central portion of the present Weald to near the eastern borders of France. By itself this circumstance would not be entitled to much weight, but as it has been shown that the physical conditions under which such a result is possible, are in themselves probable, we may not unreasonably view them to a certain extent in the relation of cause and effect, and consider that the probabilities in favour of both are increased by the corroborative testimony thus afforded.

EXPLANATION OF PLATE XV.

The following sections show the dimensions and position of the Thanet Sands at intervals in their range from east to west,—from the point where they are best marked to that near to which they disappear beneath the London Clay. After a range of a few miles further west, they thin out altogether (fig. 3, p. 236). In soft strata of this description the pit-sections are rarely permanent, although there are some which are at present good and illustrative. The sections, therefore, selected to serve as types are those which appear most permanent, two of them being coast-sections and not liable to any very great change, and the others being works opened to supply a constant demand and likely to continue to be worked for many years. All the sections are actual ones, except that of Woodnesborough Hill, which is planned from surface-outcrops and wells, and is introduced to show the relation of the sands at Richborough to the outcrop of the Chalk, and the probable thickness of the Thanet Sands. The same observation applies to a small portion in the middle of the Upnor section No. 4.

Sect. 1. Gives a view of the end of the Isle of Thanet cliffs adjoining the valley of the Stour. Pegwell Bay is about two miles west from Ramsgate. Cliffs of chalk only are continuous round the other parts of the so-called island. At the point *a* in section, a remnant, 3 to 4 feet thick, of the basement bed of the Thanet sands, with the usual layer of green-coated flints, reposes upon the chalk. Between that point and *b* the cliff is a good deal obscured by debris and the slopes made for the road which descends to the beach; and at *b*, where the section can again be resumed, the cliff is composed entirely of the tertiary sands and drift, so that the junction of the chalk with this mass of Thanet sands is not seen. From the dip of the strata at *a*, the high level there of the small portion of Thanet sands, and the position of the main mass at *b*, it is probable that a fault occurs between these two spots; I have not, however, seen it exposed.

From *b* to the cliff end at *c* the section is continuous, and shows perfectly well probably all the series of the Thanet sands except the very highest and lowest beds. The lowest part, towards *b*, consists of about 10 feet of light-coloured, grey, and greenish clayey sands with traces of Plants and of a *Ditrupa* or *Dentalium,* and, continuing in the direction of *c*, pass up into 12 feet of more argillaceous and greener beds, then into 10 feet of laminated darkish grey sandy clay with a few fossils, succeeded by 8 feet of grey clayey sand, drying white, and with numerous small fossils. This is overlaid by 15 feet of dark clayey laminated beds with a considerable number of well-preserved fossils. This last stratum and the remaining upper beds are described more in detail at p. 250, fig. 4. On the beach between *s* and *b* are numerous blocks of the sandstones and earthy concretionary limestones, many of which are very fossiliferous. At *a* the Tertiary strata dip about 2° W.S.W., and at *s* about 4° S.W.

Sect. 2. The branch-railway from Minster to Deal passes at the foot of the low hill on which Richborough Castle stands. A ballast-pit adjoining the line exposes the section here figured. The Thanet sands are seen rising at an angle of about 2° to 3° from beneath the sands of the middle division of the lower London tertiaries; there are here, however, so few distinctive features between them, that the separation is not at first easily recognized; a careful search will, however, detect a few peculiar fossils in the middle series, and in the Thanet sands the fossils are abundant, but very friable, at point *a*. For details of this section see fig. 5, p. 251. Between this and section No. 1 there is only the valley of the Stour with its marsh-lands. The strata in both places dip towards this valley.

Proceeding southward there is a tract of flat ground without sections, and the surface then rises to the ridge of low hills which run from Sandwich to Wingham and Canterbury. On the eastern extremity of the range stands Woodnesborough Church, in descending from which towards Sandwich the sides of the lane exhibit a tolerably good section of the Thanet sands with fossils, and overlaid by the sands of the middle division. On going down the hill in the other direction, the chalk is seen cropping out from beneath the Thanet sands: this part of the section is rather shortened; it represents a distance of 1¼ mile. The height of the hill is only approximate.

Sect. 3. This is the finest section of the Lower Tertiaries in the London district. Herne Bay is about 1½ mile west from the spot where this section commences. At a short distance east of the town, the London Clay rises and forms a sloping and grass-covered cliff for nearly a mile; the talus then becomes less and the section clearer, showing a considerable mass of the London clay, with few or no fossils, except casts of fragments of wood in iron pyrites. A little way further, the sands (3) forming the upper division of the lower London tertiaries rise at a small angle (2° to 3°) from beneath the London clay; they abound in fossils, but in an extremely friable state, except where preserved in the tabular calcareous blocks, *a*, or in concreted portions of the conglomerate, *b*. (For a description of this bed and its fossils see my paper "On the Basement-bed of the London Clay," in the Quart. Journ. Geol. Soc. vol. vi. p. 265.) This division is underlaid by the middle group, which is here composed of three closely allied strata, consisting at *c* and *d* of an upper bed of argillaceous greensand, a middle one in which brown clay predominates, with a few small flint-pebbles, and abounding in traces of vegetable remains, and with many fragments of lignite, and a lower division marked by coarse green sands; but as these beds trend towards *d* [the left-hand *d* which should have been *e*] they appear rather less argillaceous, and as a very light green sand, the line of demarcation between them and the Thanet Sands being, in consequence, at the end of the cliff towards the Reculvers very indifferently marked. Fossils are rather scarce; the few however that occur are the same as those found in stratum 4 at Richborough. This group, as well as "4" in the Upnor and Woolwich sections, will be described more in full in the next part of this paper. Owing to the great similarity in mineral character between the lower part of this middle division and the upper part of the Thanet Sands in these cliffs, their line of separation is often very indistinct.

Immediately east of the Bishopstone ravine the "Thanet Sands" rise from beneath the middle group (4). The first bed consists of yellowish sands with only a few patches of shells, but with numerous soft impressions, and varying in thickness from about 15 to 20 feet. Beneath them is a nearly continuous, tabular, light grey, hard, concretionary, calcareous sandstone, 1 to 2 feet thick, with few fossils, but often covered with large vermiform casts. Next follows 4 to 6 feet of light-coloured argillaceous sands with a few fossils. Below this a darkish grey semi-indurated clayey sand crops out, and is well exposed between high and low water mark. It abounds in characteristic and well-preserved fossils of the Thanet sands, by far the most abundant shell being the *Cyprina Morrisii*. This stratum forms the base of the cliff nearly to the Reculvers, and is throughout marked by the same fossils : at the same time, the top bed of the Thanet sands, which at first contains only a few shells, becomes more fossiliferous, and near there abounds in well-preserved but very friable shells, chiefly the *C. Morrisii*, together with the *Cucullæa crassatina, Thracia oblata*, and many others comparatively rare (see list, p. 248). The cliff ends at the Reculvers; the marsh-lands separating this spot from the Isle of Thanet then intervene; at Birchington the cliff rises again, but consists of chalk without any capping of tertiary strata. The relation, however, of the Thanet sands to the chalk was shown by a well dug at the Reculvers some few years since. I was informed that the chalk was reached at the depth of about 70 feet, after traversing sands which became more clayey in descending, and with shells in patches throughout. This position of the chalk is shown on the left of the section.

Sect. 4. Just below Upnor the hills approach close to the left bank of the Medway, and the numerous pits opened for ballast-sand exhibit some good sections of the lower tertiaries. (For a description of Stratum " 3," see paper before cited, Quart. Journ. Geol. Soc. vol. vi. p. 263.) The middle group " 4 " is considerably expanded, and consists almost entirely of sands; the upper bed is fossiliferous and of a light yellow colour, and the lower bed is of a very light tinge of yellowish green, with subordinate beds of small flint-pebbles, but without fossils. Between these two sands are a few feet of dark grey laminated clays and sands, full of *Cyrena cuneiformis, Melania inquinata*, and some other fresh or brackish water shells. The Thanet sands rise from beneath the sands " 4 " at the pit (at *b*) just behind Upnor village, but the characters of the two groups are here so much alike, that it is not easy at first to distinguish them apart, especially as neither contain fossils. They may then be traced at intervals along the river-bank, by Upnor Castle, to a chalk-pit on the foot-road to Stroud, where the lowest beds are seen reposing on the chalk, with the usual green-coated flints at their base. They are here much mixed with fine greensand, and are also without fossils. The dip at Upnor is about 3° N.E.

Sect. 5. This is a well-known locality and has been frequently described, chiefly however with reference to the upper beds, which abound in the so-called Woolwich shells. (For particulars of this section and its fossils I beg to refer to Dr. Buckland's paper, Trans. Geol. Soc. vol. iv. p. 284, and to the Rev. Mr. De la Condamine's paper in the Quart. Journ. Geol. Soc. vol. vi. p. 440.) The Thanet sands are here fine-grained, siliceous, and without organic remains, if we except traces of plants (in fragmentary casts and impressions), and the cast of the *Pholadomya* mentioned by Mr. Morris (see text, p. 265). The upper part of these sands are nearly white, very loose, and almost purely quartzose; in descending they become tinged ash-grey and yellow, and mixed with a small proportion of argillaceous matter, and with a perceptible quantity of greensand in their lower part. The basement-bed as usual is an impure greensand, with green-coated flints, and is only reached occasionally on the floor of the pit. The view here given is one at right angles to the road, and was exposed a few years since; this part of the pit is not now worked, and the sands are almost entirely sloped over. The present works are just round the end of this section. The Basement Bed of the London Clay is given with a query, as I am not yet sure whether the bed here so marked may not be an upper member of the middle division.

In the above sections the principal masses only of drift are shown. In No. 2 there is a drift in the valley between Richborough and Woodnesborough Hill. In No. 3, besides the drift marked on the top of the cliffs, there are some detached masses on the lower cliffs between *d* and the Reculvers. In No. 4, patches of a mixed drift occur occasionally in places on the slope of the hill above *b*, and a thick mass of brick-earth drift is worked at the base of it. The same, with gravel and mammalian remains, is largely developed at the foot of the chalk hill to the left of the section.

Description of some FOSSIL SHELLS *from the* LOWER THANET SANDS. By J. MORRIS, F.G.S.

SANGUINOLARIA EDVARDSII, n. sp.   Plate XVI. fig. 1.

Testâ ellipticâ, compressâ, inæquilaterali, transversim striatâ; anticè attenuatâ, posticè rotundato-truncatâ; umbonibus prominulis.

An ovate-lanceolate, inequilateral shell, somewhat compressed, marked by numerous fine, sharp, raised striæ, which are more prominent towards the lateral margins; anterior extremity attenuated, posterior extremity rotundato-truncate. Width rather more than twice the length.

Named in compliment to Mr. Frederick Edwards, of Hampstead, to whom we are indebted for much information on Tertiary Palæontology.

Herne Bay. Specimen figured, from Mr. Edwards's Collection.

GLYCIMERIS RUTUPIENSIS, n. sp.   Plate XVI. fig. 2.

Testâ transversâ, elongatâ, subæquilaterali, subconvexâ, transversim striatâ; lateribus rotundatis; margine medio subdepresso, margine cardinali calloso; umbonibus obsoletis.

A transversely elongated, nearly equilateral, and somewhat convex shell, with rounded extremities, the dorsal and ventral margins parallel; both valves having a slight depression in the middle, which extends to the ventral margin; lines of growth numerous, sharp. Width 2½ times the length.

This shell is distinguished from *G. angusta*, Nyst, by its more equilateral form, and by the dorsal margin being less angular, and the posterior extremity more rounded.

The species of this genus are very rare in a fossil state, having been only found at present in the Tertiary strata. The one above described is the most ancient known form, the other belongs to the Crag of Belgium and England.

Herne Bay. Mr. Edwards's Collection.

PANOPÆA GRANULATA, n. sp.   Plate XVI. fig. 3.

Testâ ovato-oblongâ, transversâ, inæquilaterali, granulatâ, transversim irregulariter striatâ vel undulatâ; margine medio subcompresso; lateribus rotundatis; umbonibus minimis, incurvis.

An ovate, elongated shell, with rounded extremities; somewhat cylindrical; the middle of both valves depressed near the ventral margin, which is rather straight; surface minutely granulated, and transversely striated and undulated. This shell is difficult to distinguish from the *P. intermedia*, Sow., and appears to be intermediate in general form and character to that species and the *P. corrugata*, Sow. (Dixon's 'Fossils of Sussex'); the ligamental and ventral margins are straighter, and the shell more compressed ventrally than *P. intermedia*. The surface is also minutely granulated, which character has not been observed in the other species.

The difference of habitat may, however, have modified the forms assumed by these shells, producing only local varieties.

The *P. intermedia* of Nyst appears to be distinct from the English forms.

Herne Bay.   Mr. Bowerbank's Collection.

PHOLADOMYA KONINCKII, Nyst.   Plate XVI. fig. 4.

(Nyst, Coq. Foss. Belgiques, p. 50. t. 1. f. 9.)

It has been considered advisable to refigure this shell, as it has not been previously described as occurring in England; and especially, as this species has been sometimes mistaken for *P. margaritacea*, Sow. But, from comparison with authentic specimens, we have considered this to be a variety of *P. Koninckii*, Nyst, a species very characteristic of the Lower Tertiaries of Belgium.

Herne Bay.   Mr. Prestwich's Collection.

CYTHEREA ORBICULARIS, Edwards, MSS.   Plate XVI. fig. 5.

Testâ tenui, orbiculari, depressâ, lentiformi, subæquilaterali, vix transversâ, concentricè striatâ vel sublamellosâ; umbonibus minimis, subrecurvis; lunulâ vix notatâ.

A slender, orbicular shell, with faintly marked concentric striæ or lines of growth, becoming occasionally lamelliform; the umbones are small and slightly recurved; the sinus in the pallial impression is obtusely angular; the lunule is nearly obsolete.

This species varies slightly in form, being sometimes transversely oval, the beaks much nearer the anterior margin, the posterior side more compressed, the cardinal margin straighter and less angular, than in the typical form.

This shell appears to be distinguished from *C. Bellovacina*, Deshayes, by the posterior margin being shorter and less angular, and the general form being more orbicular and symmetrical.

Herne Bay.   Mr. Edwards's Collection.

ASTARTE TENERA, n. sp.   Plate XVI. fig. 6.

Testâ subtrigonâ, depressâ, tenerâ, inæquilaterali, concentricè irregulariter rugosâ; latere postico compressiusculo; umbonibus submedianis; lunulâ ovatâ, profundâ, lævigatâ; marginibus crenulatis.

A somewhat trigonal and rather fragile shell; the posterior side being slightly compressed and angulated; the surface marked with concentric symmetrical ribs and intervening furrows in the young state, which become irregular both in form and distance in the adult shell, giving it a rugose appearance; the intermediate furrows are faintly striated; the beaks somewhat acute, and recurved over the lunule, which is elliptical and smooth; the ligamental area excavated; the margins of the shell are crenulated.

A species readily distinguished from the *A. rugata*, Sow., of the London Clay by the general form, thinner shell, and less rugose surface of the valves.

Herne Bay.   Collections of Messrs. Edwards and Bowerbank.

LEDA SUBSTRIATA, n. sp.   Plate XVI. fig. 7.

(Compare *Nucula striata*, Lam., Desh. Coq. Foss. t. 42. f. 4–6.)

This shell, collected by Mr. Prestwich from the Thanet Sands at Richborough Castle and Pegwell Bay, is difficult to distinguish from *Nucula* (*Leda*) *striata*, Lam., which it resembles in general form, but is rather longer in a transverse direction, and the striæ differ a little and are interrupted towards the posterior margin in some of the specimens examined.

PECTEN PRESTVICHII, n. sp.   Plate XVI. fig. 8.

Testâ tenui, compressâ, radiatim obsoletè costatâ; costis 30–36, subsquamosis; interstitiis obliquè irregulariter striatis; auriculis inæqualibus, radiatis.

Shell thin, compressed; margin orbicular, with a rectangular beak; radiated with 30–36 very slightly raised ribs, distantly imbricated, the intervening furrows twice as large as the ribs, irregularly and obliquely striated; ears unequal, with three or four radiated costæ.

Richborough Castle.   Collected by Mr. Prestwich.

SCALARIA BOWERBANKII, n. sp.   Plate XVI. fig. 9.

Testâ elongatâ, turritâ, imperforatâ; anfractibus 9–10, ventricosis, rotundatis, suturis distinctis, longitudinaliter costatis; costis 18–20, subacutis, interstitiis transversim striatis; anfracto ultimo carinifero; aperturâ rotundatâ.

An elongated, turreted, rather thick shell, with nine to ten ventricose volutions, longitudinally costated; costæ eighteen to twenty, somewhat acute, and slightly oblique, the ribs as well as intervening furrows transversely striated; the last volution carinated.

The ribs on the lower volutions are sometimes divided and more irregular than on the upper ones.

This species is closely allied to, if not identical with, a shell obtained by Sir C. Lyell from the Lower Tertiaries of Belgium (*Système Landenien* of Dumont).

Herne Bay.   Mr. Bowerbank's Collection.

TROPHON SUBNODOSUM, n. sp.   Plate XVI. fig. 10.

Testâ turritâ, ovato-fusiformi, transversim tenuissimè striatâ, anfractibus convexis, subcarinatis, supernè angulatis, carinâ subnodosâ; aperturâ ovatâ; columellâ recurvâ; canali breviusculo.

Shell turreted, ovately fusiform, transversely striated, and faintly decussated; volutions convex, upper part subangulated and nodulous; aperture ovate, with a short, open and recurved canal.

Herne Bay.   Mr. Bowerbank's Collection.

AMPULLINA SUBDEPRESSA, n. sp. (not figured).

Imperfect specimens of a shell (from Pegwell and Herne Bays) have been obtained, which bear considerable resemblance to *Globulus (Ampullina) depressus*, Lamk. sp., from Barton; but the spire is not so elevated, and the umbilicus is much more open; it is possibly only a local variety.

CRISTELLARIA PLATYPLEURA*, n. sp.   Plate XVI. fig. 12.
Diam. $\frac{1}{16}$ inch.

Testa ovata vel subcircularis, posticè rotundata, anticè angulata; margo acutus, cristâ pellucidâ instructus: loculi 9, plani, irregulariter arcuati, ultimus anticè excavatus; suturæ valdè costulatæ; umbo densus, prominens; apertura rotunda, margine granulato.

In a young state this *Cristellaria* is ovate, and has its cells more regular, and the umbo and ribs less thickened and distorted.

CRISTELLARIA WETHERELLII, n. sp.   Length $\frac{1}{13}$ inch.

Testa oblonga, anticè acuta, basi spiraliter involuta, rotundata; margo arcuatus, acutè angulatus; loculi 12, lævigati, angusti, antici infernè marginati, ultimus subconvexus; suturæ planæ, pellucidæ; apertura rotunda, margine radiato.

In the young state this *Cristellaria* is subovate, the umbo being almost central; but in the more advanced stage of growth, the chambers having gradually left the spiral for an almost straight direction of growth, the inner or inferior margins of the cells cease to join the umbo, and the form of the shell becomes elongate. One old specimen quite assumes the form of a *Marginulina*.

The *Cristellaria* from Mr. Wetherell's collection, and belonging to the London Clay, figured by Mr. Sowerby in the Trans. Geol. Soc. 2nd ser. vol. v. pl. 9. fig. 19, represents one stage of growth of this species.

ROSALINA MARIÆ, n. sp.   Plate XVI. fig. 13.   Diam. $\frac{1}{50}$ inch.

Testa suborbiculata, depressa, rugosa; supernè sex-lobata, vix umbilicata; subtus umbilico lato, aperturis subvalvulatis circumdato; margo rotundatus; loculi 6, subconvexiusculi, irregulariter triangulati, ultimus anticè valdè convexus.

POLYMORPHINA AMPULLA, n. sp.   Plate XVI. fig. 14.
Diam. $\frac{1}{40}$ inch.

Testa subglobosa, lævigata, supernè in rostro brevi producta, basi obtusa; loculi pauci, convexi; suturæ lineares; apertura rotunda, excentrica, radiata.

[It is not at all improbable that Boys and Walker, as well as Montagu, have figured and described several of the Foraminifera of the Thanet Sands of Sandwich as recent forms.—T. R. J.]

* These new Foraminifera are described by Mr. T. Rupert Jones.

EXPLANATION OF PLATE XVI.

Fig. 1. Sanguinolaria Edvardsii, *Morris*.
Fig. 2. Glycimeris Rutupiensis, *Morris*.
Fig. 3. Panopæa granulata, *Morris*.
Fig. 4. Pholadomya Koninckii, *Nyst*.
Fig. 5. Cytherea orbicularis, *Edwards*.
Fig. 6. Astarte tenera, *Morris*.
Fig. 7. Leda substriata, *Morris*, magnified.
Fig. 8 *a*. Pecten Prestvichii, *Morris*.
Fig. 8 *b*. ———— ————, portion magnified.
Fig. 9. Scalaria Bowerbankii, *Morris*.
Fig. 10. Trophon subnodosum, *Morris*.
Fig. 11. Ovoidal bodies filling tubular cavity in sand (see p. 247).
Fig. 12 *a*. Cristellaria platypleura, *Jones*, magnified.
Fig. 12 *b*. ———— ————, edge view, magnified.
Fig. 13 *a*. Rosalina Mariæ, *Jones*; under surface, magnified.
Fig. 13 *b*. ———— ————, edge view, magnified.
Fig. 14 *a*. Polymorphina ampulla, *Jones*, magnified.
Fig. 14 *b*. ———— ———— ————, seen from above, magnified.

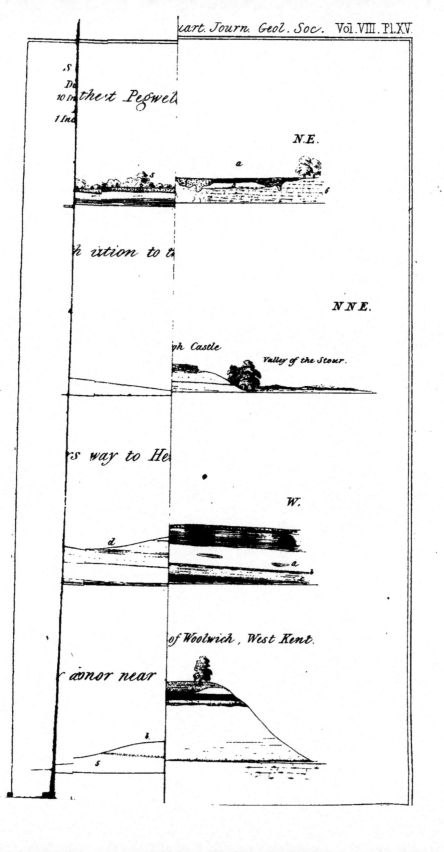

N.E.

a

b

NNE.

h Castle

Valley of the Stour.

s way to He

W.

d

a

b

c

of Woolwich, West Kent.

a nor near

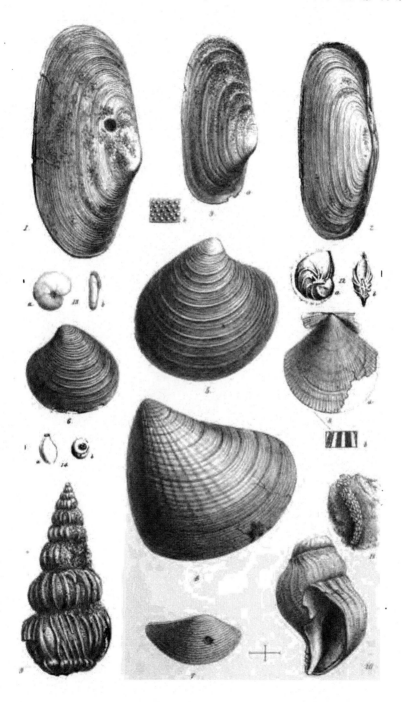

Achilles lith

F. Greenough

THANET SANDS FOSSILS.

MÉMOIRE

SUR LA POSITION GÉOLOGIQUE

DES SABLES ET DU CALCAIRE LACUSTRE

DE RILLY (MARNE),

PAR

M. JOSEPH PRESTWICH.

EXTRAIT DU BULLETIN DE LA SOCIÉTÉ GÉOLOGIQUE DE FRANCE,
2ᵉ série, t. X, p. 300, séance du 21 février 1853.

Le calcaire lacustre et les sables blancs de Rilly sont d'un grand intérêt pour le géologue, non seulement à cause de l'assemblage très remarquable de fossiles qu'ils contiennent, mais encore par la difficulté qu'ont éprouvée les observateurs à déterminer rigoureusement la position d'une telle faune dans la série des sables inférieurs du bassin de Paris. On doit se rappeler la diversité des opinions à ce sujet. Ayant eu occasion de visiter plusieurs fois depuis 1840 le gisement des couches de Rilly, et ayant observé quelques phénomènes nouveaux, ou d'une autre manière que les géologues qui m'ont précédé, j'ai l'honneur de soumettre à la Société les faits tels que je les ai aperçus, dans l'espoir d'ajouter quelques éclaircissements propres à faciliter la détermination de l'âge des couches dont il est question.

Une belle collection des fossiles du calcaire de Rilly a été d'abord faite par M. Arnould, de Châlons-sur-Marne; mais c'est M. Drouet qui, en 1835, a attiré l'attention générale sur une faune

Sm

alors toute nouvelle pour le bassin de Paris; plus tard (1), en 1838, M. Charles d'Orbigny (2) a indiqué d'une manière précise la position des sables et du calcaire de Rilly au-dessus de la craie et au-dessous des lignites, position à l'égard de laquelle tous les géologues paraissent actuellement d'accord. Mais M. Ch. d'Orbigny, et, comme je le pense, tous les autres géologues, ont considéré le calcaire lacustre et les sables situés au-dessous comme ne formant qu'un seul groupe de couches d'eau douce. M. de Boissy, dans sa monographie intéressante, paraît partager l'opinion de M. Ch. d'Orbigny que ces couches sont subordonnées à l'argile plastique, et inférieures à l'étage des lignites (3). M. d'Archiac a regardé ces couches comme un équivalent d'eau douce de la glauconie inférieure dans laquelle il avait d'abord compris les sables de Bracheux (4). Actuellement il place ces derniers plus haut dans la série des sables inférieurs, et par conséquent au-dessus des couches de Rilly (5). M. Melleville fait de la division inférieure des sables inférieurs un seul groupe, comprenant les sables, le travertin, les glaises et les lignites de Rilly, sans donner l'ordre exact des couches constituantes (6). M. Rondot (7) fait observer que l'âge du calcaire lacustre est nettement précisé, étant au-dessous des lignites et au-dessous du sable blanc, mais il ne dit pas s'il considère le sable comme appartenant au même dépôt que le calcaire lacustre ou non.

M. Hébert, qui a particulièrement étudié cette question, et qui a si bien précisé les divers dépôts des terrains tertiaires inférieurs des environs de Paris, nous a donné en 1848 ses vues toutes nouvelles sur les rapports du calcaire lacustre de Rilly avec l'argile plastique et la glauconie inférieure (8). A ce sujet, il a encore ajouté en 1849 et 1850 des détails pour appuyer les opinions qu'il avait d'abord avancées (9). D'après ses recherches à Rilly et aux environs, il conclut que, non seulement les sables et le calcaire de

---

(1) *Bull. Soc. géol.*, 1re sér., vol. VI, p 294.

(2) *Id.*, 1re sér., vol. IX, p. 321.

(3) *Bull. Soc. géol.*, 2e sér., vol. IV, p. 178; et *Mém. Soc. géol.*, 2e sér., vol. III, p. 267.

(4) *Bull. Soc. géol.*, 1re sér., vol. X, p. 174-175.

(5) *Hist. des progrès de la géologie*, vol. III, p. 606 et 683.

(6) *Bull. Soc. géol.*, 1re sér., vol. IX, p. 323; et *Ann. des sciences géol.*, vol. II, p. 3-13.

(7) *Ann. de l'Acad. de Reims*, 1842-1843.

(8) *Bull. Soc. géol.*, 2e sér., vol. V, p. 398-406.

(9) *Id.*, 2e sér., vol. VI, p. 725, et vol. VII, p. 338.

Rilly sont antérieurs et indépendants des lignites et de l'argile plastique, mais qu'ils sont même antérieurs aux sables marins de Châlons-sur-Vesle et de Bracheux (1). Il place ces derniers plus bas dans la série des sables inférieurs que ne le fait M. d'Archiac, et si l'on ne peut pas les séparer de la glauconie inférieure, ce qu'il pense difficile à admettre, alors les sables de Rilly seraient les couches les plus anciennes de la période tertiaire ; mais si la glauconie inférieure est indépendante des sables de Bracheux, rien ne s'opposerait, dans sa théorie, à ce que cette couche ne fût synchronique du calcaire lacustre (2). Suivant M. Hébert (3), les sables marins (de Châlons-sur-Vesle) se sont déposés dans des dépressions creusées dans les sables et marnes lacustres par une irruption qui du nord amenait des eaux marines, et ainsi s'explique le phénomène qu'il décrit, des sables de Rilly se trouvant au même niveau que les sables marins des environs de Châlons-sur-Vesle et de Chenay (4), et que ces couches de Rilly, Romery et Sézanne n'étaient que des restants d'un dépôt d'un lac d'une surface de 20 lieues, et qui s'étendait des environs de Reims à Sézanne, entourés et enveloppés par les sables marins ; car M. Hébert avait déjà très bien démontré que le calcaire pisolitique du Mont-Aimé appartient à la partie supérieure du terrain crétacé. Et puis il conclut qu'au commencement de la période tertiaire ce calcaire a été émergé, et qu'il en est résulté un lac où il s'est déposé d'abord de la silice pure à l'état de sable cristallin, puis un calcaire marneux, où se sont conservés des végétaux et des coquilles (5).

C'est là aujourd'hui l'état de la question. Pour moi, il m'a toujours paru que les caractères lithologiques et la structure physique des sables et du calcaire de Rilly démontrent l'indépendance de ces deux couches, dans laquelle opinion des observations ultérieures m'ont confirmé. Les sables décidément ne sont pas un dépôt chimique. En les examinant à la loupe, on voit qu'ils sont composés de grains quartzeux transparents et *anguleux*, mais dont les angles sont émoussés, sans mélange de corps étrangers. Ils ont, en effet, l'aspect ordinaire de sable quartzeux fin, seulement beaucoup plus fin qu'à l'ordinaire, comme s'ils avaient été lavés. Le calcaire lacustre, au contraire, est composé essentiellement de marne, avec

---

(1) *Bull. Soc. géol.*, 2ᵉ sér., vol. VI, p. 711, 725 et 727.
(2) *Id.*, *id.*, vol. VII, p. 340.
(3) *Id.*, *id.*, vol. VII, p. 338.
(4) *Id.*, *id.*, vol. VI, fig. 1 et 2, pl. V, et coupe, p. 714.
(5) *Id.*, *id.*, vol. V, p. 407.

des masses de concrétions calcaires, et il *empâte des grains de sable quartzeux*. Donc, minéralogiquement, il n'y a aucun rapport entre les sables blancs et le calcaire lacustre, et il n'y a que la dernière de ces couches qui puisse être un dépôt de sources. Il y a aussi une ligne bien tranchée entre les deux couches. Non seulement il n'y a point de transition entre elles, mais dans la sablière de Rilly la surface des sables blancs au-dessous du calcaire lacustre se montre ondulée et irrégulière (voyez fig. 1).

Fig. 1.

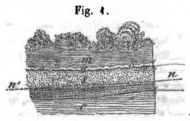

c **Craie.**

s **Sable marin inférieur, 5 à 6m.** { Sable blanc avec des cailloux et des parties ferrugineuses.
Sable blanc impur.
Sable blanc.

a **Sable marneux jaunâtre.**

m **Calcaire travertin, 4 à 5m.** . . { Calcaire en gros blocs, mêlé de marne et avec beaucoup de fossiles.
Marnes calcaires avec peu de fossiles.

n n′ **Base de la sablière. — Au-dessous de cette ligne la superposition est prouvée par des puits.**

Reste à savoir s'il y a quelque rapport paléontologique entre ces couches. Jusqu'à présent on n'a pas trouvé de fossiles dans les sables blancs à la sablière de Rilly; mais cependant les ouvriers ont fait savoir depuis longtemps qu'en creusant plus bas dans cette couche ils avaient rencontré des traces de coquilles, un peu au-dessus de la craie (1). Cette partie inférieure des sables a été explorée il y a deux ou trois ans en faisant des tranchées pour la route qui mène de Rilly à Montchenot. Je m'y suis trouvé en septembre 1850 avec M. Morris, qui peut, mieux que moi, constater les phénomènes paléontologiques.

(1) M. Rondot a fait mention de ce fait en 1842, mais sans en discuter l'importance. (*Ouvrage cité*, p. 12.)

Fig. 2. — *Coupes près de Rilly, sur la route de Montchenot (Marne).*

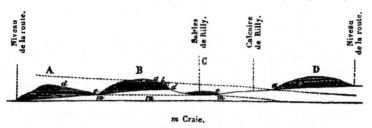

m Craie.

La première couche est à peu de distance à l'ouest de Rilly, et puis deux autres se suivent de près, au point où la route tourne au nord et en montant un peu. (Voyez A, B et D, fig. 2.) Dans deux de ces endroits (A et B), ainsi qu'à l'endroit C, on trouve assez abondamment des traces de coquilles, mais elles sont difficiles à conserver, n'étant que des empreintes très fragiles. On peut néanmoins assez bien distinguer leurs caractères pour voir que leur facies est le même que dans les sables de Montchenot et de Châlons-sur-Vesle.

Voici la description de ces coupes de haut en bas.

Coupe A. — *d.* 10 pieds de sable blanc avec des couches minces, subordonnées, d'argile grisâtre ; en l'absence de l'argile, on passe en descendant à 4 pieds de sable blanc (*e*) un peu agglutiné et en partie ferrugineux, qui contient deux lits de cailloux roulés, du silex, et de la craie. Dans cette partie inférieure se trouvent beaucoup de moules de coquilles marines.

Coupe B. — *a.* Calcaire marneux, lacustre, blanc et sableux. Il a 2 pieds d'épaisseur.

b. Argile grisâtre avec des couches minces de sable blanc, 5 pieds. On a ensuite 2 pieds de sable argileux blanc (*c*), contenant des bandes de sable ferrugineux endurci avec empreintes de coquilles marines, et puis 10 pieds de sable blanc (*d*) avec des plaques très minces d'argile bitumineuse et quelques cailloux.

Coupe C. — *e.* 5 pieds de sable blanc avec des couches minces, qui sont ocreuses et ferrugineuses. A la partie supérieure il y a un lit de 6 pouces d'épaisseur de cailloux de silex roulés, empâtés dans un grès ferrugineux très tendre, qui contient des empreintes de coquilles. Ces coquilles se trouvent encore dans la partie de cette couche qui est en contact avec la craie.

Coupe D. — *a.* De même que *a* dans la coupe B. — 12 à 18 pieds d'épaisseur.

En D on ne voit pas la superposition du calcaire *a* sur les sables blancs qui doivent se trouver un peu plus bas ; en A et en C on voit la superposition immédiate des sables sur la craie, qui est marneuse et sans couches de silex.

Le calcaire lacustre en B et en D est plus sableux qu'à Rilly, et je n'y ai pas trouvé de fossiles, mais aussi je n'ai eu que bien peu de temps à en faire la recherche.

Une chose essentielle à observer dans ces couches, c'est le caractère variable des sables. L'argile, les cailloux, et puis les fossiles s'y trouvent en couches minces et non continues. Comme base, c'est un dépôt de sable blanc auquel les autres caractères sont subordonnés. Par exemple, dans la partie *d* en A, le sable est mêlé avec beaucoup d'argile, mais en B cette même partie de la couche passe en l'absence de l'argile à un sable presque pur. En outre en C, la partie *e* est plus ferrugineuse et plus coquillière qu'en A, et les cailloux se trouvent autrement disposés.

La sablière de Rilly, exploitée pour le beau sable blanc qui sert à la fabrication des glaces, est située à quelques centaines de mètres au sud-est de ces coupes, et l'identité des couches dans l'un et dans l'autre endroit me paraît complète. Il y a la même superposition sur la craie, les mêmes lits de cailloux roulés et de couches minces ferrugineuses et fossilifères ; enfin la puissance de ces couches est à peu de chose près la même. La seule différence consiste en ce que l'argile est plus abondante dans les couches en A et en B que dans la carrière de Rilly ; mais ce caractère n'est pas constant et il est même peu important, de même que celui qui résulte de la présence de l'oxyde de fer. Les deux caractères constants de ce dépôt sont la présence des sables quartzeux plus ou moins blancs, et les lits de cailloux de silex mêlés. Ceux-ci se trouvent dans toutes les couches de ce dépôt entre Rilly et Chamens, au lieu que ceux-là ne se montrent que quelquefois. La sablière de Rilly n'est qu'un point où ces sables inférieurs sont plus purs qu'à l'ordinaire. Le test des coquilles n'est jamais conservé, et les fossiles, n'étant que des empreintes, ne se trouvent que là où le sable est un peu endurci, ou par l'oxyde de fer, ou par un ciment siliceux. Le grès ferrugineux dans lequel on les trouve est si tendre, que, des divers échantillons que j'ai remportés avec moi en Angleterre, et que j'ai apportés dernièrement à Paris, il ne restait que deux morceaux sur lesquels M. Deshayes a pu se prononcer. M. Deshayes a reconnu d'ailleurs qu'ils contiennent : 1° un fragment de coquille bivalve qui paraît dépendre du *Cardium*, n° 1, ci-dessous ; 2° le moule d'une coquille turbinée et canaliculée, probablement du genre *Fusus*. Outre ces deux coquilles, j'ai noté sur place des empreintes de *Pectunculus*, *Cardium*, et de plusieurs autres coquilles bivalves non déterminables.

Mais c'est à Montchenot où M. Hébert dit « que sa position est nettement établie » au-dessous des marnes blanches lacustres (1), que le sable blanc de Rilly montre ses rapports paléontologiques avec les sables de Châlons - sur - Vesle. La coupe que donne M. Hébert se montre parfaitement bien en suivant le bout de la vieille route de Reims, en bas de la côte à Montchenot. La nouvelle route fait un petit détour. Entre les deux routes, le sable a été autrefois exploité. Il y a des couches d'un gris blanc très tendre, formant de gros blocs ; et dans ceux-ci j'ai trouvé des moules et des empreintes de coquilles. M. Deshayes a eu la complaisance de m'en faire la détermination suivante, sur quelques morceaux que je lui ai montrés :

1ᵃ Un *Cardium*, confondu avec le *semigranulatum* de Sowerby, mais qui en est parfaitement distinct ; il se trouve aussi à Bracheux, à Abbecourt, à Brimont et à Châlons-sur-Vesle.

2° Une *Lucine*, voisine de l'*uncinata*, constituant une espèce nouvelle ; elle est à Brimont et à Châlons-sur-Vesle.

3° *Psammobia rubis*? Lam. ; elle est aussi à Brimont.

Dans un autre échantillon que j'ai, il a trouvé aussi des empreintes apparentes de Lucines et de Corbules.

Quoique les espèces déterminées ne soient pas nombreuses, il me paraît qu'elles sont assez distinctes pour montrer toujours que les sables de Rilly appartiennent à un dépôt marin, et, suivant toute probabilité, aux sables marins de Châlons-sur-Vesle et de Brimont, qui, dans ce pays, sont les seules couches marines qui se trouvent au-dessous des lignites, et avec les fossiles desquelles les quelques spécimens ci-nommés sont en parfait accord.

Il y a cependant une difficulté à cet égard, car M. Hébert a fait observer qu'à Chenay on voit le calcaire lacustre au-dessous des sables de Châlons-sur-Vesle.

Je n'ai pas fait plus tôt cette communication à la Société, parce que, avant de la faire, j'avais l'intention de visiter cet endroit à mon voyage en Champagne, au mois d'octobre passé, et je regrette de n'en avoir pas eu le temps. Je ferai observer néanmoins que, comme M. Hébert dit que les sables au-dessus du calcaire lacustre à Chenay ne sont pas fossilifères, ils peuvent

---

(1) *Bull. Soc. géol.*, 2ᵉ sér., vol. V, p. 402.
(2) *Bull. Soc. géol.*, 2ᵉ sér., vol. VI, p. 710.

appartenir à la couche de sable blanc qu'il place ailleurs, à la base des lignites, et qui est aussi souvent non fossilifère. Alors les sables blancs, qui à Chenay sont au-dessous du calcaire, correspondent, comme le sable de Rilly, aux sables fossilifères de Châlons-sur-Vesle. Il faut remarquer qu'ici aussi ce n'est que la partie inférieure qui est fossilifère. Si cependant ces sables supérieurs de Chenay appartiennent aux sables de Châlons-sur-Vesle, comme le pense M. Hébert, et sans connaître cet endroit, je ne peux pas me permettre de discuter la question avec lui, alors il faudrait croire que le calcaire de Rilly est une couche lacustre intercalée à la partie supérieure de ces sables. Mais du moins ce qui me semble certain, d'après les observations que je viens de rapporter, c'est que le calcaire de Rilly a été précédé d'un dépôt marin, et que sa faune terrestre et d'eau douce, si curieuse, n'a pas été la première de celles qui aient apparu dans la période tertiaire.

A l'égard des caractères géographiques de la surface du pays à l'époque du dépôt du calcaire de Rilly, je ne puis admettre que ce dépôt se soit fait comme on l'a supposé, dans un grand lac ayant une étendue de Reims à Sézanne, c'est-à-dire de vingt lieues, ou dans l'estuaire où a été formée la série de couches qui constituent le groupe des lignites et des sables, car je ne conçois pas comment alors quelques unes des espèces de fossiles qui se trouvent à Rilly ne se trouveraient pas dans ces autres couches, ou comment il n'y aurait pas des fossiles des lignites dans la couche de Rilly. Or, au contraire, il n'y a pas une seule espèce commune entre ces couches.

Le groupe des lignites résulte d'un charriage de sédiment assez abondant — de l'affluent d'une rivière importante — au lieu qu'à Rilly tout indique qu'il y a eu peu de mouvement dans les eaux et que le charriage était faible; car, à l'exception des grains de sable siliceux empâtés dans le calcaire et provenant des sables au-dessous, il n'y a dans la masse principale du calcaire lacustre presque pas de mélange de corps étrangers ou de boue argileuse; d'ailleurs le bel état de conservation des coquilles terrestres, qui n'ont pas été altérées par une longue exposition à l'action atmosphérique, et qui généralement ne sont ni usées ni brisées, démontrent que le transport n'a pas été long, ni effectué par une grande masse d'eau — une rivière. L'absence de toute trace de poissons et d'*Unio* est encore un fait négatif en faveur de cette hypothèse. Le carbonate de chaux formant la base et même presque la totalité du calcaire de Rilly a toute l'apparence d'un dépôt de source local — d'un travertin — qui se serait formé dans un petit lac, un étang, ou une mare, alimenté ou par de l'eau jaillissante à travers le sable, ou par un ruisseau formé par quelque source calcaire sur des hauteurs voisines. Comme il se trouve tant de coquilles terrestres à Rilly et de feuilles à Sézanne, la dernière de ces vues me paraît la plus probable.

En effet, si nous étudions le caractère de cette faune, nous verrons que des 45 espèces de coquilles il y en a 30 qui sont terrestres, 3 qui peuvent vivre sur terre ou dans l'eau, et 12 seulement qui habitent l'eau ; et ces 12 espèces appartiennent à 5 genres qui, à l'exception du Cyclas, sont tous des gastéropodes pulmonés, d'où il est probable que l'eau n'était ni profonde ni d'une grande étendue.

Des 30 espèces terrestres la plupart appartiennent à des genres dont les espèces vivantes n'habitent pas même des terrains marécageux, mais fréquentent au contraire un sol sec et des côtes calcaires. Ainsi des 7 espèces d'Hélices, il y en a 2 qui appartiennent au groupe des Caracoles qu'on trouve à présent sur les terrains secs et élevés. Les Clausilies, dont il y a 2 espèces, sont des coquilles qui se trouvent souvent en foule sur nos collines crayeuses. Il en est à peu près de même pour les Cyclostomes dont il y a 3 espèces qui, pour la plupart, habitent les endroits secs et chauds. Les *Pupa* dont il n'y a guère que 10 espèces fréquentent les bords de l'eau, aussi bien que les lieux frais et abrités des hauteurs. Parmi les genres qui habitent plutôt les endroits humides, mais pas exclusivement, on peut citer les Achatines dont il y a 4 espèces, et les Vitrines représentées par 1 espèce. Les Auricules, dont il y a 3 espèces, sont amphibies. Des 5 genres de coquilles d'eau douce, le Cyclas, dont il y a 5 espèces, vit dans les rivières lentes et dans les étangs où ils s'enfoncent dans la vase. Les Physes peuvent vivre dans les terrains marécageux, mais c'est plutôt tout à fait dans l'eau qu'il faut les chercher. Les Paludines fréquentent surtout les rivières et les ruisseaux.

Quoique en consultant la liste très complète que donne M. de Boissy (1), on soit frappé de la grande proportion de coquilles terrestres qu'il y a à Rilly, il faut faire attention néanmoins que les individus de ce groupe sont rares en comparaison de ceux qui vivent dans l'eau. Les fossiles qui se trouvent en plus grande abondance sont les Physes et les Paludines ; toutes les coquilles terrestres sont, en comparaison, plus ou moins rares. Celles-là étaient évidemment en possession du terrain, et celles-ci n'étaient que des étrangères. Cependant, quoique amenées accidentellement, comme elles sont en bon état de conservation, il est probable, non seule-

---

(1) *Mém. de la Soc. géol. de France*, 2e sér., vol. III, p. 267

ment qu'elles n'ont pas été apportées de loin, mais aussi que leur fossilisation a eu lieu avec rapidité.

Il me paraît donc, d'après ces caractères généraux des principaux genres de fossiles d'après leur état et d'après leur mode de conservation, qu'il y a eu une terre émergée non loin de Reims et d'Épernay, où le calcaire pisolitique et la craie formaient des hauteurs avec le terrain sableux des sables de Châlons-sur-Vesle à leur base (1). De ces collines calcaires il coulait des ruisseaux alimentés par quelques sources fortement chargées de carbonate de chaux et formant des mares ou petits lacs locaux placés sur les sables inférieurs, dont les grains quartzeux ont été charriés et mêlés avec le dépôt calcaire. Après les averses, les coquilles terrestres, qui vivaient sur les bords des ruisseaux et sur les côtes voisines, auront été emportées, et, comme les feuilles qui les accompagnent à Sézanne, fixées rapidement par le carbonate calcaire avant qu'elles aient eu le temps de se décomposer. Ces conditions d'eau limpide, aérée et chargée de carbonate de chaux ont aussi sans doute contribué à la grande taille des Physes et de quelques autres coquilles.

Il reste encore à expliquer comment il se fait que ce n'est que dans les endroits où se trouve le calcaire de Rilly que les sables quartzeux marins au-dessous sont si blancs et si purs. Si l'on examine la partie inférieure de ce calcaire, on verra qu'il n'y a pas de couche d'argile capable d'empêcher les eaux qui déposaient le calcaire de s'infiltrer à travers les sables sous-jacents et d'échapper ainsi par voie souterraine, au lieu de s'écouler par une voie à la surface, si toutefois il y avait dans les environs des endroits plus bas que ceux où étaient placés ces petits lacs, ce qui ne présente pas de difficultés. Il résultera de cette manière de se décharger que l'eau du lac aurait été dans un état de repos propre à laisser déposer le carbonate de chaux dont elle était chargée. Quoiqu'elle eût pu perdre ainsi tout excès d'acide carbonique, cependant l'exposition à l'atmosphère et puis les matières organiques et la présence des mollusques auront été cause qu'il en sera resté toujours une certaine quantité en dissolution avec de l'air atmosphérique ; de manière que cette eau, passant par une infiltration continue dans les sables placés au-dessous du dépôt lacustre, aurait exercé une force oxydante et dissolvante en même temps avec les effets mécaniques ordinaires du lavage. Donc on peut bien concevoir qu'un tel phé-

---

(1) Peut-être même n'y avait-il qu'un seul lac, le Homery, passant par Rilly, à Châlons-sur-Vesle ; mais il me paraît que le calcaire de Sézanne était déposé dans un autre lac à part.

nomène ayant lieu à travers une masse de sable quartzeux, mêlé avec un peu d'argile et de calcaire, avec des tests de coquilles et des traces de matières végétales, rouillés en place par l'oxyde de fer, la matière fine argileuse serait emportée et les autres corps décomposés et dissous par le passage de l'eau, ne laissant que la partie la plus grossière et insoluble de cette couche perméable, c'est-à-dire le sable à grains de quartz hyalin, qui, ainsi débarrassé de matières étrangères, se présente de ce beau blanc et dans cet état de pureté si remarquable qu'on voit à Rilly. Quoique les sables marins de Châlons-sur-Vesle soient d'une grande étendue, ce n'est que là où ils sont recouverts par le calcaire lacustre qu'ils présentent ce caractère; d'où il faut conclure qu'il y a quelque rapport comme celui que nous venons de suggérer entre les deux faits.

PARIS.— IMPRIMERIE DE L. MARTINET,